D0754554

CONVERSATIONS WITH A DEAD MAN

CONVERSATIONS

with a

DEAD MAN

The Legacy

of

DUNCAN
CAMPBELL SCOTT

MARK ABLEY

Douglas & McIntyre

Copyright © 2013 by Mark Abley
13 14 15 16 17   5 4 3 2 1

All rights reserved. No part of this book may be reproduced, stored in a retrieval system or transmitted, in any form or by any means, without the prior written consent of the publisher or a licence from Access Copyright, www.accesscopyright.ca, 1-800-893-5777, info@accesscopyright.ca.

Douglas & McIntyre (2013) Ltd.
P.O. Box 219, Madeira Park, BC von 2H0
www.douglas-mcintyre.com

Printed and bound in Canada

Edited by Audrey McClellan
Jacket and design by Carleton Wilson
Indexed by Stephen Ullstrom

Cataloguing data available from Library and Archives Canada
ISBN 978-1-55365-609-8 (cloth)
ISBN 978-1-77162-008-6 (ebook)

We gratefully acknowledge the financial support of the Canada Council for the Arts, the British Columbia Arts Council, the Province of British Columbia through the Book Publishing Tax Credit and the Government of Canada through the Canada Book Fund for our publishing activities.

The epigraph from Armand Garnet Ruffo's "Poem for Duncan Campbell Scott" (from *Opening in the Sky*, Theytus Books, 1994) appears by permission of the author, and the epigraph from Margret Laurence's *The Stone Angel* appears by permission of Random House Canada.

PHOTO CREDITS: *The Thomas Fisher Rare Book Library, University of Toronto*: plates i (bottom); ii (top left); ii (bottom); iii (top).
Library and Archives Canada: page 6, PA-165842, e010752290, *Yousuf Karsh photo*; plates i (top), C-056072, *Jarvis photo, Harry Orr McCurry collection*; ii (top right), 1987-054, e010678738, *Yousuf Karsh photo, Yousuf Karsh fonds*; vii (bottom), PA-023095, *Department of Mines and Technical Surveys*.
Duncan Campbell Scott fonds at the *Archives of Ontario*: plates iii (bottom), C275-2-0-2 (S7569); iv (top), C 275-1-0-5 (S 7666); iv (bottom), C275-2-0-1 (S 7546); v (top), C275-1-0-6 (S 7528); v (bottom), C 275-1-0-6 (S 7650).
United Church of Canada Archives, Toronto: plates vi (top), 93.049P/1363bS; vi (bottom), 93.049P/1385N; vii (top), 93.049P/850N.
Blaire Russell photo: viii.

For the survivors
And in memory of those who did not survive

Portrait of the poet as a tired old man: in this image from 1933, Duncan
Campbell Scott stares out at the young photographer Yousuf Karsh.

Contents

So it came to be a sort of companionship for him, this haunting voice; and sometimes one could have seen him in his garden stretch out his hand and smile, as if he were welcoming an invisible guest. Sometimes the guest was not invisible, but took body and shape, and was a real presence; and often Paul was greeted with visions of things that had been, or that would be, and saw figures where, for other eyes, hung only the impalpable air.

—Duncan Campbell Scott, "Paul Farlotte"

Who is this black coat and tie?

...They say he asks too many questions but
doesn't wait to listen. Asks
much about yesterday, little about today
and acts as if he knows tomorrow.
Others don't like the way he's always busy writing
stuff in the notebooks he carries. Him,
he calls it poetry
and says it will make us who are doomed
live forever.

—Armand Garnet Ruffo (Ojibwa), "Poem for Duncan
    Campbell Scott"

When did I ever speak the heart's truth? Pride was my wilderness, and the demon that led me there was fear. I was alone, never anything else, and never free, for I carried my chains within me, and they spread out from me and shackled all I touched.

—Margaret Laurence, *The Stone Angel*

I wrote this book because I had formed the strong impression that the people currently living were paying insufficient attention to the dead.

—Niall Ferguson, *Civilization*

1

Even Beyond the End

THE MORNING FELT LIKE any other; I saw nothing uncanny in the cold grey light. The new year was still waiting for its first storm. A smell of fresh-brewed coffee wafted into the living room where I lazed on the sofa, annoyed by the political news in the paper, an overweight cat by my side. The coffee promised to be ferocious; I thought I'd earned it by clearing up my chaotic study and dragging the Christmas tree out to the kerb. Now the driveway was speckled with needles and the bare tree lay on its side, waiting to be collected along with the other forlorn conifers that had held so much promise three or four weeks earlier. Occasional wisps of snow drifted onto its branches from the low sky.

I heard the faint noise of a car's horn from a nearby street. But otherwise the world kept silent. If my computer was still humming in the study upstairs, I didn't notice it. I put aside the news section and picked up the sports pages. Alas, the Canadiens had lost again…

Only the tabby cat gave a sudden hint that anything had changed. Normally a lethargic ball of fur except at mealtimes, she hissed, leaped off the sofa and dashed toward the back door. I followed her with my eyes, wondering if I'd squashed her tail or if she'd suffered a nightmare of pit bulls. Then I heard a soft cough, little more than a clearing of the throat.

"That's strange," I thought. "Don't I have the house to myself?" My wife and younger daughter had gone into town an hour ago. I glanced toward the fireplace, where we'd burned a few logs the night before. And there he was, standing on the small green carpet beside a magazine-laden coffee table, looking straight at me.

I gave a shout. Had I left the front door open? How could anyone manage to sneak into my home? Not that he looked like the standard image of a burglar. He seemed the picture of respectability, as defined by a formal style unusual for the present day. He wore a three-piece grey suit, a striped tie and black shoes that had been so perfectly shined, I expected them to reek of polish. The anxiety lines of late middle age stretched across his forehead and inched down toward his thin-framed glasses and his pale eyes. Questions darted through my mind: Who is he? Why isn't he wearing a winter coat? If he's here to sell me something, whether salvation or real estate, why didn't he ring the doorbell? What gives him the right to lurk in my living room without an invitation? Above all, why didn't I notice his arrival?

"Good morning," he said. His voice was a discreet baritone. "Mr. Abley, I believe? I imagine you are surprised. I myself am a little taken aback."

"I don't understand," I said. "I—"

"Please allow me to introduce myself. My name is Duncan Campbell Scott. I was a poet. You may have read some of my work."

When I was a boy I believed in phantoms, but I've been a grown-up for longer than I care to recall. I thought I'd put away the childish things that used to fascinate me: sasquatches, sea serpents, extra-terrestrials, ghosts. I have never held out much hope that human beings will eventually travel through time as we now do through space. Yet there was no getting around it: this visible, audible presence standing near me belonged to the past. Looking at the man's austere face, I had a momentary sensation of time sweeping past me in a cool rush of air.

I felt a sudden need to hold on to what I knew was real. Without realizing it, I had already stood up. Was I still in the world of the living? I took a couple of steps toward the dining-room window, needing to make sure the back garden had not undergone some strange metamorphosis of its own. But there it was, large and unruly, carpeted this winter by less snow than normal—if "normal" has any meaning in our unravelling climate. A jay was calling harshly in the cedars. Across the white lawn, a blind squirrel wandered in search of the cashews and walnuts my daughter had thrown for it to find.

I turned back, trembling. "You can't be real," I said. Even as I spoke, the words rang hollow in my ears.

"I suppose that may depend on what you mean by real." His eyebrows rose slightly. "It's true I have been dead for many years. Please do not be alarmed—I am here for a particular reason. But I will not ask you to do anything unnatural. I will not dictate new poems, and you must not fear that I plan to take up some sort of permanent residence in your house."

I could feel the blood pounding too quickly inside my head. In his manner, his clothing, his precise way of speech, this man was a refugee from another century. The knowledge that this could not be happening—never, under any circumstances—matched an absolute certainty that it was.

"Would you like—are you able to drink a cup of coffee?" I asked.

"No, thank you. I wish I could. Help yourself, it smells delicious."

I didn't want to turn my eyes away from him. What other apparitions might emerge? Could a whole tribe of early Canadian poets materialize in the living room, driving all three cats to distraction? But I needed to get a grip on my thoughts, and a mug of strong coffee might help.

"This is ridiculous," I said aloud to myself as I opened the refrigerator in search of milk.

"No, although I agree it is unlikely," came his voice from the dining room. He had followed me part of the way, his footsteps making no sound on the hardwood floor. "But evidently not impossible. I have been told of extremely rare precedents. You see, I very much wanted to undertake this journey. I have petitioned on many occasions. And now, unexpectedly, my wish has been granted. Hence this—" he paused slightly "—this visit."

Petitioned. Are there political campaigns and protest movements even in the afterlife? But I thought of this question only later, when the drink in my hand was not coffee but Scotch and I was replaying the morning's events in a troubled mind.

"Did you ask for me in particular?" I said. It's astonishing how quickly the mind adapts to the unforeseen: while I still knew the conversation could not possibly be taking place, I had already entered into it. Yet my hands were trembling. Some coffee spilled onto the counter and I reached for a cloth from the sink. "Or is this merely a random encounter?"

"Perhaps you should take a few sips before you sit down again," he replied. There was a quiet command in his voice, an air of cool mastery, and I did as he suggested. By the time I returned to the living room, he was perched on a dark blue armchair, leaning forward, his long fingers pressed together in a pose of concentration.

"You need not be afraid of me," he said. "I did indeed ask to meet you— or someone like you, to be more precise—and I have no power to harm you in any way. Harm is the last thing on my mind. I must admit, although the admission is a painful one, I am in need of assistance. I dare to hope you will be willing to use your influence on my behalf."

"But how can I help someone who has been dead for, for—"

"Since December 1947," he replied. "Before you were born, I believe."

"Of course," I said a little sharply. It's true I have aged a good deal in recent years, but I don't like to be mistaken for a senior citizen.

"I will explain. There are certain things I must explain, and others that I am forbidden to mention. You must not ask me any questions about the afterlife, for example. Certain things will become clear in the course of our discussion, but I am not allowed to describe"—he waved his left hand towards the front window—"the modes of existence in the other realm. Or non-existence, I should say. I realize these words may sound rather cryptic."

The coffee was beginning to take effect. I felt a little giddy: a man who had died in 1947 was sitting in a Montreal living room, speaking in a normal voice, asking for help. "So what *can* you explain?"

"Well. As people have long suspected, the final failure of the body does not bring about the immediate death of consciousness. That process happens only gradually. Those of us who were blessed with intellectual gifts or a strong power of will often maintain a cohesive personality, if you like, for a significant length of time. And there are paths by which news of the material world does reach us. But the news tends to arrive in a fragmented form, and it becomes garbled in the telling. Even if we can be confident that a certain event has taken place among the living, we often have no idea *why* it has occurred. And so we exist, insofar as we exist at all, in the dark. Do I make myself clear?"

"Not really," I said. My mind was racing with a thousand ideas, a thousand questions.

Scott glanced away. His eyes lingered for a few moments on an Aboriginal painting I bought years ago in a small frontier town in Western Australia. Though it looks abstract at a casual glance, it tells a story of three women gathering food by a waterhole in the desert. "I'm sorry. But again I must ask you not to inquire too closely about the circumstances of our, so to speak, our condition. The important point for you to grasp is that—to the very limited extent in which we survive at all—we remain ourselves." He reached up and stroked his long, sharp nose. "Our character does not change. Our memories endure, and sometimes they act as a blessing. At other times, a curse. But we do not acquire, as my dear wife used to hope and believe, any new powers of knowledge or perception that were denied to us while we lived. My second wife, I mean to say. In short, the physical realm moves on. We do not."

"So for you, the world remains how it existed in 1947?"

"For the most part, yes; 1947 and before. I have not the least idea who sits in the House of Commons now, whereas I could tell you countless details about the men who served there in the 1920s. When you die, Mr. Abley, you will find that images and facts exist in a sort of weightless realm, as though deprived of gravity. Explanations depend on context, and in the afterlife we have no context, no communication as you would understand it. Strange tales have begun to reach us, for example, about the extraordinary power of new electric devices and the disappearance of books. Your shelves"—he gestured at two overcrowded bookcases—"show me these tales are not all true. That is reassuring. On a much wider scale, I hope I'm correct in assuming the atom bomb has not become a weapon in common use?"

"That's right," I said. "Touch wood. I mean, nuclear weapons haven't been used in combat since 1945. But we live in the constant knowledge they could explode at any moment. Could blow up the whole planet, in fact. At least nine nations have them. But so far, so good."

"The whole planet," he repeated. He appeared to be struggling with the idea. "Amazing. I grew up in a time of cavalry and muskets. Buffalo herds still roamed the plains. Sailing ships plied the North Atlantic. As a young man, when I stepped off the wooden sidewalks on my way to and from the office, I had to dodge the horses—terrifying creatures, I always thought. How dazzled we were by the advent of electric streetcars! Whereas now… But let me return to the purpose of my appearance. My first appearance."

This time I was the one to raise my eyebrows.

"Indeed," he said, noticing. "I have been granted the privilege—the licence, if you like—to pay you a number of visits, assuming several will be needed. I suspect they will. So I trust the novelty of meeting me—I do not presume to call it a pleasure—will outweigh any burden of imposition. I imagine your writing time is limited by necessity. Mine always was. Few of us can follow our vocation as we might desire."

My writing time? My vocation? I took a long last swig of coffee before its heat faded. Somewhere beyond the dining-room window, a chickadee gave a couple of sharp nasal calls before releasing its jaunty song into the winter air. Scott inclined his head and, for the first time, I saw his thin lips break into a smile.

"A great many years have gone by since I was able to hear that song," he said quietly. "Or any form of music." His gaze seemed distant now. I had the impression he was listening to a melody belonging to some other time and place. But after a few moments he straightened his shoulders.

"Come," he said, more to himself than to me. "That won't do. I must not indulge in nostalgia for either birdsong or Brahms." I saw his eyes stray around the room again, pausing for a moment at the djembes my wife had placed in front of our old, out-of-tune piano. To reach the keyboard and the piano stool, we have to move three African drums aside. Scott's expression flickered, perhaps with amusement, perhaps with distaste. Then he looked me again in the face. "We need to discuss why I am here."

"So you know I'm a writer," I said. "How did that piece of information reach you? You mustn't think I'm famous or anything."

He sidestepped the question. "My request, and you'll understand I have been asking this for a considerable length of time—not that the concept of time among us is the same as it is for you—was to be given the chance to rectify a serious injustice. This requires making a case for myself. My former self. I asked to converse with a Canadian poet who has also enjoyed some success in the field of journalism. I trust you recognize yourself in that description?"

I nodded.

"Very good. My hope has been to find a writer," he went on, speaking more quickly, "who will be able to appreciate my work from the inside, as it were. I mean my real work, of course."

"I've read a little of it," I told him. "Not for a long time, though."

"There's never enough time, is there?" He made this observation in a matter-of-fact tone, with no ironic edge that I could detect. He had, after all, nothing to gain by irritating me.

"Not until I retire, anyway. If writers can ever afford to retire."

Scott leaned a little further forward in the chair. He rested his chin on his right hand, exposing a pair of silver cufflinks. "A few cheques would be pleasant to receive, I'm sure. Appreciation, even more so. But there's nothing unusual about neglect. Some of the great poets of history were ignored or slighted in their lifetimes. Think of poor Keats…"

His voice trailed off into silence. He seemed to be gathering his forces, as though preparing to take a deep breath. Thinking of his triple-barrelled name, I suddenly recalled old collections of verse—those brown, musty-smelling volumes, redolent of secondhand bookstores and damp basements, that were published long before the postmodernists, before even the modernists, in an age when some people took the phrase "Canadian literature" to be a contradiction in terms.

"Mr. Abley, my situation is both more singular and more urgent. To come clean with you, I require the help of an author capable of refuting the lies that I understand are now attached to my name. An author who, having read my work attentively and understood the calibre of man I was, will want to publish a long essay, perhaps more than one, powerful and eloquent enough to dispel the rumours and correct the mistakes."

It sounded like a well-prepared speech. There was, I was beginning to realize, a certain desperation behind the formality of his words, a look of supplication in his steely gaze. He was a man—a ghost—on a quest. When I said nothing, he spoke more plainly: "Someone who can restore my reputation. Someone who can clear my name."

"Your name is under a cloud?"

"Under a cloud! My name is mud. Are you not aware of this?"

I was aware of very little about Duncan Campbell Scott. As a teenager, studying literature at the University of Saskatchewan, I had read a handful of his poems. I knew that a small group of poets had flourished in Ottawa at the end of the nineteenth century, and that he and his close friend Archibald Lampman were prominent among them. But in my youthful hunger to keep up with the writers of the moment, I had paid little attention to the sleek melodies of the late Victorians. Finding my models elsewhere, among poets who turned away from regular metre and rhyme, I struggled to emulate the masters of a jagged, angular style. Scott already belonged to history; I wanted to belong in the future. Decades would pass before I came across his name again: in 2009 the literary journal *Arc* asked me to judge its annual prize for the best collection of poetry written in the Ottawa region. It was called the Lampman-Scott Award, and none of the living poets whose slim paperbacks landed in my mailbox wrote in a style remotely similar to Scott's or Lampman's. For an award recognizing new work, the name of the prize seemed almost archaeological.

In the twenty-first century, of course, few people willingly choose to read poetry of any description, and only professors of English and graduate students of Canadian literature are likely to be familiar with Scott's writing. But why would his name be mud? Something was tugging at the back of my mind, a doubt, a suspicion, although I could recapture no details. Had he been implicated in some posthumous scandal? Were there women, were there boys, was there financial misdealing? Was there a Parliament Hill murder he feared I might recall?

"I'm sorry."

"No, I'm glad," he replied. "I'm very glad. You have the freedom of innocence. You will not approach my work in a tainted frame of mind. Your reading will not be corrupted by the, well, the malignant reputation I seem to have acquired."

"You'd better tell me," I said. As it happens, I'm a cancer survivor, and the word "malignant" echoed in my ears.

He nodded. "Let me first describe the legacy I thought I'd left behind. As poets, you and I do not expect financial luxury or great renown, do we?" He was speaking now with a kindly air, and even at the time, amid my lingering shock at his presence, I sensed he was working hard to win my sympathy. My allegiance. "Ours is still a young country, and it prefers to assign fame elsewhere. Sportsmen, starlets, tycoons—very well. Political leaders—so be it. But I believe we poets should command, at the very least, respect."

I suddenly noticed that his hands had begun to shake.

"Mr. Abley, I was a respected man. A highly respected man. I did not grow up amid wealth, with all its pleasures and temptations. The chance to enter university never came my way—I began to earn my daily bread at the age of seventeen. Yet many years later, the University of Toronto saw fit to grant me a doctoral degree. Queen's University followed suit."

He paused for a moment, as if rehearsing a text in his mind.

"Why did they pay me this honour? Because of my poetry, first and foremost, but in full knowledge of my other work too. Together with my friend Pelham Edgar, I edited a series of history books entitled *The Makers of Canada*. I helped to establish the Dominion Drama Festival, and for many years I was the secretary of the Royal Society of Canada. Eventually I served as president of that society and also of the Canadian Authors' Association, where I tried to ensure writers would receive fair copyright protection. Near the end of my life I did what I could, through the limited resources of the Canadian Authors' Foundation, to find money for writers in distress. I still had decades to live when Vincent Massey described me in print as 'one of the most distinguished men of letters in Canada.' In this country we do not have a poet laureate, but—"

"We do now," I said.

"Really? I am pleased to hear it." The expression on his face lightened. "Did you know that John Masefield, the poet laureate of Great Britain, declared that the experience of reading one of my early poems 'set me on fire,' as he put it, and left him determined to take up poetry himself?"

"I had no idea."

"Ah. Well, perhaps Canada is maturing at last. In my day its philistine tendencies were all too obvious. Its puritanical bent, too. Yet to return to my point: I can say in all honesty that if the office of poet laureate had existed in this country when Robert Borden or Richard Bennett was the prime minister, I should have been, let us say, high among the candidates. Or even Mackenzie King, though he might have preferred to appoint his infernal dog to the post."

"I believe you." Indeed, I suddenly felt like adding the word "sir."

"I saw eleven books into print in my lifetime. Mostly collections of poetry, but a fair number of short stories as well, and some non-fiction. Of course that figure does not include the private pamphlets and the little chapbooks, nor all the editing work I did on poor Archie Lampman's behalf. I have reason to believe other volumes of my writing may have appeared since 1947: selections, reprints, letters, that sort of thing. I learned—of course you will want to verify the wording for yourself—I learned that shortly after my death, the magazine *Saturday Night* published a tribute to me under the headline 'Great Poet, Great Man.'"

"*Saturday Night*," I said with interest. "That takes me back. I used to write a lot for the magazine. In fact I spent a couple of summers in Toronto working as an editor there."

"Did you indeed! It still thrives, I trust?"

"No, not for many years. There wasn't enough advertising. It's tremendously difficult for general-interest magazines to flourish in this country, or even survive. They're casualties of what people call progress."

Scott nodded. I suspect he would have enjoyed a good exchange on the subject, and it took some effort for him to maintain his focus. But he had not journeyed back from the shadowlands to discuss the dubious prospects for the Canadian magazine industry.

"You will understand me, Mr. Abley, when I say I used to be at peace in the afterlife. 'Great poet, great man'—not being a saint, I cannot pretend I was immune to such flattery. It has a consoling quality. I felt my work had not been in vain. And I worried about this a little, for I recognize there had been an element of drift in my life. As I wrote in one of my better poems, 'Why are there tears for failure?' If you will allow me to quote myself briefly:

Catch up the sands of the sea and count and count
The failures hidden in our sum of conquest.
Persistence is the master of this life;
The master of these little lives of ours;
To the end—effort—even beyond the end.

"And so time passed. But after many years, I'm not sure of the exact number, rumours began to reach me, stories—distressing stories. Stories suggesting that in place of the modest amount of recognition I had rightfully earned, my name had become notorious. I might even use the word infamous."

He paused, watching me closely to see how I would respond. I kept my face blank.

"I was never a good sleeper in the physical world, and now it has become difficult for me to rest in the afterlife. People casually say 'Rest in peace'—if they only knew!" A bitterness had made its way into his voice, and the furrows stood out in his pale forehead. "You see, as my life drew to a close, I was comforted by the knowledge that I had left a certain legacy— a legacy of service to Canada, and of service too, in a modest way, to the English language. In my poetry I sought to honour its traditions and its greatness. Yet I stood ready to serve my country in the hours when duty called. The long hours. In certain respects my daily life was a sustained answer to that call. Because of my attachment to duty, there were times when the imaginative voice fell silent within me."

"Your daily life?" I said. "Your attachment to duty? I don't understand. I don't really know what you're talking about, apart from your writing."

He stared at me in silence for a little while. I realized that these last remarks too had been a carefully prepared address, and that my offhand reaction was not what he had foreseen. Did I imagine seeing his upper lip tremble? But he kept his feelings under control.

"You will find out soon enough, I imagine."

"If I agree to act on your request."

"Exactly."

An SUV hurtled down the quiet street, taking the corner in front of my house too fast. Scott peered out in silent curiosity—vehicles in his day had a very different shape and speed. Yet he would not digress.

"And these rumours are what brought you here today?"

"They are," he said. "I could mention several examples, not that enough of them are clear in my mind. The details are jangled and obscure. But there was one event in particular. Let me describe the pain it caused me, even in the afterlife where one feels and sees through a glass darkly, as it were. Forgive the Biblical phrase—I mean no blasphemy. If you worked at *Saturday Night*, I suspect you may be acquainted with a magazine named *The Beaver*."

"Sure," I replied. "I've written for it as well. Only now it's called *Canada's History*. There were problems with its somewhat risqué name—search engine problems, I mean."

Scott peered at me hard. I realized this was his way of expressing puzzlement. "What could be risqué about our national animal?" he asked. "And what in the world is a search engine?"

"It's a little complicated to explain." I sensed that to embark on a description of new technology would lead nowhere. "Don't worry. I know the magazine you mean."

"Well. I have had to make a pest of myself. I have posed far more questions, you understand, than are welcomed in the realm of shadows." He gave a brief sigh. "But I recall seeing the first issue of *The Beaver*; it appeared in 1920 or so. I thought it was a magazine of genuine promise. Its devotion to history showed how far, so to speak, our country had come. Some years earlier I had written an essay on the three hundredth anniversary of Quebec City in which I said, 'We begin to be civilized when we celebrate and cherish the past.'"

"In that case, I'm not sure Canada is civilized yet. History is taught less and less in our schools. Nor is there any consensus on whose version of history young people should learn."

"I see." My interruption did not please him. "Or perhaps I don't. Surely you have an accepted version of history?" He struggled to recapture the flow of his story. "But speaking of *The Beaver*: 'A journal of progress,' the first editors called it. Very well. To my shame, to my horror, I have found out on good authority that quite recently their successors asked a panel of well-known figures to choose the ten worst Canadians of all time."

"Instead of the ten best."

"Precisely. The worst. It may be conceded that Adrien Arcand is a suitable name to appear on such a list—one of Quebec's most odious politicians. He was imprisoned during the recent war as a great admirer of Hitler. Kanao Inouye likewise. A devilish traitor. He grew up in Kamloops, returned to his parents' home in Japan and tortured some of the Canadian boys who were captured when the Japanese took Hong Kong. A few months before my death he was executed for treason. Good riddance, I say. I wasn't told the other names on the list. But tell me, why do I grovel in such company?"

"I'm sorry?"

"Why, Mr. Abley, why have I been publicly identified as one of the ten worst Canadians of all time?" His voice quavered again. I realized that only by a strenuous effort of will was he holding himself together. "It is an insult—an affront to the principles by which I lived, the values I worked to uphold. It is a gross caricature."

"I'm stunned," I said.

I was also perplexed. Surely the experts hired by *The Beaver* did not bear a consuming grudge against nature poems composed in a traditional form. If Scott had been embroiled in some peculiarly awful scandal—fraud, blackmail *and* murder? underage prostitutes of both sexes?—wouldn't I have read about it? His cheeks were slightly flushed. I thought it best not to press him.

"So now you know," he said. "Now you know. But now you have also met me. You see the man I am—the man I was—and you can imagine how I have suffered of late."

I nodded slowly.

"Let us turn to more cheerful matters. I am pleased to find you've read a little of my work, and I hope you will now want to see more. I don't suppose my poetry might still be for sale in one of Montreal's bookshops?"

"That's not very likely," I replied. I could have stated the truth more bluntly.

"No, of course. A public library, then. I live in hope—rather, I don't live in hope."

I smiled briefly. If it was a joke, it wasn't a very good one. He hurried on.

"I would like you to gain acquaintance with my poems and short stories, a few of my essays too, if you have the time. After some further conversations like this one, you will be equipped to write a defence—for discerning readers in your own time, I mean, as well as those in the future. Thankfully the educated men and women of my day knew nothing of the accusations, the lies." A short hesitation. If I hadn't been watching him closely, I might have missed the shade that came over his eyes. "But I realize you will also need to understand—better than I do, perhaps—why I now endure humiliation. I have an inkling, of course, and I can make certain remarks to you as a result. A sort of explanation, I mean. An apologia, though not an apology. Perhaps we can enlighten each other on my next visit. Are you prepared to make some inquiries?"

"What if you don't like what I find?"

"I must take that risk," he said. "You are your own man, and I have no reward to offer. No purse of gold. No seed grain or cattle, so to speak. But consider: unless I expected vindication, I would not have made these persistent attempts to revisit the world of light. My request having finally been granted, I can now be confident of meeting you again. I mean to continue until my name is cleared."

"I assume there must be certain things you preferred to hide," I said carefully. "Things that have come to light since 1947."

A couple of seconds passed before he answered. "Whatever may have come to light, I hid nothing. No more, I mean to say, than it was my duty to conceal, in the interests of the work I performed. The work I *faithfully* performed. I once wrote an ode to Canada in which I expressed my love of this country and my hope for its future. In it I spoke of our mountains, our great forests, our farmlands, and also of the marvellous birds and wildflowers that bring joy to the human soul. I asked the great power of the universe—you may use the word God if you like—to 'Purge us of Pride,' to 'Give Mind to match the glory of the gift,' and also to 'Give great Ideals to bridge the sordid rift / Between our heritage and our use of it.' I saw how that heritage

24

could be spoiled, you see. I asked for 'wisdom in the midst of our elation,' knowing full well that 'freedom brings the deepest obligation.' When my poems were collected in a single volume, it seemed appropriate to place this ode at the front." He paused. I wasn't sure how to respond. Finally he carried on. "And having done this, having poured out my noblest patriotic feelings and shaped them in verse—that I should now be called one of the worst Canadians of all time—at first I thought it must be a bad joke."

He fell silent.

"But it wasn't," I said at last.

"No. And now I cannot rest. If you are disposed to clear my name, you will learn," and now his eyes were shining a little brighter behind his spectacles, "'I am a man more sinned against than sinning.'"

"I recognize the quote. *King Lear.*"

"Like so many other lines in Shakespeare, it rings true."

"And these attacks have been driving you mad?"

He inclined his head and said nothing.

I stood up, holding out my right hand. He raised himself too, a little awkwardly, as if having use of a body again was a challenge as well as a novelty. The lines on his forehead appeared less prominent now. He stood tall, as though a weight had been lifted from his jacketed shoulders, and straightened his tie. "I regret not being able to give you my hand," he said in a friendly tone. "But my appearance is a kind of illusion. Not my presence, which I assure you is just as real as that splendid deciduous tree outside your window. A maple, I believe?"

"Yes, it is. It'll need to be trimmed in the summer. But are you giving me any particular deadline? I do have other commitments."

"Of course. The winter is now at its height, I suppose. Shall we say I hope to return in March, when, if you're lucky, Montreal may be feeling the initial stirrings of spring?"

"No problem. I don't suppose I'll have had the chance to write anything by then, but I promise I'll have done some research. And I'll have read your work."

"I appreciate your candour." He leaned toward me and spoke in an unnecessarily low voice. "It might be best if you don't say a word about my visits to anyone. Not even your family. There could be a risk of—well, complications. Is that agreed?"

I nodded.

"Thank you, Mr. Abley. Your decision is gratifying. I am obliged to you."

"No, thank *you*, Mr. Scott. Dr. Scott, I mean."

I meant to tell him how extraordinary it was to come face to face, voice to voice, mind to mind, with a man from my great-grandparents' generation—a Victorian, in fact—but in an instant, without warning, he was gone.

2

Heart's Blood on the Feathers

OVER THE NEXT TWO months I did the research he wanted.

I learned that the dead man who had stood in my dining room and sat in my blue armchair had been born in 1862, in a parsonage at the corner of Queen and Metcalfe, a couple of blocks from what would soon be called Parliament Hill. In those days Ottawa was a lumber town of some 12,000 people, still unready to be a national capital. Duncan Campbell Scott would spend nearly all his adult life there, watching the raw settlement grow into a lively city with aspirations to grandeur. A very discreet man, he wrote little about his childhood. But it's clear he was often moved around—his father, William Scott, a Methodist minister, served various churches in eastern Ontario and Quebec. Growing up in a succession of half-built small towns, the boy had no chance to form lasting friendships. He learned to rely on his inner resources.

His mother, Janet MacCallum Scott, came from a family of Gaelic-speaking Highlanders. Among the few details recorded about her is that she had to comfort her little son on a summer Sunday when Duncan had been playing outside his father's church and burst into the service in loud tears. "Oh mummy, look!" he cried. "I've been bitten by a harlot!" Her brother Duncan MacCallum, who held a professorship in obstetrics and gynecology at McGill University, was a forceful advocate of vaccination—then a controversial practice in Quebec—and of total abstinence from alcohol. Reverend William Scott was of the same opinion: in 1860 he published a volume entitled *The Teetotaler's Hand-Book*.

The younger Duncan hoped to follow his uncle into the field of medicine. But clergymen did not earn large salaries, and William Scott could not afford to give his son a university education. What he *did* have was a useful connection to the prime minister of Canada. "Nobody deserves more at my hands than you," Sir John A. Macdonald wrote to William Scott in November 1879. "I shall have great pleasure in helping your son to a position in the public service at an early day." Macdonald was as good as his word—patronage in Ottawa was direct and immediate during Victorian times. Before Christmas, the boy had a job.

For more than fifty-two years Duncan Campbell Scott would work in the federal civil service. Having started off as a junior copy clerk, accepting dictation from his superiors, he mastered bookkeeping, becoming a first-class clerk and his department's chief accountant. He gained an intimate knowledge of the system's inner workings by seeing how and where money flowed. He was discreet, efficient, ambitious. But accountancy was not the most important thing in his life. In the mid-1880s, after he met Archibald Lampman, a young writer with a dead-end job elsewhere, he turned his hand to poetry. Both men gained pleasure and inspiration from the canoe trips, short and long, they took together. Rumour had it that Scott also harboured an unfulfilled love for Lampman's sister Annie.

Sometimes dreamy in his poetry, the accountant was meticulous and exacting on the job. Rising smoothly through the ranks, he eventually reached the heights of Deputy Superintendent-General—deputy minister, we'd say now. In the eyes of his peers and superiors, he performed his duties superbly. His public life was a triumph, but in private he grew intimate with sadness. Archibald Lampman lost a battle with heart disease at the age of thirty-seven; other friends also died young; and for much of his adult life Scott was estranged from his mother and sisters.

Through all this he earned a good living from the government and wrote poems and short stories as and when he could. It was a busy, seemingly blameless existence. Scott was never one to loosen his tie and go pub-crawling with other writers, yet despite the severity of his manner he became a mainstay of the city's small artistic community. His rambling house on Lisgar Street—built in 1887 to his own specifications, and expanded to twelve rooms in 1926—boasted a small tower and an unusual wealth of windows for a late Victorian building. As the years went by he filled its walls with paintings and drawings by the likes of David Milne, Clarence Gagnon and Pegi Nicol. By the standards of Ottawa, seldom a hotbed of artistic novelty, his taste was daring and assured. A three-storey affair in dark brick, the house was an easy stroll from Sparks Street, Ottawa's commercial thoroughfare, and also from the Houses of Parliament. Scott worked first in the Langevin Block, facing Parliament Hill, and then in the East Block, before the department's headquarters moved in 1913 to the Booth Building on Sparks Street.

He wrote little about Ottawa. The main exception is an awkward, uneven novel that remained unpublished until long after his death. When he attempted to ground his writing in the places he saw every day, the results were occasionally embarrassing: "Across the stream float faintly beautiful / The antiphonal bells of Hull…" He set most of his short stories in the past; most of them, too, in rural Quebec, where he had lived as a teenage boy and which he continued to visit as a young man, often in Lampman's company. The lakes and mountains of the Eastern Townships gave him, he once remarked, "my first impression of romantic scenery." He was among the earliest writers of fiction in English Canada to pay respectful, vivid attention to the lives of French Canadians.

Scott's literary talent blazed brighter in his poems. Margaret Atwood, when she edited the *New Oxford Book of Canadian Verse* in 1982, granted him eleven pages; only two authors in the entire collection have more. The best of his poems combined precise observations of the natural world with a shrewd grasp of human character and a superb rhythmic sense. Classical music was a passion for him. He had learned the piano in his Methodist boyhood—both his sisters became music teachers—and he continued to play it well as an adult. The big, high-ceilinged music room at the back of his house contained a grand piano.

For the young Scott, music was the food of love: his wife, Belle Botsford, was a professional violinist from Boston. Lady Aberdeen, the consort of the governor general, had been so impressed by a recital in January 1894 that she asked Belle to remain some days longer in Ottawa and perform at an evening reception in Rideau Hall. The shy civil servant filled in as her accompanist. As they rehearsed, they fell in love. Months later Miss Botsford became Mrs. Scott. "Canadian Government Attaché Marries a Well-Known Violinist," the *Boston Globe* announced.

Belle was a proud, headstrong American. One of Scott's close friends called her "a stunning redhead, with wonderful warmth and vividness of personality." Another used the word "imperious." Apart from giving solo violin performances, often of the more showy and difficult pieces in the repertoire, she ran a concert company under her own name. At least, she did so before her marriage—like nearly all women of the time, she sacrificed her own career to that of her husband. Not entirely, however: in 1905, eleven years after she married Scott, she made her London debut under her maiden name. The handbills for her recital at the Aeolian Hall on New Bond Street stated that Madame Belle Botsford, even then, came from "Boston, USA."

Forced to live in Ottawa, a much smaller city than she was accustomed to, she replaced most of her musical ambitions with social ones. In the last years of the nineteenth century and the first years of the twentieth, Belle compiled elegant scrapbooks of her dinner cards and party invitations. To look at them now is to imbibe a distant aftertaste of the gilded age. A cocktail party here, a bridge afternoon there, an invitation to the governor general's "At Home"…The social columnist who called herself Amaryllis, writing in *Saturday Night,* described an Ottawa lunch party in honour of George Washington's birthday at which "Mrs. Duncan Campbell Scott's loyalty showed itself in a massive brooch, holding a miniature of George Washington, in the form of a hatchet." Some who failed to make the social grade—or didn't care about the social whirl—regarded Belle as a snob.

She gave birth to one child, a daughter born in 1895. Elizabeth Duncan Scott was the light of her parents' lives. From a very early age she wrote poems, made up stories, drew clever pictures of cats. She also had a gift for music. At the age of eleven, she died of scarlet fever.

Belle's social climbing came to an abrupt stop with her daughter's death, and the bright extravagant frocks gave way to black. She did not play the violin again in public. In 1913 Rupert Brooke, a dashing young writer touring from London, called on the Scotts and found the Lisgar Street house "queerly desolate." He liked Scott, describing him as "the only poet in Canada," but added, "Poor devil, he's so lonely and dried there: no one to talk to." He was exaggerating, but not by much. When Scott, having driven his guest out to a country club, raised his whisky and soda and said, "Well, here's to your youth!" Brooke nearly broke into tears.

In her later years Belle became a chain-smoker, more and more irritable. She filled some of her days with charitable work. In 1929 she died.

Scott had continued walking the few blocks from his home to his office in the months after Archie Lampman died; he had continued walking to the office in the months after Elizabeth died; he continued walking to the office after Belle died too. And in 1931, by now a well-known figure in Ottawa, he surprised the city by marrying the niece of his friend and neighbour Arthur Bourinot. Elise Aylen was also a writer, at least an aspiring one, a shy, small, round-faced woman with a love of ancient history and a keen interest in mysticism. She had little desire to make an impression on society. Elise was forty-two years younger than her husband, and she looked after him devotedly. In his old age Scott could at last repair the breach with his sisters that had opened wide soon after he married Belle; his mother had died unreconciled.

He retired in 1932, a few months short of his seventieth birthday. As the Western world sank into the Great Depression, Scott had the time and ease to devote to the poetry and music that had long been his private delights. He and Elise sailed to Italy and Britain; he wrote poems about Ligurian olive groves, Swiss birdsong and Shropshire hills, while she worked on a lengthy novel about Anglo-Saxon England in the age of the Venerable Bede. The couple spent their winters in the mild and genteel comfort of Victoria, Vancouver, even Arizona. After they bought a painting by Emily Carr, she gave them another and sent a handwritten letter expressing thanks for "the beauty & pleasure Dr. Scott has given to Canada through his poems." He was named a Companion of the Order of St. Michael and St. George; an influential critic, E.K. Brown, became a dear friend and saw to the growth of his literary reputation. Now, despite his lifelong reticence, Scott was glad to meet visiting painters, musicians and authors. A string quartet would occasionally perform in the music room. He was eighty-four when the literary editor of the *Toronto Globe and Mail,* William Arthur Deacon, described him as "a figure of incarnate courage."

"To those who knew him well," wrote his friend Arthur Bourinot, "he never seemed old. If any man has ever drunk the waters of eternal youth it was he. His spirit never failed, faltered or aged." Scott wrote and published nearly to the end, seldom looking back on the government department where he had worked so much of his life.

~

THAT DEPARTMENT WAS INDIAN Affairs.

Scott oversaw the residential schools. He expanded their number and scope. He rewrote parts of the Indian Act, making attendance in departmentally approved schools a requirement for all Aboriginal children on reserves. Having spent four years as the superintendent of Indian education, he knew that most of these schools were shoddily built havens of infectious disease. But, as a prudent guardian of the government's finances, he resisted calls to fund the schools more generously. After a promotion in 1913 put him in charge of the entire department, he set out to destroy the traditional Longhouse system of governance at Six Nations, the most populous reserve in the country. He crafted legislation that prevented Indian bands from hiring their own counsel; instead they had to rely on lawyers handpicked by his department. He enforced laws that made it a criminal offence to take part in spiritual ceremonies like the sun dance. He did much else besides. It was a time when the population of Canada was expanding fast, yet the number of Aboriginal people stood at its lowest level ever.

He was a poet. At the visionary height of English Romanticism, Percy Shelley had described poets as "the influence which is moved not, but moves," and as "the unacknowledged legislators of the world." A century later, in Canada's Department of Indian Affairs, a poet was the immovable influence, the acknowledged legislator. So effectively did Duncan Campbell Scott perform his job that for a whole generation of Aboriginal people, his was the defining voice of Ottawa, the government's stone face. When they dared to submit a complaint or make a request, his was the declining

signature scrawled at the foot of the letter. His power was so great that activists today accuse him of genocide.

This is not a word he would have recognized. It was coined in 1944, with
reference to the horrific slaughter of Jews still occurring in Nazi-controlled
Europe. Scott died three years later, just as "genocide" was beginning to
gain a wide currency. Yet in our time, as dozens of websites reveal, his name
is often linked to the term. In 2012, for example, a staff member of *Obiter
Dicta,* the newspaper of Osgoode Hall Law School in Toronto, wrote: "The
Indian residential school system was a government initiative intended to
achieve 'aggressive assimilation.' Ultimately, the aim of the Indian residential school system was cultural genocide. Dr. Duncan Campbell Scott in
1920 referred to my ancestors as an 'Indian problem' that Canada needed
to rid itself of."

Ashley Stacey was quoting a speech Scott gave before a committee
of the House of Commons looking at proposed amendments to the Indian Act. He had drafted those amendments. They gave his department
the power to deprive any Indian in the country of his or her treaty rights,
granting in their place "involuntary enfranchisement." These abstract poly-
syllables meant that Scott and his fellow civil servants would henceforth
enjoy the power to decide who was and was not an Indian. In his eyes, an
enforced loss of identity seemed a trivial price to pay for the privilege of
becoming a Canadian citizen with the power to vote, to own property, to
reside anywhere in the country—and not to spend one's entire life at the
mercy of Indian Affairs. Speaking to the politicians with greater bluntness
and fewer qualifications than he would allow himself in print, Scott said:
"I want to get rid of the Indian problem…That is my whole point. Our
objective is to continue until there is not a single Indian in Canada that has
not been absorbed into the body politic, and there is no Indian question,
and no Indian department, and that is the whole object of this Bill."

Today those remarks have an ugly ring. Behind Scott's sharp words,
however, is the conventional wisdom of his time: Indians needed to be assimilated into the mainstream of society. They had no other option; they
could have no better hope. In the department's annual report for 1920, Scott
expressed this belief in more measured language: "The ultimate object of

our Indian policy is to merge the natives in the citizenship of the country."
This was not a controversial statement—nearly all Canadians shared his
conviction. Many still do, although they may be cautious about saying so
too loudly. Assimilation was, and to them continues to be, an ideal.

The prime method of achieving this goal was the network of residential schools. By 1920 more than eighty of them existed; many others would
be founded in the years to come. These institutions, which lay scattered
across several provinces and both territories, were particularly common
in Western Canada, where most of the department's money was spent.
Roman Catholic and Protestant churches promoted the schools as charitable and missionary projects; they met some of the costs; they provided
the staff. The churches were partners of the government, and often pushy
ones. After all, they were out to save souls. The idealists among the teachers believed they had a mission to rescue Aboriginal children from the grip
of heathen beliefs, to give them a new outlook on the world, and to equip
them to survive amid the hurly-burly of modern society. Only a few of the
teachers were idealists.

From Vancouver Island to Nova Scotia, the Department of Indian Affairs laid out the rules and oversaw the system. The department also fur-
nished much of the money, paying churches on a per capita basis according
to the number of students in a school. Whether they were operated by
Catholics, Anglicans, Methodists or Presbyterians, the residential schools
all followed a single overarching principle: by making it impossible for
Aboriginal children to eat their own food, speak their own language, wear
their own clothes, master their own traditions, practise their own religion,
live with their own parents and learn from their own elders, the school
would allow those children to be "absorbed into the body politic." Once
they had abandoned their culture, once they no longer thought of themselves as Indian, they would no longer pose the Canadian government a
problem.

The word jars. For Scott to announce there was a single "Indian problem" or "Indian question"—and to further declare he and his government
knew the answer—betrays an astonishing level of confidence. Or naiveté.
Or just plain arrogance. In the aftermath of all the white papers, debates,

speeches, consultations, reports, documentaries, hearings, memoranda, books, conferences, editorials and royal commissions looking at indigenous issues over the last forty-five years, only the foolhardy would dare to suggest there is a single answer. Indeed, are there even problems? At least until the growth of the Idle No More movement, the most popular response to indigenous concerns appeared to be denial: in June 2012 an Ipsos Reid survey found that two-thirds of all respondents across the country agreed that "Canada's Aboriginal people are treated well by the Canadian government." An even larger number said they believed the government gives Aboriginal people too much money.

Weariness has set in. Impatience, too. Only the activists and a few historians, it seems, look back in anger. Most Canadians prefer to let bygones be bygones. Over the past few years, the nation's public history has turned into a feel-good affair of soldierly celebrations, smiling anniversaries and flag-waving at reconstructed forts. TV ads, websites and brochures entice us to visit these forts with promises that we can travel "back in time to the rugged, adventurous days of the fur trade" or "follow interpretive guides as they lead you through the tumultuous past." Better not to look too closely at what the tumult entailed. We speed along divided "highways of heroes." The unheroic byways of history are becoming overgrown.

When they can be roused to peer into the past and think about Aboriginal issues, one of the few points most non-Aboriginal Canadians reluctantly seem to agree on is that the residential schools—the spine and hallmark of Scott's policy—proved a sad failure. The full scope of that failure, though, is still not widely understood. I suspect a lot of people imagine residential schools in much the same way they might regard the "prosperity certificates" that the Social Credit government issued to every citizen of Alberta in the 1930s: a misguided effort, conceived and carried out in a spirit of goodwill, that fell short of its worthy aims. "The past is a foreign country," L.P. Hartley's novel *The Go-Between* begins; "they do things differently there." Were the residential schools merely a sign of that difference?

In truth, the failure of the system goes much deeper than many Canadians have brought themselves to acknowledge. The Social Credit effort to challenge the banking system petered out with little impact. But the schools are another story. They existed for well over a century; they had a pivotal, life-changing effect on dozens of First Nations, hundreds of communities, hundreds of thousands of people. Their impact has not yet reached an end. Christopher Powell, a sociologist at the University of Manitoba, recently argued that "the Indian residential school system, in both its stated intent and its observable effects, meets the definition of genocide specified in the United Nations Genocide Convention of 1948. Article 2 of that convention defines genocide as certain acts 'committed with intent to destroy, in whole or in part, a national, ethnical, racial or religious group, as such,' and includes in the specified acts, 'forcibly transferring children of the group to another group.'"

Genocide again. Can a more terrible charge be laid against a nation? In his article, Powell cited the single most damning phrase Scott is said to have uttered: that the purpose of the residential system was "to kill the Indian in the child." Many other commentators have quoted the same words. In June 2008 Stephen Harper used the phrase when he stood in the House of Commons and apologized for the mistreatment of Aboriginal children in the residential schools: "Some sought, as it was infamously said, 'to kill the Indian in the child.' Today, we recognize that this policy of assimilation was wrong, has caused great harm, and has no place in our country." The prime minister was, for once, applauded by members of all parties.

But the offending phrase is not Scott's. He never used those words. Neither did any other Canadian official. The quotation can be traced back to a somewhat different statement uttered by a high-ranking officer in the U.S. Army, Richard Henry Pratt, the nineteenth-century superintendent of a residential school in Pennsylvania: "All the Indian there is in the race should be dead. Kill the Indian in him, and save the man." The sentiment is an alarming one, though in his day Pratt was known as a friend of the Indians. In 1996 the final report of the Royal Commission on Aboriginal Peoples accurately quoted the first of Pratt's sentences, and paraphrased the second with "child" replacing "man." After the report's publication, the revised phrase began to circulate on the Internet. It soon became notorious and was widely attributed to Scott. An article that appeared in Postmedia

News in 2012, for example, stated that the residential schools "for 150 years operated on a government mandate to 'kill the Indian in the child,' in the famous words of Duncan Campbell Scott, the head of the Department of Indian Affairs from 1913 to 1932."

Perhaps the mistake doesn't matter too much. The wording of a single phrase is infinitely less important than the fruits of a long career; and overall, Scott's work has come to appear the embodiment of a national calamity. The policies he tirelessly worked to implement were designed to produce graduates who could never go back to a traditional way of life—and to that limited extent, they succeeded. Unfortunately, the schools succeeded at little else. They broke but could not rebuild; they maimed but could not create. The coercive methods employed throughout the system were supposed to unleash a flow of young Indians adept with teaspoons and shovels, shoelaces and Bible verses, and eager for absorption into the Canadian mainstream. They did not. Yet since the phrase "to kill the Indian in the child" has entered public consciousness as a repulsive symbol of Canadian policy in general and of Scott's moral turpitude in particular, it bears repeating that he said no such thing.

The residential schools were imbued by Christianity from the start. Catholics, who ran a slight majority of institutions, wanted to save their charges from both paganism and Protestantism; the Protestants were equally keen on preventing innocent boys and girls from falling into the clutches of the Pope. Either way, the language of salvation would also be the language of instruction: English. (Only a few residential schools existed in Quebec, and for a relatively short period.) Children across the country suffered beatings and humiliation if they were caught speaking their own tongue. A century ago more than fifty indigenous languages flourished in Canada, some of them as different from each other as English is from Chinese. Teachers and administrators in the residential schools referred to all these languages as "Indian dialect." Generations of children grew up associating their family's language with physical and mental pain. Most of the languages are now in serious, perhaps terminal, decline.

Apart from conversion and assimilation, the schools had other aims as well. The buffalo having been massacred to near-extinction, and the

prairies having been thrown open to agriculture, the Blackfoot, Assiniboine and Plains Cree could no longer survive as hunters, so the schools
in Alberta, Saskatchewan and Manitoba tried to turn boys into farmers.
Schools elsewhere attempted to fit Indian boys for other jobs: loggers, car-
penters, mechanics. Girls were taught housewifely duties like laundry and
sewing. The government, instead of paying the schools for their upkeep
and repairs, their cleaning and fresh vegetables, wanted the students to
look after such matters themselves. In practice, this meant that much of
the children's time went into maintaining the institutions where they were
forcibly confined.

The Ojibwa writer Basil H. Johnston was among the victims. In the
1940s he suffered sexual and physical abuse at the Spanish School in northern Ontario, abuse that for many years he kept secret even from his wife.
"We had all been damaged in some way," Johnston wrote six decades after
his school experience, when the shame was losing its terrible power at
last. "Even those who had not been ravished suffered wounds, scars, and
blemishes to heart, mind, and spirit that would never fully heal. Those who
suffered most damage were the little four-, five-, and six-year-old boys and
girls, cast into these prison-like institutions when they were just out of
babyhood. Little outcasts they were, cast out of their communities, homes,
families; motherless, fatherless, unwanted, unloved. They had nothing.
What they needed was love … For such, there was no childhood."

The administrators of the system never pretended to offer love. It was
hard, especially for the Protestant schools, to recruit and retain staff who
were willing to work for a low salary in a distant corner of Canada. Both
the Protestant and Catholic systems ended up hiring a large number of
unqualified teachers, and academic standards, such as they were, suffered
accordingly. In 1905, when Scott was the chief clerk of Indian Affairs, his
annual salary stood at $2,500 (over $70,000 in today's money). It was more
than eight times higher than the $300 salary earned by teachers in many of
the residential schools.

Throughout Scott's career, and for many years after, most of the schools
did not offer high-school programs; there was no attempt to equip even
the brightest students for college or university. The very idea would have

struck many Canadians as bizarre. Indians did not have the right to vote in a federal election until 1960. Nor, in Scott's day, could Indians enter into a contract, make a legal will, or obtain a licence to conduct a business without the federal government's approval. For in legal terms, an Indian was a child. The Indian Act, which became law in 1876, shortly before Scott's arrival in the department, was explicit: "The term 'person' means an individual other than an Indian, unless the context clearly requires another construction."

Indians were not persons. Yet the residential schools were meant to impart a spirit of self-reliance. This was a paradoxical task, given that the children had no choice but to attend; those whose self-reliance led them to escape faced severe punishment as soon as they were recaptured. Some ran away and were not recaptured: they froze or starved to death.

These policies and practices would endure, with minor variations, throughout much of Canada's history. Having begun on a small scale in the nineteenth century, the residential system grew and grew, gradually acquiring the weight of inertia. After the Second World War, even when Scott's successors in Indian Affairs hoped to abolish the network, the Catholic church in the West applied strong political pressure to make sure its schools survived. The failures of the system had become common knowledge long before the last residential school, originally an Anglican-run establishment in the Touchwood Hills of south-central Saskatchewan, closed down in 1996. By then its long-time supervisor, William Starr, was serving a prison sentence for the sexual abuse he had inflicted on boys between seven and fourteen years of age. Soon after the final bell rang and the heavy doors clanged shut for the last time, the school was demolished. About 230 men would eventually receive a settlement from the federal government for the abuse that Starr had perpetrated over many years. At least six other men were unable to do so. They had committed suicide.

⁓

THE TRADITIONAL WAYS WERE dying: Scott believed this. Nearly everyone believed it. The past was nomadic; the future was agricultural and industrial; he trusted it would also be imperial. The poet in him had started off as something of a cultural nationalist, keen to evoke Canadian landscapes, proud to write on Canadian themes. Yet the poet in Scott was at the mercy of his political convictions, his public faith. As an old man in 1939, he fulfilled a commission to celebrate a royal tour by delivering a servile ode in which he promised the people of this country would "do our part in high and pure endeavour / To build a peaceful Empire round the throne." The CBC broadcast the poem from its Halifax studios as the king and queen were sailing out of Halifax harbour back to an England on the brink of war. Three months before Scott died, he semi-facetiously wrote to a friend, "Why don't you order a poem on some special subject, say the marriage of Princess Elizabeth, if the CBC would pay me for it!" Against what he had called, in his ode, the "ageless, deep devotion" of Canadians to the Crown, he found it only natural to believe that Aboriginal cultures, languages and ways of life were doomed.

The surprise, or paradox, or twist of the knife is that while doing his utmost to enforce government control over indigenous people, Scott made them the subject of his most vibrant writing. Of the eleven pages Margaret Atwood found for him in the *New Oxford Book of Canadian Verse,* eight are devoted to poems about Indians. These items form a small minority of his total output; they also show his talents at their best. When John Masefield spoke at a memorial service held for Scott in St. Martin-in-the-Fields, London, the British poet laureate declared that Scott had been deeply impressed by many of the Indians he had met: "Admiration is a great help to understanding. In his poems and stories about them we are brought, perhaps for the very first time, to a living knowledge of what they are."

A colder view is possible. Perhaps Scott was simply using Indians for his own literary gain. In her book *The Laughing One: A Journey to Emily Carr,* Susan Crean condemned him as a "thin-blooded bureaucrat" who "rather perversely…wrote lyric poetry that idolized the very vanishing race whose affairs he was governing." His job gave him access to rare material, thanks to which he could make Aboriginal stories and customs appear picturesque. Yet this is not the whole story. In the early twentieth century how many other writers, anywhere in the English-speaking world, would have written an ode in praise of indigenous names?

> They flow like water, or like wind they flow,
> Waymoucheeching, loon-haunted Manowan,
> Far Mistassini by her frozen wells,
> Gold-hued Wayagamac brimming her wooded dells:
> Lone Kamouraska, Metapedia,
> And Metlakahtla ring a round of bells.

The bells of Metlakahtla, though, were tolling an Anglican tune: this isolated Tsimshian settlement on the Pacific coast lay under the rigid control of its founder, an evangelical missionary named William Duncan who called traditional First Nations beliefs "demoniacal."

The general assumption was that the people from whose mouths such evocative names had sprung did not have long to live. "Indian Place-Names" begins in a very different spirit from the lines quoted above: "The race has waned and left but tales of ghosts…" The names, and perhaps the tales, are all that will survive. One of Scott's most accomplished sonnets, "The Onondaga Madonna," describes "This woman of a weird and waning race"; her infant child, presumably the son of a white man, is "The latest promise of her nation's doom." He wrote the poem in 1898, a year in which his department's report from the Six Nations reserve in southern Ontario, where Canada's Onondaga lived, noted that "The general health has been unusually good during the year" and "The Indians are constantly improving their homes by better ventilation." Scott the civil servant had to worry about ventilation and epidemics; Scott the poet preferred to contemplate doom.

"The Onondaga Madonna" tackles assimilation as a subject. It is tougher and more complex than the bulk of his work, which features regular appearances by mists, flowers, exclamation marks, and beauty with a capital B. The sonnet's bleakness recurs in other poems that touch on what Scott saw as the degraded condition and miserable fate of Aboriginal people. In his late poem "A Scene at Lake Manitou," for instance, an Ojibwa woman sits below some cedars and watches her adolescent son die. Against the illness that had also killed his father, the white men's medicine and religion are of no help. Desperate, the woman reverts to her old beliefs and tries to win the help of the lake's spirit by throwing her most treasured possessions into the water: a gramophone, a little sewing machine, her blankets... The boy dies anyway. Bereaved and alone, yet still defiant, the woman stares at a line of distant, burned-out trees. The image comes to symbolize her people's destiny:

> Standing ruins of blackened spires
> Charred by the fury of fires
> That had passed that way,
> That were smouldering and dying out in the West
> At the end of the day.

The image recalls a sentence in a biography Scott had written many years earlier of John Graves Simcoe, the first governor of Upper Canada: "The Indian nature now seems like a fire that is waning, that is smouldering and dying away in ashes." More distantly, it echoes some heartbroken lines that commemorate his daughter's death:

> The dew falls and the stars fall,
> The sun falls in the west,
> But never more
> Through the closed door,
> Shall the one that I loved best
> Return to me...

Elizabeth had brought "the beauty of sunrise" into the poet's life. Now the sun had gone. Writing to his friend Pelham Edgar a few weeks after her death, Scott said: "In no merely rhetorical way I say it seems impossible for us to go on." But he went on. Indeed, he lived another forty years in the rambling house on Lisgar Street, where the music room would always contain, along with the grand piano and the painted landscapes, a few of his daughter's favourite toys.

The Deputy Superintendent-General of Indian Affairs would not have put it quite this way in his terse memos to the minister, but his imaginative writings suggest what he believed his day job entailed: managing the final years of a doomed people. They were smouldering. They were dying out. They were falling in the west.

~

A SLIGHT TREMBLING IN the air. A cultured voice from the next room. "Mr. Abley. We meet again. I trust you are well?"

I'd been expecting him to reappear for weeks, and trying to prepare myself. What could I say to a man responsible for policies that had inflicted so much pain and caused so much grief? But with no means of knowing when he might come back, I found it impossible to stay at a pitched height of readiness for long. I took one practical measure: searching out a few of the most crucial statements, printing them, and putting them in a folder on the coffee table. As the March days passed, I began to wonder if his January visit had been merely an extended fantasy, a long and vivid hallucination. Winter faded like a snowprint in the sun. When at last he did return, late on a sunny afternoon while I was standing in the kitchen, waiting for the kettle to boil and starting to think about the dinner I'd promised to cook for my family, I was taken by surprise.

"Doing okay, thanks. And you?"

Duncan Campbell Scott was gazing out of the dining-room window, a look of amusement on his face. The discreet tie, the suit, the tab collar and the polished shoes appeared the same: a little too elegant to be understated, a little too understated to be elegant. "The dead are always—okay. We do not suffer from heartburn or gout. Or tooth decay. You might say it's an advantage. One of the few."

"Indeed." I took a teabag out of its package and disposed of the cold tea lingering in the bottom of the pot. Now that he had arrived at last, I felt suddenly reluctant to converse with him. How could I bring myself to tell the man—the ghost—that the work he did for Indian Affairs appalled me?

"I'll wait until you've poured your tea," he said in the manner of a casual friend. "Don't hurry. But tell me, what has become of all the snow? Your garden is looking astonishingly green, or should I say brown." He waved a long hand toward the damp dead leaves that occupied the flowerbeds and lay scattered over the lawn. "Unless I'm sadly mistaken, you are still in March."

"Most of the snow has been gone for a while," I told him. "Last week the temperature went up to 27 degrees—I mean 27 Celsius. That must be about 80 Fahrenheit. The other day when I was coming home I saw violets in my neighbour's hedge."

He shook his head. "Extraordinary. The weather in Montreal is hardly different from the weather in Ottawa. I recall no such thing in March."

"No, you wouldn't," I said grimly. "But this is the twenty-first century, and the world's climate is changing fast. Deserts are expanding, coral reefs are dying, and governments refuse to do a thing to stop it. Especially Canada's, I mean. Scientists are warning that soon the Arctic Ocean won't have any summer ice, and not much in the winter either. Polar bears will probably go extinct." I paused: he was looking stricken. I realized I had transferred my anxiety about his visit into a rant. "I'm sorry, I shouldn't be troubling you with all this."

"No more summer ice in the Arctic!" he said. "I suppose the Eskimos must be alarmed."

"I'm glad you remember the Inuit," I replied. "They're a remarkable people, and some of them are prospering. You'd be amazed how successful they've been with their sculptures and prints. Their artwork has been bought by some of the finest museums in the world."

"I recall Diamond Jenness praising their ingenuity. Not that I felt one could always trust the opinions of an anthropologist."

"Jenness was right," I said. "He lived among them and he knew them well. But of course climate change will transform their whole way of life."

"Of course. No doubt that's how it has to be." Scott's voice had acquired a resigned tone. "The way of the modern world—it means a series of difficult adjustments. What is the general state of the Indians today, I wonder?"

Having carried my tea into the living room, I had just taken the first sip.

Now I saw an opening. I put the mug down on the coffee table and looked him in the eye.

"A series of adjustments," I repeated. "But those adjustments don't have to be inhumane. They don't have to be brutal. Change can happen when indigenous people are ready and willing. They have a say in the matter too. Or they do now. It's their life, after all. When you were in charge of the Indian department, you simply told them what they had to do—you never gave them a choice. On some of the western reserves, they were prisoners—for years they couldn't leave the reserve without a pass from the local Indian agent. The government treated the adults like children and it treated the children, well, not much better than animals."

I saw his eyebrows rise, but I carried on.

"We stole everything from them: their traditions, their languages, their economy, their self-respect. Not to mention their land. It's no wonder that when *The Beaver* asked him to nominate one of the worst Canadians of all time, Will Ferguson made the choice he did. As you said on your previous visit, the name Duncan Campbell Scott is mud."

Even though this hadn't come out as gracefully as I'd hoped, it was enough to reduce him to a dismayed silence.

"I know that isn't what you wanted me to say." I could feel my heart pounding in my chest. "But I've done some research. And I've found out things about you that strike people today as shameful. Unforgivable."

"Tell me." His voice was quiet, his hands pressed together at the fingertips.

"You outlawed the potlatch on the west coast. Well, I realize you didn't do it personally, but you chose to enforce the repressive laws on the books. You did the same for the sun dance on the prairies. And it's not as though you were a bishop or a businessman—you were a poet. How could a poet set out to destroy another culture? Or think of the residential schools. You oversaw them for what, four years? Then you got a promotion and were named deputy minister—"

"Deputy Superintendent-General," he interrupted, his tone frosty.

"Whatever. So really, you stayed in charge of the schools for another nineteen years. The department was yours. You held these people's lives in the palm of your hand. And the schools were hellholes. They were places of abject misery. Sites of unforgivable pain."

"I notice you're employing the past tense," he said. "Have all the schools been closed?"

"Yes, thank goodness, although the last of them stayed open for nearly fifty years after your death. I think lots of Canadians have trouble believing it now. How did this disaster happen? We can't believe our own forefathers could have done this."

"Done what, exactly?"

"Well, perpetrated the abuse that Aboriginal children suffered."

"Are you accusing all your forefathers of abuse? Rather excessive, surely. But tell me."

I took a long swig of tea and opened the yellow folder on the coffee table. The first page in it was a quote from *They Came for the Children,* the interim report issued in 2012 by the Truth and Reconciliation Commission of Canada. It reads less like a standard official document than like a short and devastating book, in which Scott's photograph appears on an early page. The young Yousuf Karsh had captured the retired civil servant in an anxious pose, leaning forward with his brow vertically furrowed, his chin resting on his left hand, his right hand on his hip. One side of his face caught the light; the other remained in shadow. *They Came for the Children* includes a few statements by Scott, each more damning than the last. But that afternoon I didn't quote any of his own words back at him. Instead I cleared my throat and read a statement that appears at the beginning of the report:

"Residential schools disrupted families and communities. They prevented elders from teaching children long-valued cultural and spiritual traditions and practices. They helped kill languages. These were not side effects of a well-intentioned system: the purpose of the residential school system was to separate children from the influences of their parents and their community, so as to destroy their culture. The—"

"Yes," said Scott.

I blinked. "I beg your pardon?"

"Yes," he repeated. "Of course the system had other purposes too. But you promised, or threatened, to speak about abuse. What you've just read, although phrased in a polemical style, is not inaccurate. Where is the abuse in preparing Indian children to take their place in a modern economy, whether on a farm or in a factory? Where is the abuse in making sure they acquire a proper facility in one of the two languages of our nation? Where is the abuse in giving them the opportunity to win a place in Canadian society?"

"I hadn't finished," I said. "Please allow me to read the next two sentences."

He bowed his head slightly.

"The impact was devastating. Countless students emerged from the schools as lost souls, their lives soon to be cut short by drugs, alcohol, and violence."

"And other students emerged with a very different result," he said. "If anything, they *found* their souls. They were glad of the experience. Does this report quote any of them?"

"Yes, it does. But just because a few students encountered decent teachers, met with good treatment and turned into lifelong Christians, that doesn't outweigh the tens of thousands who were treated like dirt. Like dirt. And you knew it."

"Your evidence?" he said.

"Do you remember the name Peter Bryce?"

"Of course I do. A doctor and a malcontent. A man who bore a crippling grudge."

"If you say so," I said evenly. "But he was also a distinguished physician—the first Canadian to be named president of the American Public Health Association. When he was the chief medical officer of your department, he made a tour of the residential schools in the West. That was in 1907, I believe." I reached into the yellow folder again, to be sure of my facts. "He explained how and why tuberculosis was rampant. He described the constant overcrowding, the lack of ventilation, the filth, the unsanitary conditions. He showed how the staff in a lot of schools made light of the problems and minimized the dangers of infection. Why, when *Saturday Night* got hold of a copy of Bryce's report, they said it exposed 'a situation disgraceful to the country.' They observed that 'Indian boys and girls are dying like flies' and said that the percentage of soldiers who die in warfare is no greater than the percentage of Indian children who die in residential schools."

"That may depend on the kind of war," Scott said.

"And I suppose you'll say it also depends on the species of fly."

"No. Of course not. Mr. Abley, I did what I could. In retrospect it wasn't enough—could it ever have been enough? But within the department, Bryce's report was not altogether dismissed. We did take certain actions to improve matters. We did. For some years we were able to improve the quality of the school buildings, as Bryce and several others had suggested. We enhanced the sanitation, the heating, the lighting, and so on. But then the Great War came, and the money for all such projects disappeared. Do you seriously believe I could have asked my minister to go before the cabinet and say that improving the heating system at Indian schools in northern Saskatchewan should have a higher priority than equipping the Canadian Army with rifles?" He paused and looked at me searchingly, as though trying to assess whether I believed him. "And often our efforts were blunted by the churches. Thwarted by them, even. I can now speak more openly about all this than I could while I was active in the department. I remember the principal of a Catholic institution in Alberta—Father Balter, that was his name, at the Saddle Lake school. Does he appear in the papers you have before you?"

I shook my head.

"He assured us that the main cause of tuberculosis was heredity, not infection, and he said it was a duty of charity and humanity to save the soul of 'a weak child whose sojourn here below will not be very long.' I remember that phrase for particular reasons of my own. The improved ventilation that Bryce kept calling for was irrelevant to Father Balter—he didn't seem to care if the students died, as long as they were baptized first. So instead of turning away Indian children who were infected with the disease, he welcomed them into the dormitories at Saddle Lake. That's the type of man we had to deal with, you see. We never had as much direct control over the operations of the schools as people even in my day liked to think. I am beginning to get a sense of what people think in yours."

"Bryce called the residential schools a national crime."

"I don't believe he used those words in the report of 1907. That was what he said in a polemical booklet, published after he had left the service of the government many years later."

"A booklet," I pointed out, "in which he accused you of 'transparent hypocrisy.' He also said you showed 'active opposition' to his recommendations."

The publication of "A National Crime" in 1922 marked a rare occasion when Scott was named and personally blamed for the miserable state of the residential schools. Civil servants, then and now, are not accustomed to such exposure. But after a passing flurry of dismay at Peter Bryce's charges, the attention of the press soon moved elsewhere. The department and the churches continued on their way. Indeed, the residential system expanded.

"I was not opposed in principle to everything Bryce recommended," Scott said, his voice tight. "I merely saw that his ideas could not all be put into practice. If the doctor had had his way, the schools might as well have been turned into sanatoria. He was a great proponent of the fresh air cure. But did he ever prepare a budget for a national system?"

"So you were happy to let the children die instead of spending a little more money."

"No, Mr. Abley, I was not happy. For many years I was seldom happy. Of course children do die…You will recall I was answerable, not to an ill-tempered physician, but to the government of Canada. When Bryce presented his report in 1907, I was serving as the department's accountant; I did not yet have overall responsibility. We had to do a thousand things, more than a thousand things, with the limited resources at our disposal. My task was to ensure the money that we were allotted was spent wisely and well. Had I been a member of Parliament, I could have agitated for more generous financing. But as a public servant, I left agitation to others. I recall an occasion when the principal of the Crowfoot School in Alberta asked for our permission to admit yet more students. This would have enabled him to receive further money from the department. That is to say, from the people of Canada. He assured us he could take care of the extra pupils, although we had reports in our files stating that his school was already overcrowded and more than half the students in it were suffering from tuberculosis. What were we to do?"

I thought he was asking a rhetorical question. As the seconds passed, I realized he was not.

"You could have said no."

"And by so doing, we would have made an enemy of the principal in question, the Catholic church in Alberta, and some of the province's leading politicians. Now multiply this case by fifty or sixty. Do you begin to see what I was up against?"

"But this doesn't excuse you, Mr. Scott. The fact remains: this is your legacy. You oversaw a system of horrific cruelty, a system where sickness was normal, where death was rampant and where huge numbers of Indian children were abused with impunity. How could you? How could you? Will you take no responsibility?"

Scott closed his eyes briefly. He looked tired and remained silent for a time. Then he sighed, moved his hand to his neck as though to adjust his collar, and spoke in a low, resigned voice: "I don't know if I will bother to come back, given all you have said this afternoon. I always disliked this type of argument, and I would rather not subject myself to any more of them. It's a pity that amid your strenuous efforts to find out the worst about me, you did not trouble yourself to look for other evidence. Other qualities. You have searched no further than the obvious and the shrill. I don't suppose any author in my time knew so much about the Indians of Canada or described their plight with so much sympathy. Yes, sympathy! If you were to read my poem 'At Gull Lake: August, 1810,' you would find the lines:

> Quiet were all the leaves of the poplars,
> Breathless the air under their shadow,
> As Keejigo spoke of these things to her heart—"

I interrupted him: *"In the beautiful speech of the Saulteaux."*
He blinked.

"I know," I said. "You described an Aboriginal language as beautiful. In your poem 'The Forsaken' you introduced the Ojibwa word for a cradle, *tikanagan*. I'm familiar with your poem about the splendour of Indian place names too. In the Gull Lake piece you made Keejigo the central figure, and obviously you had no liking for the foul-mouthed Orkney trader who calls her a bitch. I love the monologue where she says:

> The crane hides in the sand hills,
> Where does the wolverine hide?
> I am here my beloved,
> Heart's blood on the feathers
> The foot caught in the trap.

Scott shifted uneasily in his chair. There was a sudden vulnerability in his gaze. "So you *have* been reading my poetry," he said.

"As you see. As you hear. And your stories too."

"And you realize there was more to me than what the propaganda suggests. More than the insulting names I have been called."

"Propaganda? That's a loaded word. But yes, of course. Look, Mr. Scott, I respect your poetry. I wish I'd read a lot more of it when I was young. I could have learned some useful lessons for my own work."

He stood up. The small muscles in his face were quivering. "I need to consider what you have told me," he said. "May I take a little time?"

"Of course," I said again.

He bowed slightly. "Then farewell, Mr. Abley."

And abruptly he was gone, leaving me to cook dinner in a bewildered silence. I burned the onions. I overdid the salt. I cut my thumb peeling a potato. My wife came home and wondered what had happened, and I couldn't bring myself to say.

3

Treatment That Might Be
Considered Pitiless

ATTAWAPISKAT—A CREE EXPRESSION FOR "the people of the parted rocks"—was a word well known to Duncan Campbell Scott, although it doesn't appear in his poem "Indian Place-Names." In the fall of 2011 Attawapiskat became known to the Canadian public too, as the disastrous state of housing in that isolated community briefly turned into a national issue. The media chartered flights to James Bay and descended on the town, reporters and broadcasters competing with each other to highlight both the physical squalor of the place and what they found to be its residents' psychological distress. The images they gathered seemed more shocking than surprising—Canadians were scarcely unfamiliar with the news that people living on many First Nations reserves suffer from miserable housing and poor social conditions, although very few members of the general public yet recognized Chief Theresa Spence. The uninsulated shacks, wood-frame tents and bucket toilets of Attawapiskat had been inadequate long before the TV cameras arrived, and they would remain inadequate long after the cameras had left. The blatant poverty that filled the nation's screens for a few days provoked the usual mixture of dismay, annoyance and numbness. After such knowledge, what forgiveness?

The desire to remain innocent, the impulse not to know, has a long precedent. Leaked to the press, P.H. Bryce's report alerted newspaper and magazine readers to the grim state of children's health in the residential schools; but the report produced no lasting changes in Scott's department.

This was, in part, because of the high respect Christianity enjoyed and the subtle, pervasive power its leaders exercised. While a government could always be attacked, the mainline churches stood above serious reproach. If the cabinet of the day, whether Conservative or Liberal, had any complaints about how the Department of Indian Affairs chose to spend taxpayers' money, it also had more pressing issues to confront, and the recipients of its Indian policies suffered in silence. Forcibly deprived of their children, forbidden to practise their spiritual traditions, required to obey the edicts of a colonial regime, Aboriginal people had no power and no public voice. What politician would risk his career on their behalf? The routines of the department carried on; Scott and his fellow officials could always reassure the government that public servants were doing the best they could under difficult conditions. When required, reasons for failure could always be propounded.

"As has been experienced for many years past, tuberculosis continues to be the most formidable of all maladies from which the Indian race has to suffer." The words are those of Frank Pedley, who preceded Scott as Deputy Superintendent-General of Indian Affairs, writing in 1913 the last of his annual reports to the minister. (Scott may well have worked on the report with him.) Pedley went on: "Undoubtedly the lamentable state of affairs is due to the inability of the Indian to thoroughly comprehend and adequately put into effect the primary laws of sanitation." He could make this claim even though the most terrible disease "the Indian race has to suffer"—an interesting morsel of syntax—had the nickname "the white man's plague." Tuberculosis conjured up images of tenements, poverty, joblessness, but also of artists and writers whose imaginations flamed even as their bodies failed, allowing them a brave Romantic death; and nobody blamed Anton Chekhov or Emily Brontë, John Keats or Robert Louis Stevenson for failing to grasp the basic laws of sanitation. Such authors were coughing, gasping individuals, whereas "the Indian" was a silent abstraction. Of course, until Aboriginal people were dispossessed of their lands, they had inhabited North America for thousands of years without enduring the tuberculosis, smallpox, cholera and other sicknesses that European settlement brought in its wake. Some of the early explorers and adventurers from across the Atlantic expressed surprise at how well-fed and healthy were the indigenous North Americans they met.

Compared to Frank Pedley, who performed his duties in an Ottawa office building, white men who worked among Aboriginal people sometimes saw more clearly—up to a point. In 1896 John MacLean, a Methodist missionary from Scotland who had spent many years in the company of the Blackfoot, published a book entitled *Canadian Savage Folk: The Native Tribes of Canada*. Whatever might be said about his title, the author was far more sympathetic to Aboriginal people than were most of his peers. MacLean did not set out with the clear intention of blaming the victim. He could use the phrase "native culture" without irony or apparent condescension, and he recognized that "the new mode of life on a Reserve, dwelling in filthy houses, badly ventilated, has induced disease." Among the other causes of sickness he witnessed were "the idle manner of living, being fed by the Government, and having little to do; the poor clothing worn in the winter; badly cooked food."

Then, in the same sentence, his tone began to shift: "the consciousness that as a race they are fading away, and the increasing strength of the white race, has caused such a depression of spirit that many of them may be said to die of a broken heart." MacLean could see all too well what was happening to Blackfoot families: "The mortality among the children from diseases common to the white children is very great." But his belief system impelled him to discover further explanations for the people's troubles: "The two chief causes…are immoral diseases and depression of spirit." If they embraced Christianity—"the savage folk have learned through its teaching to forsake the dreary paths of error and superstition"—Indians could perhaps avoid the perils of extramarital sex and mental illness alike. Otherwise, in spite of the poorly ventilated houses, the inadequate clothing, the lack of work and the bad food, their deaths would be their own fault. One of MacLean's subchapters bears the title "The Doomed Race."

AS A YOUNG MAN, Duncan Campbell Scott lost his faith in the fervent beliefs that inspired John MacLean and other Protestant missionaries, his
father included. He began to drink alcohol—modestly, never to excess—
and he moved toward a belief in what he would describe, in his final book,
as the "unperverted earth-spirit lying at the core of all life." He seldom
quoted from the Bible. Yet in some crucial ways he remained his father's
son. William Scott was a competent writer (he published pamphlets and
books on educational, religious and social topics); he had once worked as
an editor; and, like MacLean, he took a personal interest in Indian matters.
Long before his son was born, William Scott had spent years at the St. Clair
Mission near Sarnia, trying to convert the Ojibwa.

By 1876 he was the president of the Montreal Conference of the Methodists, and in that capacity he prepared an appeal to Queen Victoria, "pray-
ing for redress of wrongs" committed against Mohawks and Algonquins in
the Lake of Two Mountains area west of Montreal. The Sulpician priests,
who owned an enormous tract of land in the region, were refusing to acknowledge the rights of Indians who had, indisputably, lived there for
generations. In recent years many of them had renounced Catholicism
and joined the Methodists. As French-Canadian families moved into the
area, some Indians were arrested for chopping down trees on the Sulpician estate. Others had their livestock killed and their belongings stolen by
settlers near the French-speaking town of Oka. In December 1875, as the
result of a court order obtained by the Sulpicians, the Methodist chapel
was demolished. William Scott took up his pen in the Indians' defence.

The queen did not answer.

Six years later—the Sulpician church at Oka having burned down in
the meantime—the controversy remained unsettled. The Department of
Indian Affairs asked the aging clergyman to study the issue. By now Duncan Campbell Scott was a young clerk employed by the federal government, and William Scott enjoyed the imposing title Superintendent of the
French and Indian Missions of the Montreal Conference of the Methodist Church. His ninety-page "Report Relating to the Affairs of the Oka
Indians" displayed a complete reversal of opinion. William Scott said he
still held the Indians' best interests at heart. Yet after a detailed study of

documents going back to the mid-seventeenth century, he backed the claim of the Sulpicians: the French Crown had granted them the land outright, a decision by which the British Crown had to abide. Therefore the Indians were squatters. Scott urged them to abandon Lake of Two Mountains for a new reserve in Ontario. The government of Canada, he was at pains to observe, "has not failed to use all proper and lawful efforts for the benefit of the Oka Indians. Whatever may be said to the contrary, there is abundant documentary evidence that the Indians have all along been made aware of their dependent position." The land belonged to white men. Indians had no title to it. They lived in the area only at the Sulpicians' mercy, and the laws of property could not be changed in their favour.

This argument did not go unchallenged. Another Methodist minister, John Borland, fired back a forty-page reply in which he called the report "a painful surprise." Borland noted that the Methodist church had asked William Scott "to watch over and promote the interests of the Oka Indians to the utmost of his power. Instead of which, it looked as if—and using his position for the very purpose—he had betrayed those interests to his bitterest enemies." Borland charged that Scott had failed to place himself "as an effectual barrier between the suffering Indians and their cruel op-pressors"—language very unusual for 1883—and he rejected any idea of "a wholesale deportation of the Indians from Oka." Neither the church nor the government were swayed. Watching the dispute from Ottawa, Duncan Campbell Scott would have absorbed some critical lessons about the basis of Canadian law, the powerlessness of Indians, and the need to make hard choices regardless of previous sympathies.

In the end, 133 Aboriginal people did leave the area, as William Scott had urged. The community they founded near Parry Sound survives today under the name Wahta Mohawk Territory. But the majority of Indians took Borland's advice and remained at Kanesatake (to use the Mohawk name), even without any title to the land. The conflict over property ownership simmered for generations and flared into violence in the summer of 1990, when the town of Oka tried to expand its nine-hole golf course by chop-ping down the majestic pine trees overlooking a Mohawk cemetery. A Quebec police officer died in what came to be known as the Oka crisis; it involved a lengthy confrontation between the Canadian Army and Aboriginal warriors, as well as a blockade of one of the main bridges connecting the island of Montreal with the mainland. In the French-speaking town of Châteauguay, a Mohawk warrior was burned in effigy. The fury unleashed by these events contributed to the federal government's decision to create a Royal Commission on Aboriginal Peoples. A permanent solution to the land dispute remains as absent in our own day as in William Scott's.

⌒

EVEN WELL-MEANING AUTHORS LIKE John MacLean would not, could not, face the implications of what they had seen. To hold the government or the churches responsible for the clear suffering of Aboriginal people would have required them to make an unfathomable mental leap. Using figures provided by the Canadian Association for the Prevention of Tuberculosis, Peter Bryce estimated that at the beginning of the twentieth century, the disease was killing Aboriginal people at a rate nineteen times higher than non-Aboriginal Canadians. The department could explain this only by pointing, in Frank Pedley's phrase, to "the inability of the Indian." Scott, the chief accountant at the time, preferred to cut back on expenditures rather than authorize new spending; when he took over as Deputy Superintendent-General, he told Bryce that annual medical reports would no longer be required.

In his annual report for 1910 Pedley wrote: "That indifference to human life and suffering which characterized even highly civilized nations, until Christian doctrine took possession of them, still to no small extent pervades the Indian population, who manifest a certain apathy as to the prolongation of a life which affords comparatively few interests and enjoyments." Under his watch, and soon under Scott's, the department did its best to keep those enjoyments to a minimum. What other observers praised as the stoicism of Indians, Pedley described as apathy and indifference. Their lives were being cut short, he admitted, by tuberculosis and "infantile mortality." But the deaths of so many young children could not be the government's fault; instead they were the sad result of "premature

marriages, which result in weakly offspring," and "ignorance of inexperi-
enced mothers." Pedley had arrived, by accident or design, at a very useful
strategy. If the Indians were doing well at anything, the department and the
churches deserved credit for lifting them up into civilization. If they were
doing badly, their own primitive nature was to blame.

This rhetorical strategy, or sleight-of-hand, lingered on for many years.
Growing up in southern Alberta in the 1960s, I can remember being informed by Baptist elders that the buffalo had vanished from the prairies
because the Indians shot them all. (MacLean had been charmingly evasive
on the subject, remarking only that some Indians "died during the famine
of 1878, when the buffaloes left the country.") As a small boy in Lethbridge
I was told that Indians were the authors of their own misfortune; they
had been stupid or crazy enough to wipe out the animals on which their
livelihood depended. Decades would pass before I learned that the disappearance of the buffalo was at least partly a policy, an act of will. In 1875
Lieutenant General Philip Sheridan—soon to become the commanding
general of the U.S. Army—asked Congress to authorize the slaughter of
the remaining herds; he saw their extinction as a weapon to force the Plains
Indians into submission. As long as buffalo herds roamed the West, Indians
would pose a threat to settlement. When the Texas legislature debated a
measure to outlaw buffalo hunting on tribal lands, Sheridan intervened to
praise the white poachers as heroes who deserved a medal, "engraved with
a dead buffalo on one side and a discouraged-looking Indian on the other."
On one famous occasion he declared, "The only good Indians I ever saw
were dead."

That phrase quickly took on a life of its own. A future president, Theo-
dore Roosevelt, alluded to it in 1886 when he said: "I don't go so far as to
think that the only good Indians are dead Indians, but I believe nine out
of ten are, and I shouldn't like to inquire too closely into the case of the
tenth." He called Indians in general "reckless, revengeful, viciously cruel."
The defeat of General Custer at the Little Big Horn had occurred a decade
earlier; the massacre of the Sioux at Wounded Knee still lay in the future.
Thomas J. Morgan, who was appointed United States Commissioner of
Indian Affairs in 1889, was forthright: "The Indians must conform to 'the

white man's ways,' peaceably if they will, forcibly if they must. They must adjust themselves to their environment, and conform their mode of living substantially to our civilization. This civilization may not be the best possible, but it is the best the Indians can get. They can not escape it, and must either conform to it or be crushed by it."

When Duncan Campbell Scott was a novice poet and a young clerk, the men who wielded power in both Washington and Ottawa looked on the indigenous peoples of the prairies as a menace. Canada's Department of Indian Affairs took no responsibility for the Métis—"half-breeds," to use the parlance of the time—but when the Métis rose up in 1885, the Cree allies of Louis Riel and Gabriel Dumont played a key role in military victories at Duck Lake, Frog Lake, Battleford, Fort Pitt, Cut Knife and Frenchman's Butte. "Civilization and savagery were in striking contrast," wrote John MacLean after witnessing Chief Poundmaker's final surrender, "a picturesque scene, never to be repeated on the Western plains, the last protest of the lords of the prairies, and the closing chapter of the history of the red man of the West as master."

On both sides of the 49th parallel, the aftermath of resistance was grim. Praising the hanging of eight Cree warriors after the revolt had subsided, Sir John A. Macdonald told a subordinate: "The executions of the Indians...ought to convince the Red Man that the White Man governs." To enforce the point, the children attending the new residential school in Battleford were brought to the gallows to watch the prisoners die. The surviving Aboriginal people across a vast region, forced onto reservations (the American term) or reserves (the Canadian one), learned they must either adopt agriculture or starve.

What the government in Ottawa called "the evil counsel" of Riel had led some of the Plains Cree into armed rebellion against the Crown. As soon as order was re-established, the government redoubled its efforts to make Indians abandon their traditional culture. The basis of that culture had been the buffalo; now there were no buffalo to hunt; therefore their culture was an irrelevance. Worse, it was a handicap.

❧

TODAY SOME PEOPLE CONTINUE to look on indigenous cultures as an obstacle to progress. Interviewed on CBC Radio's *The Sunday Edition,* Frances Widdowson, co-author of the 2008 book *Disrobing the Aboriginal Industry,* informed Michael Enright that even if the now-geriatric Indian Act were scrapped or transformed, a crucial difficulty would remain: "The core problem is that you have a people that still retains a lot of features from the hunting and gathering period." In that book, Widdowson and Albert Howard claim that Aboriginal people suffer from "undisciplined work habits, tribal forms of political identification, animistic beliefs, and difficulties in developing abstract reasoning." By hanging on to tradition, they have "not developed the skills, knowledge, or values to survive in the modern world." Their languages are utterly inadequate for modern society, and any efforts to maintain these languages do "a disservice to native people." Widdowson and Howard are dismissive of attempts to integrate traditional beliefs into the school curriculum; in their minds, such work amounts to "honouring the ignorance of our ancestors."

This last phrase—one of the chapter titles—is particularly offensive to many Aboriginal people. (It's also a sarcastic echo of *Heeding the Voices of Our Ancestors,* a book by the indigenous scholar Gerald Taiaiake Alfred.) Widdowson and Howard contend that Aboriginal people today are preyed upon by lawyers, professors and consultants who gain financial benefit from their plight; this is the "aboriginal industry" they set out to disrobe. Yet as far as the authors are concerned, much of the lamentable state of affairs seems due to the inability of the Indian to thoroughly comprehend and adequately put into effect the primary laws of civilization.

The book struck a chord. Despite the shoddiness of many of its arguments—what the authors say about languages, for example, is absurd—the book was widely praised in the national media (a *Globe and Mail* columnist called it "impressive," a *National Post* reviewer "valuable" and "powerful"). Such commentators were happy to overlook the hardline Marxism that underlies Widdowson's and Howard's analysis, a Marxism that allows the authors to praise the residential schools. "Leaving aside the tragedy of incidental sexual abuse," they write, "what would have been the result if aboriginal people were not taught to read and write, to adopt a wider human consciousness, or to develop some degree of contemporary human knowledge and disciplines? Hunting and gathering economies are unviable in an era of industrialization, and so were it not for the educational and socialization efforts provided by the residential schools, aboriginal peoples would be even more marginalized and dysfunctional than they are today."

One of the many distasteful things about this passage is that its abstract rhetoric bears no relationship to the lived experience of human beings. As the Royal Commission on Aboriginal Peoples stated in its final report, "Children were frequently beaten severely with whips, rods and fists, chained and shackled, bound hand and foot, and locked in closets, basements and bathrooms." What boys and girls endured in the residential schools was not just a socialization effort. It was indoctrination, enforced by what plenty of observers at the time recognized as physical and mental abuse. To take but one example, Bill Graham, an inspector of residential schools in southern Saskatchewan, informed headquarters in 1907 about abuses at Crowstand, a Presbyterian school near the town of Kamsack. Graham noted that when retrieving some runaway boys, the principal of Crowstand had tied the children to ropes and forced them to run eight miles back to school behind a buggy. The department urged the Presbyterian church to dismiss the principal, but the church declined; there was no room in the wagon, it said, and the horses were not trotting fast.

In 1921, when Scott was in control of Indian Affairs, he reacted with anger after a nurse at Crowfoot School in Alberta sent a disturbing report to his department. A complaint about poor food had led her to enter the school's dining room unexpectedly. There she found four boys and five girls chained to the benches. One of the girls had been badly scarred by the strap. Scott wrote to the school's principal, an Oblate priest: "Treatment that might be considered pitiless or jail-like in character will not be permitted. The Indian children are wards of this Department and we exercise our right to ensure proper treatment whether they are resident in our schools or not."

But the department almost never did exercise its right. John S. Milloy's superb book "A National Crime": The Canadian Government and the Residential School System, 1879 to 1986 gives many examples of other reports that landed on the desks of Indian Affairs but were never acted upon. Scott could compose a chilly letter to Father Riou at Crowfoot School, but he had no power to fire an offending principal; that would be up to the church, and the church, whether Protestant or Catholic, generally refused to act. Time and again, teachers, nurses or Indian agents would inform the department of hunger, violence, overcrowding, sodomy, disease, brutality, escapes, drastic incompetence, deaths; and the department would make a recommendation, offer a suggestion or file the matter away for possible action at some point in the future. It often declined to do even that much, choosing to reply that the complaints were excessive, the charges unproven or the complainants unreliable.

The government could, and did, point an occasional finger at the churches, whose ability to manage the schools was so patently dismal. But the churches could, and did, point an occasional finger back at the government, which never gave them enough money to operate the schools in a humane or efficient way. For many years the per capita amount that Ottawa granted the churches for Indian education was about half what it provided for orphanages and homes for white children. The finger-pointing was mild and genteel. The treatment of Aboriginal children was anything but.

Scott did his best to hide this news from the public. Troubled by a complaint about the physical abuse of children in the Mohawk Institute near Brantford in 1913, he composed a memo to his minister, W.J. Roche, admitting and deploring the use of corporal punishment: "The rules governing the disciplinary action in the case of misdemeanours by pupils, are I think antiquated...I do not believe in striking Indian children from any consideration whatever." But when he wrote to the lawyers acting on behalf of the complainants, he sounded a different note: "No necessity exists for the investigation which is asked for by the Indians mentioned. That it is a popular Institute is shown by the fact that the waiting list contains the names of 80 children whose parents are anxious for them to attend." In fact the Mohawk Institute was known by many of its inmates as "the mush hole."

Ten years later, answering a question from a parliamentary reporter, Scott made the outlandish claim that "ninety-nine per cent of the Indian children at these schools are too fat." (The reporter knew of a letter that a boy in the Saskatchewan school of Onion Lake had sent to his parents; the boy had complained about cruel treatment and lack of food, mentioning that seven children had tried to run away because of extreme hunger.) Despite the official lies, at least part of the truth was available to anyone determined to look for it. In 1907 Samuel Blake, a reform-minded lawyer for the Anglican church, had told the minister of Indian Affairs that "the appalling number of deaths among the younger children…brings the Department within unpleasant nearness to the charge of manslaughter." The minister was unperturbed. The department's annual report for that year made no mention of Blake's charge, although Frank Pedley did lament "the retarding and retrogressive influences of the home upon the pupils" and the "hostility [that] results from superstition." Families, once again, were proving to be a bad influence. Failure, once again, was the Indians' fault.

Blake did not give up. He wrote to the Attorney General's office in Edmonton, seeking details about "the Indian question" in Alberta. In March 1908 a reply came from A.Y. Blain, the inspector of legal offices for the province. Blain, who had only recently moved to Alberta from Ontario, told Blake that he had now met all the members of the legislature "and made a point to get what information I could in regard to the Indian from such of the Members as had reserves in or near their districts." He had consulted other Albertans too. The results were discouraging. "I might say," Blain wrote, "that most of those with whom I have spoken are not, I would gather, very much in sympathy with the Indian, nor with the efforts to better his condition. They look upon him as a sort of pest which should be exterminated."

⌣

NOBODY KNOWS EXACTLY HOW many students died in the residential schools, or contracted diseases there before being sent home to die. Unmarked graves of Aboriginal children are still being discovered near the sites of former schools—most of the buildings have long since gone up in flames or been torn to the ground. Neither the churches nor the federal government, neither the provinces nor the individual schools kept adequate death records. The truth was relatively safe as long as it could be hidden or ignored. Yet it's clear that over the long history of the schools, many thousands of children died.

Before Scott reorganized the residential system, giving it greater administrative clarity though no more money, its institutions were split into two groups: boarding schools (located on or near reserves, and designed for younger children) and industrial schools (larger facilities located far from reserves, and aimed at somewhat older students). Day schools also existed on some reserves. In March 1902 one of Scott's colleagues, Martin Benson, wrote a private memo providing some details on the results of industrial schooling in Western Canada up until then. A total of 2,752 students had been admitted, and just over a thousand were still in residence. Of the 1,700 who had been discharged, Benson wrote, "506 are known to be dead; 249 lost sight of; 139 in bad health; 86 transferred to other schools; 121 turned out badly and 599 said to be doing well." The phrase "bad health" may have been a euphemism for tuberculosis, which was often fatal. Its ravages doubtless accounted for many of those "lost sight of." These figures were not revealed to Aboriginal people or to the press.

Overall it was a wretched picture, and it seldom looked much better on a school-by-school basis. In his 1907 report, P.H. Bryce noted that only nine out of the thirty-one students who had been discharged from File Hills, a Methodist school in eastern Saskatchewan, were still alive. Fifteen had died at the school, and another seven within a few years of returning home. Scott acknowledged in 1910 that Indian children were dying "at a much higher rate" in the schools than in their own villages. But, he added, "this alone does not justify a change in the policy of this Department, which is geared towards the final solution of our Indian Problem." The rise of Hitler lay a generation in the future, so by using the phrase "final solution," Scott was not quoting Nazi doctrine. The weak, he knew, would die; the strong, he thought, would be assimilated into the Canadian mainstream.

Indian Affairs staff hoped that before the final solution was attained, residential school graduates would succeed in improving the tenor of life on reserves across the country. The teenage boys and girls were to accomplish this by their new way of being—not only how they dressed and behaved, but also what they felt and thought. Education had a transformative power: this was a common belief in Scott's day. Elwood Cubberley—among the most significant educational administrators in the United States in the early twentieth century—wrote in his 1905 dissertation for Columbia University: "Schools should be factories in which raw products, children, are to be shaped and formed into finished products...manufactured like nails, and the specifications for manufacturing will come from government and industry." Canadian officials believed that those finished products—if they had been manufactured at residential schools—would no longer want to see themselves as Indians.

Behind the hopeful rhetoric, though, there were doubts. There were always doubts. "I have no hesitation in saying—we may as well be frank—that the Indian cannot go out from school, making his own way, and compete with the white man." When Clifford Sifton said this in the House of Commons in 1904, he was the minister responsible for Indian Affairs. "He has not the physical, mental or moral get-up to enable him to compete. He cannot do it." Sifton's successor, Frank Oliver, didn't know what to think. Perhaps Sifton was right, and "we are not able to educate them to compete, in which case our money is thrown away." On the other hand, if the Indians could "compete industrially with our own people, [it] seems to be a very undesirable use of public money." Evidently "our own people" were white. In defending the notion that Indian education was both possible and desirable, Scott had to battle some very powerful men.

What undermined the system from the start was its insistence on keeping Aboriginal people isolated from white settlers—perhaps for the security of the Aboriginals, perhaps for that of the settlers. As long ago as 1955, when dozens of old residential schools were still in operation and the government was rushing to open new ones in the Arctic, the political scientist J.E. Hodgetts observed: "If the ultimate aim was civilization and assimilation, this isolation was undesirable. The curious paradox seems never to have struck the white administrators: the Indian must obviously be forced to embrace the superior culture of the white man, and yet contact with that culture and with the bearers of that culture seemed to render the plight of the natives even worse." Hodgetts called his essay "Indian Affairs: The White Man's Albatross."

Perhaps Scott did grasp the paradox. Perhaps he was merely willing to play a very slow waiting game. In his biography of John Simcoe, he took heart from the tidy appearance of the Six Nations reserve in southern Ontario: "Where stood clustered the wigwams and rude shelters of Brant's people now stretch the opulent fields of the township of Tuscarora." It had required more than a century for the Iroquois and the settlers of European origin to "become confederates throughout a peaceful year in seed time and harvest," so much so that a casual visitor to the Grand River valley couldn't easily tell where the territorial division lay, and Scott knew it might require further centuries before the Cree, Ojibwa, Blackfoot and other formerly nomadic groups adhered to the main body of Canadian society. He was an administrator; he never had to confront an impatient electorate. He could afford to take the long view. Yet however many decades the process took, he was convinced that graduates of residential schools would stand in the forefront of progress. Exposure to civilization would have leached the savagery out of them.

That was the ideal. That was what the bishops, lawyers, business leaders and members of Parliament wanted to hear. Today, after all the details that have emerged about the residential system over the past few decades, no one could be under the illusion that schooling generally took place in a wise or humane manner. In the book *Stolen From Our Embrace*, Sto:lo elder Ernie Crey recalls that "the school was such a powerfully negative experience for my father that as a parent he used it as a kind of threat to discipline us. If I didn't behave, he told me, I would be sent to a school where children had to rise at 5:00 a.m., say prayers on their knees for hours and eat thin gruel three times a day." Through the locked dormitory windows of St. Mary's Residential School, Sto:lo children would peer out at the Fraser River where their people had fished for millennia and where they were now forbidden to go.

Neglect, incompetence, violence and disease were rampant through-out the system. Small wonder that its own promoters gradually lost faith in their work. When Scott retired in 1932, the "field secretary" of the Mission-ary Society of the Church of England in Canada wrote an appreciative let-ter from Bible House in Winnipeg, thanking him for his wisdom, courtesy and "expert knowledge of the Indian peoples of this country, and of their many problems." Then the letter shifted into a minor key: "Whatever the future may hold in store for these dependent but valorous people, it is now quite impossible to say." The confidence so evident in the early years of residential schooling in Western Canada had given way to anxiety.

"Eventually," Milloy writes in *"A National Crime,"* "the Department came to understand that the system itself was abusive…The schooling of the children, its numbing routinization and regimentation, produced in-dividuals incapable of leading an independent life, unable to thrive either in their own communities or in those of the dominant society." Yet the de-partment, and a succession of governments, kept this awareness off the rec-ord. It took decades for common knowledge to become official knowledge. Until the 1980s, nobody in a position of power would admit the profound failure of the residential system, or speak publicly about its victims. The broad outlines of Indian Affairs policy continued unchanged long after the poet had retired and, as he told a literary friend in a rare unguarded mo-ment, was "released from my fifty year imprisonment with the savages."

It's hard to say which is more striking: Scott's casual mention of Ab-original people as savages, or his definition of his career as a jail term.

∼

EASTER CAME AND WENT, and I began to wonder if he would indeed re-turn. The final vestiges of snow had vanished from shady corners of the yard, and robins made an outdoor concert on mild evenings. Had I been too hard on the man with my angry outpouring, my refusal to grant any sympathy, my use of nouns like "mud" and "dirt"?

"I see mud under your fingernails," a voice said nearby. "You have been busy in the garden, Mr. Abley."

I turned and found him standing, as before, in the living room. The afternoon light played across the creases of his face. Silently he moved to join me by a window overlooking the garden, unkempt with the furious energy of April. "O passion of the coming of the spring!" he had once written, "When all the winter of the year's dry prose / Is rhymed to rapture." The purple-blue flowers and dark green leaves of periwinkle half-hid the wire fence at the back of the yard; a cardinal sang his heart out from a branch of the white pine. Scott listened: a brief smile made his lips appear less narrow than usual.

"We do our best," I said. "My wife is more of a gardener than I am. But the place needs more attention than we ever manage to give it."

"You have not yet cleared away all the leaves that fell last year."

"No. We leave some of them. My wife says that keeping a few wild areas in the garden is helpful to the bees."

"I did the same," he said.

I turned my head in surprise. "Yes indeed," he added, "even though I lived not far from the centre of Ottawa. That's a beautiful pine. Though somewhat cast into shadow by your maple."

"It's a sacred tree. Sacred to the Iroquois, that is."

Long ago, it is said, the Peacemaker asked the warriors of five warring nations to throw their weapons into a pit where the roots of a great white pine had stood. Having done so, the warriors formed the Iroquois Confederacy. An underground river took the weapons away, and the Peacemaker put the tree back in the ground.

"I am aware of this. I was not as ignorant of Indian legends as you seem to think. Supposedly the tree is sacred because of the actions of the peacemaker—Dekanawida was his name, was it not?"

"It was," I said. "Although some people prefer not to speak that name. Out of respect."

"Do they, indeed." I noticed a steeliness in his voice. "Respect for what?"

After only a minute or two, our conversation had already veered towards hostility. "I could give you an answer," I said, "but perhaps we should bury the hatchet. So to speak."

He nodded. "I dislike confrontations, and I would shake hands with you if these hands were not a form of illusion. Shall we sit down?"

I wanted to ask him how he could see and hear if the eyes and ears before me were illusory, but I knew there would be no point. Nor could I ask him how he was. He was dead.

"Well, Mr. Scott. I've read lots more of your work." It seemed a safe beginning. Eventually I would have something unsafe to say. "A few essays and short stories, and nearly all the poems."

"And I hope you enjoyed some of what you found."

"I did. You had a wonderful ear—should I use the past tense or the present?"

"The past, I regret to say. Yes, I am proud of certain lines, certain poems—the musical element of poetry is essential, I always thought. Some of the younger poets in my day seemed to find it irrelevant."

"In my day too."

He leaned forward as though to share a confidence. "Indeed, I'm not sure the phrase 'free verse' makes a great deal of sense. But I fear my work must seem very old-fashioned to you."

"Some of it, I admit. It's hard for me to relate to the poem you addressed to the mothers of Canadian soldiers who died in the First World War—I mean, we look back on their deaths as a sickening waste, but nobody would consider them 'the Immortals that have saved the world.' You made them sound like superheroes in a video game."

He was looking blank.

"A comic book, I mean."

"At times I did have a weakness for rhetoric. Are you immune to it yourself?"

It was unfair of me to pick on one of Scott's worst pieces of writing—except that beyond its facile and sentimental fondness for the British Empire, something else had bothered me about "To the Canadian Mothers, 1914–1918" and various other poems. An air of certainty, even arrogance, clouded his impulse to tenderness and his close observation of nature. This was a writer who could, metaphorically speaking, decide who was immortal and announce who had saved the world. Such poems show little trace of doubt or hesitation.

"No, I'm not immune," I said. "It's a common weakness. And what amazes me is that you wrote so many good poems while for decades you held a senior position in the government." He gave a rueful nod. "Writers today, if they're lucky, can head off to residencies and retreats and artists' colonies. You didn't have those opportunities. I came across a novel by your friend Madge Macbeth in which she referred to the Ottawa civil service as the home of the living dead."

"Ah. Perhaps she had me in mind."

"A social rebel and a feminist. Not your type of woman, I would have thought."

"Dear Madge. She gave me an excellent recipe for apple cake. I once wrote a few verses in honour of her cook's Armenian Bliss."

I stared at him in mute surprise.

"A chicken dish, you understand."

I couldn't tell if he was joking. But I wanted the conversation to remain genial for as long as possible.

"Let me tell you about the book I just finished reading," I said. "You make an appearance in it. Elizabeth Hay, who's an excellent novelist, wrote it some years ago—*A Student of Weather* is the title. Much of it is set in southwestern Saskatchewan, an area I happen to know."

"Does Miss Hay—Mrs. Hay?—have me plough the prairies?"

"Ms. Hay," I said. He looked baffled. "No, she doesn't. The main character is a bright girl by the name of Norma Jean. One day she goes to school—this part of the novel takes place in the Depression—and her teacher, a young woman who has come west from Ontario, reads 'At Gull Lake: August, 1810' out loud. 'Mr. Scott lives in Ottawa,' she tells the students. 'People see him walking down Wellington Street and he could be anyone at all going to an office downtown. He wears the same dark suit, the same grey hat.' And then the teacher quotes four lines about Keejigo, and tells the class about unrequited love."

"Hmm. And does Miss Hay make no mention of what I did when I arrived at my office? Does she say anything about the decisions I had to make once I removed my hat?"

"No. Nothing. So maybe there's hope for you yet. So to speak."

Scott stared at me for a moment.

"I will not give up easily," he said. "And it is gratifying to think that my Gull Lake poem has touched readers far in the future. My future, that is."

"I expect it will continue to do so," I said. "I just wish I had your talent for describing nature."

Picking up a scrap of paper on which I'd scribbled a few of his lines, I began to read.

> "The moon, Capella, and the Pleiades
>   Silver the river's grey uncertain floor;
>   Only a heron haunts the grassy shore;
>   A fox barks sharply in the cedar trees;
>   Then comes the lift and lull of plangent seas…

Passages like this make me downright jealous."

"Thank you," he said with a nod of his head and a passing smile. "Archie Lampman and I used to talk about what Wordsworth had done for the Lake District—he introduced a whole new landscape into English poetry. Coleridge too, of course. The two of them made readers see grandeur and beauty where previously they had seen desolation. We thought, 'Why not do the same for Canada?'"

"And you've been praised for it. In the 1980s a New Brunswick poet named Douglas Lochhead called your work 'honest, passionate and intimate' and said that, for him, your poems more than any others 'represent the way we look at our Canadian environment.'"

"I would blush with pleasure," Scott said, "if I could only blush. I'm very pleased to hear that. It reminds me, in the last year of my life an Irish immigrant sent me a letter saying, 'Do you mind me telling you to your face that if I were asked to name one writer whose work most fully holds what, for me, a comparative stranger here, is the authentic feel of Canada, I should name Duncan Campbell Scott.' John Coulter, he was called. I—"

"John Coulter," I interrupted in wonder. "I knew him when he was a very old man—he published a memoir at the age of ninety. Earlier he'd written a hugely successful play about Louis Riel. His daughter Clare became one of the best actors in the country."

He frowned for a moment, presumably at my choice of word. "Did she really? That's delightful to hear. I dedicated a poem to her when she was a little girl."

We sat and stared at each other, equally astounded by the sudden flash of connection. For a moment I forgot what I would need to say to him.

"The authentic feel of Canada," Scott repeated. "Sometimes in the wilderness, it was as if my soul could expand. A canoe brings enormous freedom. Mind you, the wilderness can also induce fear…I don't know what your own beliefs are, Mr. Abley, and I wonder if you might quibble at my use of the word 'soul.' But I can tell you that Lawren Harris and Alex Jackson were among the leading artists who agreed with me. Emily Carr, too. Daily life in a city acts as a constraint on the imagination. Do you not find this?"

"At times, sure. And I love Thoreau's line 'In wildness is the preservation of the world.' But I can also be excited by the sights and noises of city life. If you could walk today through downtown Montreal or Vancouver or Toronto, or even Ottawa, you'd be amazed at the mixture of foods, clothes, languages."

Scott frowned. "Alluring, perhaps. A touch of the wider world. Yet also somewhat incoherent, surely."

"It's been more than forty years," I told him, "since the Canadian government gave a special preference to British immigrants. To white immigrants from anywhere, in fact. The colour of urban Canada is not what it used to be, except in the corridors of power."

"I see. Even in my day a good deal of mixing took place in the larger cities. Winnipeg, for instance—the Gateway to the West, they liked to call it. Icelanders and Jews. Ukrainians and French. Some Germans lived in the vicinity too. Not to mention the proud Scots who founded the place. The triumph of Canada is that once they had settled here and made this country their own, all these people were loyal to the Crown. They became Canadians. They assimilated."

Made this country their own. I wondered whether to challenge him on the point. Instead I took an oblique approach.

"You know, I was in Winnipeg a few weeks ago," I said, leaning forward and watching him closely.

"An interesting place, I always thought. Despite its failures of beauty."

I wasn't sure I'd heard him right.

"Beauty, or duty?"

"Its somewhat discordant appearance, I mean. When a Scottish journalist named Bob Edwards got off the train there and looked around, he said, 'So this is Winnipeg. I can tell it's not Paris.' Not that Winnipeg was any uglier than a few other cities I could name. Tell me, has the country finally begun to appreciate the virtues of good architecture?"

I was puzzled. It seemed as though on his third visit Scott wanted to chat, wanted to digress.

"We have some beautiful new buildings and some others that are very—striking, for better or worse. You'd be astonished if you could see what's happened to the Royal Ontario Museum and the Ontario College of Art. But overall, let's say civic beauty is still a work in progress."

"I understand." Scott paused. I could have sworn he sighed. "So what did you want to tell me about Winnipeg?"

"I was there for a literary festival," I said. "It occupied most of my evenings, but the days were free. And one morning the friend I was staying with—she's a social worker—took me to the head office of CancerCare Manitoba. They have a lecture theatre where experts come and give talks to doctors and nurses and medical students. My friend kind of sneaked me in."

"Sneaked me in," he repeated. It must have been a novel turn of phrase for him.

"Yes. But that day, the talk wasn't given by any of the usual experts—not by anyone directly involved in the practice of medicine. It was given by a judge, Murray Sinclair."

"A good Scottish name."

"Absolutely. As well as serving on the bench, he teaches law at the University of Manitoba. He's widely respected across the country."

"I imagine so."

"He has another name too," I said. *"Mizanay Gheezhik*—meaning 'the

73

one who speaks of pictures in the sky.' My Ojibwa pronunciation isn't what it should be."

Scott was silent.

"Of course it's a good idea for medical professionals there to be familiar with Aboriginal issues, because Winnipeg has more indigenous residents than any other place in the country. And Murray Sinclair is not only a judge, a professor and an Ojibwa elder—he's also the head of the Truth and Reconciliation Commission of Canada."

He remained silent. I forged ahead.

"That commission is at work as we speak. Its mandate is to find out everything it can about what really happened in the Indian residential schools, and to see if there can be some kind of reconciliation at the end of all the truth-telling. The commission has its headquarters in Winnipeg. But it's been holding sessions in a variety of places to listen to the testimony of survivors. I've read the report it released in 2012. I expect its final report will be even longer and more detailed."

Scott had recovered his voice, though now it had a tense edge again. "And why should there be such a commission at this point in history, many years after the last school was closed?"

"Well, it's part of the compensation package the federal government and the Assembly of First Nations agreed to. The deal was not only that the survivors would receive some money—it's also that a commission would be set up, giving them a chance to speak. To share their story. And besides, it's important for Canada as a whole that these testimonies should be on the public record. Should be heard. Should be preserved. So that nothing like this could happen again."

"Hmm." Scott stirred uneasily. "And what did the Honourable Mr. Sinclair have to say in the lecture you attended?"

"He spoke about the different types of negative impact the schools had on the children who were sent there. Being victimized directly is the most obvious one. But there are others too. Judge Sinclair explained the fear of disclosure—children were threatened with consequences if they told their families what went on behind closed doors. Sometimes they were afraid to return to their communities, especially girls who had been violated and were now pregnant. When they did get home, boys and girls found they were inadequate at the traditional skills and tasks—they'd never had a proper chance to learn. And of course the children suffered a loss of faith, a loss of trust, a loss of belief in their parents and the extended family."

I paused for a second, giving my words a chance to sink in.

"Judge Sinclair said that he and the two other commissioners hear these stories by the hundreds. And they feel the suffering each time."

"The Honourable Mr. Sinclair has evidently done well in the world. May I ask what the current state of affairs is for the majority of his fellow Indians?"

"Interesting you should say that," I replied. "Another thing he mentioned was the intergenerational effect of the schools. Because it's not just the survivors who were scarred. He used the phrase 'residual impacts in the lives of their children.' And even grandchildren."

"You must enlighten me."

"Well, he showed a film presentation about an Inuvialuit elder from Tuktoyaktuk. The man—"

"From where?"

"Tuktoyaktuk, on the Arctic Ocean. I suppose it had a colonial name in your day. Today we take it for granted that most of the communities in the far north go by their Inuit names. Anyway—until the day of the hearing the man had never spoken about his experiences at residential school. His own wife didn't know what he'd been through. He recalled being put on a plane one morning, flown south and, like all the children, given a number. In a sense that's all he was: a number. For Judge Sinclair, the most powerful moment of the man's testimony came when he said, 'I'm not Number 142. I'm Paul Voudrach.'"

"I don't see what any of this has to do with—what was your phrase?—intergenerational effect."

"Paul was sexually abused in the school. Later in life he contemplated suicide. But the point is, when he became a father, he mistreated his own children. He admitted, you see, he didn't know how to be a parent. Judge Sinclair said that when they testify, at least 80 percent of the survivors talk about how they went on to behave, or misbehave, with their own families in later life. So the shame they experienced as children gets compounded by the shame and guilt caused by their own actions."

Scott sniffed. "I'm surprised at how you keep on using the word 'survivors.' Admittedly an Indian school could be a difficult place for children, but it's not as if they'd been through the trenches serving their country in the Great War."

"Isn't it?" I said.

He stared at me. "No. It isn't."

"All right," I said, staring back. "Let's think about what they went through. Imagine that instead of being raised by your loving parents, as you were, in the company of your sisters, you were hauled away by strange men when you were six or five or even four years old. You were terrified, because you had no idea where they were taking you. The journey was long, and when you finally arrived, you were locked up inside a large, cold building. Your hair was hacked away. The clothes your mother had made for you were stripped off and you had to put on a foreign uniform. You wore this uniform all through your childhood and adolescence. There was no alternative. There was no escape.

"In your early childhood you'd lived outside much of the time. Now you could leave the school building only when the adults granted permission. You were given a number. You were known by that number. If you dared to use your own name, or if you were caught speaking a sentence in your own language, you were beaten. 'Spare the rod and spoil the child,' your teachers said. Gradually you forgot your language. When you were sent home in the summertime, you couldn't understand your own grandparents. Nor could you tell them what you were going through.

"Back at school you were told, day after day, year after year, that you belonged to an inferior people—you had no culture of your own. You were a savage, and your teachers were civilized. They understood God; you did not. And the God they understood was a jealous God who intended to consign your own parents and grandparents to the fires of hell. A few of the teachers were kind, but only a few. Most of them were incompetent and two or three were downright sadistic. The fear of them was so great, you could never entirely relax.

"You learned to live with constant hunger—the food was bad and there was never enough of it to fill your belly. The clothes you wore were ragged and dirty. The building where you spent most of your life was dark, ugly, infested with cockroaches, and in perpetual need of repair. At night you slept under a thin blanket in a miserable bed, with children coughing all around you and no fresh air. Over the years a few of the children in your dormitory died, or perhaps more than a few—but nobody was ever allowed to talk about their deaths. The absolute rule was silence.

"Let's suppose you were one of the lucky ones. Let's suppose you somehow managed to avoid coming down with tuberculosis, and that you weren't sexually assaulted by a teacher or one of the older boys. Of course you knew this was happening to many of the other children. Everyone knew it. You lived in fear, continual fear, that one day it would happen to you.

"More than anything else, you were isolated. From the first day you arrived at the school, you were lonely. You were always lonely. But Mr. Scott, if you endured ten years of this and were able to walk out the door at the end, wouldn't you call yourself a survivor?"

I swallowed hard and glanced out the front window at the tree-lined street. I was thinking about the defence of these schools in *Disrobing the Aboriginal Industry,* and I was about to make a final remark or two about "contemporary human knowledge," "wider human consciousness" and "socialization effects." But when I looked back, Scott was no longer there.

4

Obsolete as the Buffalo and
the Tomahawk

THE MORE I LEARNED about Duncan Campbell Scott, the more I suspected he had set me an almost impossible task. His reputation, which soared in the first decades after his death, has never stood lower than it does today. In his aesthetic life, Scott valued tradition; in his public life, he revered authority. His beliefs were thoroughly in line with received opinion. The irony is that if he had rebelled in life, he might not be so vilified in death. Authors of his time in other countries who promoted racist or fascist doctrines—Ezra Pound, Knut Hamsun, Louis-Ferdinand Céline—suffered disgrace in their lifetimes. Yet today they are widely read and respected. Pound, Hamsun and Céline, of course, were not high-ranking government officials. When their fingers touched a typewriter, they wrote as gifted, flawed individuals. By contrast, when Scott sat down at his desk in the Booth Building, he did so as the unseen overlord of subservient peoples. His words reeked of power.

Posterity was kind to him for decades. Scott "is now recognized as one of the outstanding figures in Canadian poetry," reads his entry in the *Macmillan Dictionary of Canadian Biography* (1978). Five years later George Woodcock agreed: "Scott has struck a responding chord among the Canadian poets of the 1970s and 1980s who combine a post-modernist interest in formal experimentation with a deep sense of environmental awareness as a source of poetry." *The Poet and the Critic,* a gathering of Scott's late letters to and from his friend E.K. Brown, also appeared in 1983. Somehow it managed to be both a scholarly collection and a loving portrait. Although the editor, Robert McDougall, was well aware of the complications in Scott's character, he felt the elderly poet was "happy enough." In his graceful introduction McDougall evoked an "aura which surrounds this man. He is at all times attentive and hospitable to the arts." The Scott of his imagining has survived long enough to see some of his writing "become part of the education of young Canadians," and "he knows his place is secure in the canon of major Canadian writers."

Sandra Gwyn echoed that judgment in *The Private Capital* (1984), her engaging portrait of life in Ottawa during the Macdonald and Laurier eras. Gwyn portrayed a man who in his youth joined with Archibald Lampman to furnish the "oxygenic essence" of Ottawa's cultural scene, and who in his later years embodied "exquisite maturity." The chapters she devoted to Scott and Lampman pay tribute to the men as central and vibrant figures in the city's artistic history. A year after *The Private Capital* appeared, a literary press in Ottawa issued a fresh selection of Scott's work, prefaced by an essay in which the poet Raymond Souster hailed him as "the most interesting, most challenging and technically the most venturesome of the Confederation poets, a real virtuoso and the true bridge between the Victorian and the modern tradition in Canada."

From there it would be downhill fast.

The descent began in 1986, when the historian E. Brian Titley published an unflinching and unforgiving analysis of Scott's work as a civil servant. *A Narrow Vision: Duncan Campbell Scott and the Administration of Indian Affairs in Canada* introduced readers to a different kind of man than earlier descriptions had allowed for. Few of the previous writers had tried to assess Scott as an influential figure in the making and carrying out of government policy. Titley assessed nothing else, and charged that Scott used his position to do Indians a terrible disservice. He displayed no interest in his subject as an editor, a musician, a devoted friend or a bereaved father; indeed, he largely ignored Scott as a poet, too. The sources he relied on were the mountains of archival documents that had until then been overlooked, revealing the methods and results of Scott's half-century of work as a civil servant. There is much evidence, Titley observed, to indicate that throughout his career Scott "remained an almost obsessive penny-pinching book-keeper." Admittedly he had colleagues who were even less flexible, even more authoritarian, but none of them lasted as long in the department or exerted as much control.

After *A Narrow Vision* appeared, other historians and writers took their own look at Scott. The verdicts in their essays and articles were seldom positive. Titley's work had made it hard to read the poetry and fiction without recalling the departmental memos, the half-truth letters, the annual reports. For many years Robert McDougall worked on a biography of Scott. He never completed it. Perhaps the revelations about Scott's career in Indian Affairs were too painful for him to deal with. McDougall may also have found it challenging—as any author would—to write a compelling book about a reserved, upright man who spent most of his working life in a government office an easy stroll from his house.

When Canada finally began to face up to the painful legacy of Indian schooling, the fact that Scott had overseen the residential system left his reputation uniquely vulnerable. Amid all the faceless names of the Ottawa bureaucracy, he stood out: those who researched and wrote about the schools now had a name and face on which to focus their anger. He wore a suit, a tie and a tense frown in nearly all the photographs; outdoors or indoors, he looked like the sad-eyed embodiment of power. The poet and critic Stan Dragland, in his sometimes brilliant book *Floating Voice: Duncan Campbell Scott and the Literature of Treaty 9* (1994), tried to mount a defence of the man, and in the end could not. Dragland appealed for a complexity of understanding, but most people in the past two decades have made a simpler judgment. Susan Crean is typical: in her 2001 study of Emily Carr she called Scott an "infamous" man, "remembered more for his villainy than his verse."

Posterity has changed its tune. Scott has become a symbol.

The literary prize I judged in 2009 had a different name the following year. Poets in the Ottawa area would no longer compete for the Lampman-Scott Award; instead they would be eligible for the Lampman Award. A key reason for the change was that one of the previous winners, Shane Rhodes, had publicly declared he would give half of his prize money (the

Scott half, if you like) to the city's Wabano Centre for Aboriginal Health. Having done research into First Nations history, he decided: "Taking that money wouldn't have been right, with what I'm writing about." Rhodes believed that Scott's legacy as a civil servant could not be glossed over. The editor of *Arc,* the poetry journal that sponsors the prize, replied by saying, "I don't think controversial or questionable activities in the life of any artist or writer are something that should necessarily discount the literary legacy that they leave behind." Anita Lahey also declared, "To forget either side of Scott's legacy would be a dangerous act of erasure."

Even so, the award's name changed. Likewise, Ottawa's main literary festival no longer sponsors a Duncan Campbell Scott Address. But while no major prize today is named after Scott, the Canadian Pediatric Society has instituted a P.H. Bryce Award, celebrating someone whose work in public health has bettered the lives of Aboriginal children and youth.

Several Aboriginal artists in recent years have taken Scott on directly. In his poem "Hot Blooded," the Kwakwaka'wakw writer Garry Thomas Morse mocks him as a "foppish flapper of propaganda" and a "proud plucker of inviolate pride." The Secwepemc poet Garry Gottfriedson, in his "Dangerous Words Trio," has Scott declare, "I want the blood of all Indian women snipped at the arteries, drained of their ancestors." The Ojibwa author Armand Garnet Ruffo, in "Poem for Duncan Campbell Scott," evokes him with more subtle irony:

> Christian severity etched in the lines
> he draws from his mouth...
> This man looks as if he could walk on water
> And for our benefit probably would,
> if he could.

Louise Bernice Halfe—a Cree poet who was once a student at a residential school in Alberta—utters his name in a terse and memorable passage:

My father became a skin
slipped through their jail like a falling star.
Duncan Campbell Scott. Captured. Barbed wire.

And in his piece "Buffalo Spirit," the Lil'wat composer Russell Wallace took a departmental memo in which Scott warned about the dangers of Indian dancing, and recorded it as one element of a multi-layered score to which Aboriginal dancers perform. All these artists treat Scott as a master of empire, an engineer of suffering. Now the victims of empire are striking back.

In the Internet age, when lines and images are quoted, posted, misquoted and reposted at lightning speed, Scott has two enormous strikes against him. One is an error: his supposed wish "to kill the Indian in the child." The other is not an error: his declaration that federal policy was designed "to get rid of the Indian problem." That phrase has taken on a life of its own. Often it is deployed as a weapon against him. In December 2011, for example, Hemas Kla-Lee-Lee-Kla, a chief of the Kwawkgewlth—also known as the lawyer Bill Wilson—wrote a column for the *Vancouver Province*. There he charged that Aboriginal Affairs and Northern Development Canada (as the department is now called) "has not changed its policy since Duncan Campbell Scott, the deputy superintendent of the Department of Indian Affairs from 1913 to 1932, wanted to 'eliminate the Indian problem' by eliminating the Indians. It is common knowledge now that Indian reserves were just corrals for dying animals." In the last years of his life, and the first few decades thereafter, Scott wore the image of a reserved and studious poet who had accomplished much good work. Now he wears the image of a cold-blooded murderer.

Recently a further suggestion has begun to spread, both in print and online. The historian David McNab has stated that Scott's maternal grandmother was not an immigrant from the Scottish Highlands but an Onondaga woman of the Bear Clan who lived in Kahnawake, a Mohawk community just across the St. Lawrence River from Montreal. She was, he suggests, the "country wife" of a British-born administrator named Duncan Campbell Napier. If Scott did indeed have indigenous ancestry, the implications would be huge. But McNab offers no clear evidence for his claim, and it goes against the words of a letter Scott wrote to E.K. Brown: "I remember my maternal Grandmother, being held up to see her on her death-bed; then I was about five, and I can see an old face and a head with a lace nightcap; she had The Gaelic, as they say." He did not. He was a creature of the English language.

~

WHATEVER THE RESULTS OF its Indian Affairs policies, the Canadian government didn't just lurch into those policies by accident. The reserve system can be traced back to military and political decisions made by British officials in the 1820s. As for the residential schools, the first one in what would become Canada—the Mohawk Institute in Brantford—was established in 1831. (South of the border, a school for Cherokee boys had opened its doors as early as 1804.) The men who created the system in the nineteenth century had a goal in mind: to destroy indigenous cultures, languages and beliefs. Those who maintained and expanded the system in the early twentieth century shared the goal. They did not see it as a cruel desire. Achieving it, they believed, would hasten the end of savagery.

Canada's chief negotiator for several of the western treaties, Alexander Morris, expressed the high ambitions in a volume published in 1880. It would have been required reading in Ottawa for the young Duncan Campbell Scott. "Let us have Christianity and civilization," Morris wrote, "to leaven the mass of heathenism and paganism among the Indian tribes; let us have a wise and paternal Government faithfully carrying out the provisions of our treaties, and doing its utmost to help and elevate the Indian population, who have been cast upon our care." As the Blackfoot, Cree, Saulteaux and other peoples were unchristian and, in Morris's terms, uncivilized, he took it for granted that they needed elevation. He was not a cynic, and the above passage is quoted approvingly by the influential political scientist Tom Flanagan in his book *First Nations? Second Thoughts*. Morris looked forward to an era of "peace, progress, and concord" when the Plains Indians would be "happy, prosperous and self-sustaining," and when

Canadians could bask in the knowledge "that in a truly patriotic spirit, our country has done its duty by the red men of the North-West." A more revealing phrase, I think, is "who have been cast upon our care." Neither Morris nor Flanagan stops to consider who did the casting, and why.

The truth, which has only lately been recognized, is that Aboriginal peoples already practised farming on the plains before the settlers arrived. They grew small crops of tobacco, maize and, after the early nineteenth century, potatoes, and many of them were ready to adopt a partly agricultural way of life provided they could continue to hunt. In the treaty negotiations with Morris, they asked for seed grain and cattle, hoes and ploughs and wagons. Adaptability in the region's tough and wayward climate was essential, far more so than the newcomers realized. As the historian Peter Russell puts it, "Though very few missionaries and no civil servants knew anything about prairie farming, they all assumed it would provide a more reliable material support than hunting and gathering. That excessively optimistic assumption wrought great havoc in the lives of most Plains Indians confined to the reserve system." Equally damaging, the Indian agents who controlled daily life on the new reserves saw the treaty terms not as obligations but as charitable options. "Natives found themselves trapped in the circular logic of the Indian Department," Russell explains. "They could not begin farming (on the scale and in the way that the government wanted) until they had oxen, ploughs, and seed; but over and over agents refused these, until natives had begun farming, somehow, without them." If they failed, their failure only proved how helpless they were and how badly they needed to obey the government.

Scott and his fellow administrators felt it was their duty to ensure that traditional Aboriginal practices and religious beliefs would not be passed from one generation to another. The residential schools achieved that goal by forcibly denying parents and elders the care of their own children. This policy had been decided at the highest level. When the adolescent Scott began work in the department, Sir John A. Macdonald was not only the prime minister but also the Superintendent-General of Indian Affairs, a post he retained for eight years. Addressing the House of Commons in that capacity in 1883, he declared: "When the school is on the reserve, the child lives with his parents who are savages; he is surrounded by savages, and though he may learn to read and write, his habits and training and mode of thought are Indian. He is simply a savage who can read and write." Such was the power of the home. The removal of Indian children from their parents, Macdonald went on, would allow them to "acquire the habits and modes of thought of white men." Two years later, in the wake of the Métis uprising, he wanted to extend the new pass system—which imprisoned all members of rebel bands on their reserves unless an Indian agent agreed to let them out—to loyal Indian bands as well. Even though Macdonald was the prime minister, this suggestion would largely be ignored.

⌒

UNLIKE MANY OF HIS contemporaries and successors, Macdonald spoke plainly. Policy-makers in Ottawa have always liked to tell the nation they are acting from the highest motives, and more typical, then as now, was the deployment of big abstract nouns: Civilization. Education. Progress. Morality. Rhetorically speaking, these nouns flanked and buttressed each other like slabs of architecture. In the Department of Indian Affairs, it proved to be the architecture of a house of cards.

A crucial though less obvious word in the department's lexicon was "improvement." Reading through the annual reports written by Scott and his predecessors, I noticed how often that word recurs. If "reform," "efficiency" and "development" are three of our mantras, "improvement" was one of theirs. The 1879 report, for example, reads like a hopeful catalogue of improvements. "An improvement in the moral and intellectual status of the Indians generally is reported by their respective superintendents and agents"; Ontario has witnessed "a decided though gradual improvement in the general condition of the bands throughout the Province"; reports from Nova Scotia show "an improvement in the condition of the Indians generally, more especially those from the island of Cape Breton, where the Indians on several of the reserves appear to be advancing steadily in the arts of civilization"; and as for a decrease in drunkenness on various reserves, "we may also hope that it is the result of improvement in the moral character of the Indians." Such were the dreams of the department in the year Scott joined. In Quebec, alas, "the improvement in the condition of the Indians…is not so marked." As for the North-West, the Indians had little chance to improve, or be improved, for the near-extinction of the buffalo meant that many of them had starved to death.

"Improvement" could occasionally arrive by surprising means: the First World War, for instance. In the course of it thousands of Aboriginal men volunteered to fight for Canada. Scott, by then in charge of Indian Affairs, encouraged them to do so, rightly trusting they would make excellent soldiers and believing the war would speed up the slow process of assimilation. "These men who have been broadened by contact with the outside world and its affairs," he wrote in an essay of 1919, "who have mingled with the men of other races, and who have witnessed the many wonders and advantages of civilization, will not be content to return to their old Indian mode of life. Each one of them will be a missionary of the spirit of progress." Only somebody who had never worn a gas mask or seen a Flanders trench could talk so confidently in 1919 of the spirit of progress and the wonders of civilization. The war, Scott thought, "will have hastened that day… when all the quaint old customs, the weird and picturesque ceremonies, the sun dance and the potlatch and even the musical and poetic native languages shall be as obsolete as the buffalo and the tomahawk, and the last tepee of the Northern wilds give place to a model farmhouse." *Will not… will be… will have… shall be*—Scott's syntax leaves no chance of dissent. "In other words," he concludes, "the Indian shall become one with his neighbour in his speech, life and habits, thus conforming to that world-wide tendency towards universal standardization." It's hard to believe such a sentence is the work of a poet.

In most of his annual reports, Scott found cause for confidence and hope. But his final statement to his minister, written in 1931 as Canada tumbled headlong into the Great Depression, has a sombre air. True, the government could take pride in "the progress in Indian education during the past fifty years." The number of schools had more than tripled over that time, and "the improvement in the attendance regularity… shows a remarkable awakening on the part of Indian communities and parents." Apart from saluting the growth in residential schools, the report credited many Indian parents for finally agreeing to send their children to the day schools on reserves. "Fewer and fewer natives"—also described as "our wards"—"are finding it possible to live by the chase and they are turning towards education to prepare themselves for encroaching civilization." ("Encroaching" is a notable word; it implies trespass, intrusion, stealth.) Scott also wrote that the department's aim "to make the Indians self-supporting…has met with remarkable success, particularly in the Prairie Provinces." Self-supporting, of course, is exactly what indigenous people were before they became the department's children.

The congratulatory tone vanished when Scott turned to the economy. He was writing at a hard time. In and around Indian reserves everywhere, the Depression was taking its toll on employment, timber sales, fishing and trapping. Scott could not find any reason why matters were likely to improve. Besides, no amount of rhetorical bluster could hide the fact that a large number of Indians were miserably ill. Vigorous action would be required for the department to combat an epidemic of trachoma, an eye disease that was causing widespread blindness in the three western provinces. Trachoma had become prevalent in the residential schools, with the result, Scott admitted, that children who went home in the summer were likely to infect healthy families and communities. Then there was tuberculosis, still ravaging "practically all of the Indians north of the railways." The department had plans—or so the report stated—to deal with the disease, but it lacked the money to do so. Therefore, "the remedy is in the hands of the public." By "the public" he meant the Canadian mainstream, those who had the vote. Indians, not being legal persons, were excluded from the public.

In 1931, ill health and a feeble economy were combining to cloud their prospects. "It is more than possible," Scott wrote, "that many of the northern districts are now overpopulated…During the past few years fur has become scarce, the price has fallen, the forest has been invaded by white trappers, and the increased populations are quite probably more than the country can support at any reasonable level of life. It would appear that, for a time at least, there is not much hope of improvement in their condition." In short, "it may be that an actual decrease of these bands is inevitable, and some of them may be reduced to remnants of their present numbers."

This sounds like a prediction of future starvation coupled with a refusal to accept responsibility for it. The Department of Indian Affairs could do nothing about the price of fur, the invasions of white trappers, or the alarming tendency among Aboriginal women to have sex and give birth. A central question, then, is one of tone. Did Scott write those sentences, as his harshest critics would have it, in a mood of satisfaction? I don't think so. In the 1920s he had dared to suggest that white trappers should be kept out of the Northwest Territories so as to preserve the fur-bearing animals for the use of Indians; his proposal had been turned down. Yet if Scott allowed himself much inward regret at the vision of indigenous groups being "reduced to remnants," he kept his feelings out of his prose. Look at his deployment of the passive voice: "has been invaded...may be reduced." Mammals are merely "fur," Aboriginal people are "populations," and the direct relationship between the abundance of trappers and the scarcity of wildlife is left unexplored. Overall, the neutral, evasive language of the report avoids giving any impression of urgency. It also removes the plight of hungry, desperate human beings from the orbit of personal care.

In his poetry, on the other hand, Scott could evoke hunger and desperation sharply enough to make readers imagine and care for the suffering people he described. "The load of passion, violence, and sheer terror which many of these poems carry is considerable," wrote the poet and critic D.G. Jones. Take "The Forsaken" as an example. The Ojibwa woman in that poem uses her own flesh as trout bait in a winter storm so as to save her own life and the life of her sick child. The second half of the poem leaps forward in time and shows her as a very old woman, abandoned by her family on an island as winter is about to set in. Both in youth and in extreme age she is "Valiant, unshaken," and when she takes her final breath, God is with her. "The Forsaken" was much admired by the eminent literary scholar Northrop Frye. Scott, he said, "writes of a starving squaw baiting a fish-hook with her own flesh, and he writes of the music of Debussy and the poetry of Henry Vaughan. In English literature we have to go back to

Anglo-Saxon times to encounter so incongruous a collision of cultures." Frye could not have realized how offensive many readers would find the word "squaw"; the term does not appear in "The Forsaken." Neither do words like "improvement," "condition," "populations" or "overpopulated." As a poet, Scott could rise to empathy.

❧

"WHAT?" MY HEART SKIPPED a beat. "Oh, it's you."

I was coming downstairs from my study, intending to retrieve the lawn mower, and had glimpsed his trousers and impeccable black shoes before I saw the rest of the man. He was standing in the living room, watching me with close attention. Only a week had passed since our last, difficult exchange, and his arrival took me by surprise. He offered no explanation.

"You are an admirer of dandelions, I see."

"Phlox too. Not every plant out there is a weed."

"Quite so. Your ferns are especially luxurious. Are you ready to have another conversation with me, Mr. Abley?"

Scott's manner was brisk and to the point. He had once described his friend Archibald Lampman as having "a sort of stern, almost obstinate set of the mouth," which was "quite characteristic." I could see the same expression now on him. Walking on into the kitchen, I poured myself a tall glass of juice. Then I returned to the living room and sat down on a sofa riddled as usual by cat hairs.

"You haunt me still," I remarked.

"Please excuse my abrupt departure the last time I visited. I hope you are well?"

"Thank you, I am. I suppose it's futile to make any wishes for you."

"Not quite. You could wish for the salvaging of my reputation."

I had observed the use he sometimes made of silence. This time I gave him a taste of his own medicine.

"Very well. I would like to begin today by mentioning I have observed something about you in our earlier conversations—I hope you will not think it presumptuous if I raise the matter now. I realize you might take my remarks as a criticism, but there is no such intention in my mind. It is simply an observation, and one that perplexes me."

This did not bode well. I swallowed. "Go ahead."

"On two occasions, Mr. Abley, I have asked about the present condition of Indians in Canada. I am curious, you understand. I wish to know. A man does not give fifty-two years of his life to another people without—"

"But you didn't."

He blinked in surprise.

"That's exactly what you didn't do. You gave fifty-two years of your life to a department, a government, a bureaucracy. You worked on behalf of a colonial system, not the Aboriginal people themselves."

"Have you finished your little outburst?" His tone was ice to my fire. "Given the pains I took to make my visits possible, and given also the exceptional nature of these meetings—I should have thought they would strike you as something of an opportunity—one might expect you to address me in a more courteous manner."

For a few seconds we sat in an angry silence.

"You're right," I finally said. "I apologize. But I didn't want to let that idea go by unchallenged. In everything I've heard from you so far, you glide over a lot of your decisions at Indian Affairs. I wouldn't go so far as to call it self-delusion, but I think it's blatant self-justification."

"And is this not a privilege of age? Have you never felt the urge to justify certain deeds that you performed in the past?"

"Just because my beard has gone grey, it doesn't make me an old man."

"You are choosing to miss my point."

He could be relentless. No wonder he had earned so many promotions.

"Okay," I admitted, "I've done it myself. I guess it's human nature."

"Exactly," Scott said. "Given a chance, we do what we can to alter inconvenient facts, to ignore them, forget them, wish them away. All of us suffer from this habit, whether Indian or white—oh yes, in my experience the Indians were just as ready as anyone else to avert their eyes from the truth. The Iroquois drone on about their Great Law of Peace when their actions showed them to be among the most bloodthirsty tribes on the continent."

Drone on? Bloodthirsty? I bit my tongue.

"Indeed," he added, "this touches on the very point I was trying to raise when you interrupted me."

He was asking for a second apology. I thought one was enough.

"Fine. I was saying that after more than half a century of service, a man does not easily forget the work he did and the people for whom he was responsible. All those tedious annual reports. Anxiety was my constant companion...Elise quickly learned not to ask me, once I had retired, about my duties on the eleventh floor of the Booth Building. This does not mean I forgot them. As she knew all too well, I suffered from insomnia. Day in and day out, my life for several decades was bound up with the welfare of the Indians. And so it's natural I should wish to know the conditions under which they live today." My heart was beating a little faster in my chest. "Indeed it may be crucial for me to gain a better idea of this, given the charges laid against my name. But each time I've broached the subject with you, I have noticed your reluctance to answer. Perhaps it is merely a rhetorical tactic, or an effort to disguise a certain ignorance, but I sense it may be something more. Is this a fair observation?"

A wild idea sprang into my mind.

"Before I answer—and I promise, I *will* give you an honest answer—let me ask you something in return. I know you're always careful to arrive when I'm alone in the house. But is there any possibility that on your next visit I could have company? I'd love it if I could invite someone here from Kahnawake or..."

I trailed away into silence because Scott was already shaking his head. "I have explained the rules of these conversations," he said, "and the exceptionally rare privilege I was granted. The privilege was to meet a living person, a writer, just one. If I spoke to anyone else, the privilege would be instantly revoked and our meetings would be at an end."

"All right," I said. "I understand. But I want to tell you a true story. It may help you appreciate my reluctance."

He settled back in his chair, a sunbeam glinting off his spectacles.

"A decade ago, I wrote a book about endangered languages—languages that are under siege in the modern world. Some linguists say that of the six thousand or so languages that are spoken now, maybe only six or seven hundred will be alive by the end of the twenty-first century. If we get that far, of course. All the others will be effectively extinct. And I happen to think that if English and Chinese and a few other big languages are the only ones left standing, the world will have suffered a tremendous loss." I paused, in case he wanted to intervene. He did not. "On the strength of the book, I was invited to a symposium on indigenous languages that Canada was organizing for Expo 2005—a world's fair taking place in Nagoya, Japan."

"In Japan! After their atrocities in the recent war—how extraordinary."

"They've been a peaceful democracy for many years. They made a wonderful recovery after 1945."

"Well. That would be something to see," Scott said a little wistfully, as though the event were still far in the future.

"It was indeed. But the reason I'm telling you all this is that many of the Canadians in attendance were First Nations leaders. The federal government asked them to come, and it paid their way, just as it paid mine. There were linguists and teachers and Aboriginal people from other countries too. Early in the proceedings, before lunch on the first or second day, a young woman from the Canadian government gave a talk. I thought it was remarkably candid, coming from a civil servant. But she said little or nothing about Aboriginal achievements—instead she spoke about the failings of Canadian policy over the years, and she described the appalling conditions on many reserves. As I recall, she gave some facts about death rates, dropout rates, unemployment and so on."

"And?"

"When we came back from lunch, she was standing at the front of the room in tears. Before the afternoon's proceedings were allowed to go ahead, she had to make a public apology. Two elders, one of them a Mohawk chief, the other a Métis leader, held a smudging ceremony, and the woman told everyone in the audience how much she regretted her ill-advised words. I heard privately that a few of the First Nations leaders had said unless she apologized, they would go to the airport and catch the first plane home."

"And her sin was…?"

"Her sin was that as a white woman, speaking on behalf of Canada, she had exposed the failures and the ongoing difficulties facing Aboriginal people without highlighting any of the achievements. It would have been fine for the First Nations representatives to quote exactly the same statistics and make exactly the same points. But she was shaming them in the eyes of guests from all over the world. And this was unacceptable."

Scott was sitting in rapt attention. He finally stirred and shook his head. "How astonishing," he said. "Of all the things you have said in our conversations, I find this the most surprising. How vulnerable the woman must have felt, and how betrayed! I'm reminded of a sentence from the novel I wrote: 'She was one of the innocents who are slaughtered for lack of a little knowledge of the world.' This anecdote shows me, as nothing else has done, how enormously far the prevailing beliefs in Canada have shifted since my death."

"And that shift was necessary," I said.

"So you approved of this woman's public shaming?"

I hesitated. "No, I was quite shaken by it. On a personal level, she was treated in a cruel way. I felt very sorry for her. But having said that, I think I can understand. Some years ago a marvellous Cree singer from Saskatchewan, Buffy Sainte-Marie, received an honorary Doctor of Laws degree from the University of Regina. And in the speech she gave in front of all the students and professors and dignitaries, she said, 'The single worst thing ever about being an Indian is to be misperceived, all our lives, by otherwise knowledgeable people, many times even our friends.' I would say that Aboriginal people are still so marginalized in Canada, one of the few ways they can exercise power is by influencing how they're perceived. To be portrayed only as victims and losers in an international forum—in their own presence, I mean—must have seemed a huge insult."

Another example crossed my mind. In March 2012 the federal minister of Natural Resources, Joe Oliver, spoke at a Board of Trade breakfast in Vancouver. During an address devoted mostly to the government's thirst to expand mining in British Columbia—a "truly transformative" opportunity, or so he claimed—Oliver said that many Aboriginal communities are "socially dysfunctional." In response the head of the BC Federation of

Indian Chiefs, Stewart Phillip, called Oliver's remarks "incredibly ignorant" and said they showed "a colour of racism." I dislike many of the policies of the current federal regime; my sympathies are with the First Nations and environmental groups who resist the government's plans for massive resource extraction. But to accuse Joe Oliver of racism merely for using the phrase "socially dysfunctional" smacks of what conservatives love to deride as political correctness.

Scott had been sitting in silence for a minute. He looked at me and said, "So are there things you feel you are not *allowed* to say?"

"There are things I feel uncomfortable saying."

"What's that line of Alexander Pope? 'For fools rush in where angels fear to tread.'"

"Are you saying Aboriginal people are fools?"

"Certainly not. I knew them far too well. Nor am I saying you're an angel. You have made this abundantly clear. Merely that Pope's underlying meaning seems pertinent."

"Which is?"

Scott was sitting near the edge of the armchair, his fingertips pressed together. "That if they are fearful of saying the wrong thing, and doubtful of what the response might be, intelligent people often hold their tongues. I wonder if you do this. I suspect you practise a form of censorship on yourself."

It felt odd to be accused of moral failure by a ghost. I had a momentary twinge of sympathy for Ebenezer Scrooge.

"Not necessarily. I try to find the right way to get my point across. But in this particular case, I would say many indigenous people are convinced that others have spoken *for* them far too long. Spoken on their behalf. Taken their voice. The government, first and foremost—think of all those memos and reports you churned out; the page total must be in the thousands. But also academics, people in the media, so-called experts, writers—people like me, in fact. If our voices take up too much space, their voices fall silent again. That's why I hoped it might be possible for you to speak to one of them. Or just listen, that's what I mean."

"Just listen."

"Yes. As you never did in Indian Affairs."

"Do you know, Mr. Abley, as with so many things you've said to me over the past month or two, that is profoundly unfair."

"Is it really?" I said. "I've looked in the historical record. You set me a challenge, and I promised to meet it. But so far, what I've seen is not in your favour."

"Tell me. Please."

"Well, there's the testimony of Diamond Jenness."

"An anthropologist, and a gifted one. Of course he had enjoyed great privilege—a Rhodes Scholarship and all. I did not experience such good fortune and I was not an anthropologist. When I retired as Deputy Superintendent-General, he did everything he could to succeed me. His campaign did not bear fruit—the minister settled on another candidate. Jenness grew bitter. That is, he grew even more bitter."

"That may be true," I said. "But he knew you pretty well. And in 1953, when he was addressing the annual meeting of the Canadian Political Science Association, he spoke about the failures he had seen in your department during the 1920s. He stated—just a minute, let me find the exact quote here in this folder—'The Indian administration of that period was a "holding" one, more concerned with preserving the status quo than with improving the economic and social status of the Indians or with raising their living standard. The head of the administration disliked them as a people, and gave a cool reception to the delegations that visited him in Ottawa.' That would be you, Mr. Scott, and that was Diamond Jenness's word."

Scott was looking a little bruised. "How on earth does he presume to know my heart?" he said. "I never discussed matters of the heart with him. He is making an inference, pure and simple."

"I notice you're not denying his point."

"Like! Dislike! I had the honour to shape the policies and direct the procedures of the Department of Indian Affairs. True, I was responsible in the end for the general well-being and improvement of the nation's wards, but I also had to ensure the smooth functioning of my department. Each expenditure required careful thought—I could not go through money like water. The demands, the requests, the complaints never stopped. Yes, I tended to give a cool reception, as Jenness puts it, to delegations of Indians that begged us to do still more for them. Some of them were accompanied by money-grubbing lawyers. When we didn't oblige, they would rush off to curry favour with reporters and members of Parliament."

"Perhaps all they wanted," I said, "was more control over their own lives."

"You are forgetting the law. My job was to administer the law."

"But look at the effect of the law—the damage it caused to generations of schoolchildren."

Scott shook his head. "Mr. Abley, you appear to think that the work of my department mainly had to do with education. This is not so: our agents dealt with misdemeanours, road repairs, crop production, epidemics, surveyors' disputes"—I tried to say "I get the point," but he kept talking—"land sales, bridge construction, bootlegging, timber leases, insect infestations, and I could go on. Believe me, I could go on. Our office staff was limited in number, and if you added our salaries together you would find they amounted to a pittance compared to what the department spent on the Indians. Ultimately we had to answer to Parliament. Where then does affection come into play? Tell me, is the Deputy Minister of Agriculture compelled to like potatoes?"

"So first you compare Aboriginal people to fools and now you're comparing them to vegetables."

His lips trembled. He stood up and began to stride around the room. It was a curious stride, as it made no sound on the floorboards and no impression on the carpet. When he turned to look out the window at my dandelion-strewn grass, his mouth appeared set in contempt.

"Is this what has become of honest debate since 1947?" he finally said. His voice was lethally quiet. "This pathetic excuse for an argument. This refusal to answer a civil question."

"You mean your question about potatoes?"

"Of course not. I mean the question I raised a little while ago, one I have also raised on previous visits. How are the Indians of Canada faring today? Tell me, please." He had sat down again and was looking at me, unblinking.

Arms crossed, hat on his lap, the young Duncan Campbell Scott sits at the left among a group of Ottawa friends. Behind him, his friend and fellow poet Archibald Lampman is wearing a hat.

The fifty-year-old Scott, at left, sits in his garden beside the English poet Rupert Brooke, who is exactly half his age. Brooke was touring Canada in 1913; two years later he would be dead.

Scott's first wife, Belle Botsford, as a serious girl in Boston. When Scott met her, she was a professional violinist. Some of his friends found her "imperious."

The young poet Elise Aylen had become the second Mrs. Duncan Campbell Scott by the time this photograph was taken in the early 1930s.

Elizabeth Duncan Scott, aged eight, with her father in the spring of 1904. She was his only child, and three years later she would die alone in a foreign boarding school.

The light illuminates only some of the middle-aged poet in this moody portrait by the Toronto
journalist and photographer M.O. Hammond. Scott was a shy man, prone to nightmares.

En. Route___ Abitibi River

Scott sits in the middle of a canoe, being paddled up the Abitibi River in the late summer of 1905.
The boatmen are Aboriginal. Scott and the other treaty commissioners are white.

At Fort Metagami

These Ojibwa women and girls have come to Mattagami in July 1906 for the signing of Treaty 9—and the ensuing feast. Scott took this picture; a camera was one of his accessories on the trip.

The Commissioners_Fort Albany

Scott is seated at the right, in the lowest chair, in this shot of the treaty party at Fort Albany, on the coast of James Bay, in 1905. His two fellow commissioners have the other chairs.

Chief Monias — Fort Hope. Lake Eambamel

Moonias, the Ojibwa chief at Fort Hope, waits for the treaty-signing ceremony. He was worried, Scott wrote, that by signing the document he would be getting something for nothing.

At Chapleau.

Scott's friend Edmund Morris is working on a portrait of the Ojibwa chief Chessequim (or Cheesequini) near Chapleau, Ontario. Scott took this picture in the summer of 1906.

These boys at the Brandon Industrial Institute are working in the vegetable fields. Notice the white supervisor behind them. The school stands on a hill in the distance.

Brandon Industrial Institute: a forbidding sight to any Aboriginal child. This photograph dates from about 1910, when Scott was national supervisor of Indian residential schools.

Churches had a mandate from Ottawa to run the residential schools. This picture, from the Red Deer Industrial Institute in 1914 or so, shows one way the Methodist message was delivered.

Dene children at work in this undated shot from the Catholic-run residential school at Fort Resolution, Northwest Territories. The academic quality in most of the schools was very low.

Protesters at an Idle No More event on the Blood reserve at Standoff, south of Lethbridge. Scott would have been dismayed by their refusal to merge quietly into the Canadian mainstream.

"I will not ask you to apologize, whatever you tell me. I most certainly will not force you to take part in a, a smudge display."

The last phrase made him shudder slightly. I failed to stop myself: "You mean a smudging ceremony."

Again the silence was long. I wondered if he was about to take his leave. If he vanished now into thin air, would he ever return?

"I see," he said at last, "you are a pedant as well as a coward. Is there no limit to your wilful ignorance?"

"I won't try to answer that question," I said evenly. I realized I didn't want him to leave. Not just yet. "And I won't ask you for an apology either."

He parted his lips as if to speak, then closed them again.

"So look, here's your answer." I pulled out a couple of documents from the folder in front of me, one of them a feature article by André Picard that had appeared in the *Globe and Mail.* "First of all, it's important to say that there are many, many success stories. We have a national event called the Aboriginal Achievement Awards, which are televised each year. The man who founded the awards, John Kim Bell, is a Mohawk from Kahnawake. Many of his peers became ironworkers and skyscraper builders. You know what he became? An orchestra conductor. I'm sure you remember Massey Hall in Toronto. Well, John Kim Bell has stood at the podium there and conducted the Toronto Symphony. But there are countless other indigenous artists and musicians and writers—I'll tell you some stories about them, if you like."

"Not right now, thank you."

"Indigenous people have become leaders in other fields, too; more than a man like you could probably imagine."

"And?"

"And yet, overall, the news is not good." I peered down at the article in my hands. "Aboriginal people kill themselves at a rate six times higher than the Canadian average. The rates of unemployment and poverty are five times higher—we could quibble about the definition of poverty, but that will give you a rough idea. A few years ago an eminent political scientist named Janet Ajzenstat stated publicly, 'The impoverishment of Aboriginals is the greatest blot on Canada's record, and one that we do not know how to correct.' More than a third of Aboriginal people have what the government calls a 'core housing need,' meaning they live in pretty awful conditions. Their life expectancy is a decade less than everyone else's. Of course some of the gap is because their babies die at three times the rate of non-Aboriginal infants. And yet more Aboriginal children are said to be in government care right now than at the height of the residential school system. About half of all the foster children in Canada are Aboriginal."

I looked up. "Is that enough for you? Or shall I carry on?"

"Carry on. Please."

"On the subject of education, then. Only about one in every twenty-five Aboriginal adults has a university education, and only—"

"You mean 4 percent of Indians *do* attend university?"

"Yes. Well, that figure would include Inuit and Métis too."

"I'm impressed," Scott said. "That shows improvement."

"But it's not enough. Not nearly enough. Just think of the wasted potential."

"Hmm," he said. "I thought that people of your, should I say, intellectual persuasion liked to criticize my department for running a school system in which we did our best to educate the Indians instead of leaving them to forage in the bush and suffer wretchedly at the hands of white intruders with their rifles and corrupted whisky. Not to mention their sexual appetites. You romanticize the natives and their dying languages. Yet now you're saying they don't receive enough education. I am perplexed."

"Not all the languages are dying. And I suppose you could say the current situation risks being the worst of both worlds. It's very hard for traditional cultures and languages to survive, and yet the modernizing forces often have a terrible effect. Here's an image that occurred to me the other day: if the Cree and Ojibwa can't rely any more on a traditional diet, it doesn't mean they've begun to consume organic multigrain bread and fresh-squeezed orange juice. I'm sure the manufacturers of potato chips and chocolate bars and cola are very happy with life on the reserves."

"I suppose." He didn't sound entirely convinced. Neither, to be honest, was I. "Though isn't their diet their own responsibility? At any rate, you have given me a reasonably clear idea of how things stand. It doesn't sound as if those who followed me in the department have achieved any greater success than I did."

Only later, replaying the conversation in my head that evening, did I realize he had finally made an admission of failure.

"So that's where we stand, Mr. Scott. And I fear your legacy is a substantial part of it."

He ignored my second sentence.

"In short, when it comes to jobs, poverty, housing and education, the plight of most Canadian Indians is dire. And the suicide levels reflect this." I could hear the civil servant in him, mustering the relevant facts, organizing his thoughts. "May I ask about infections and other diseases?"

"It's the same old story. The rates of heart disease and diabetes are substantially higher among Aboriginals. For traumatic injuries, the rate is four times higher. And as for tuberculosis—this is the real shocker—the rate is sixteen times higher than among the Canadian population as a whole."

"Yes," he said unexpectedly. "So it's still a great scourge. It was the bane of the department when I was in charge. A disease we could never get a grip on."

"But there are effective treatments now," I told him. "Antibiotics." He was looking puzzled. I realized the word was largely unknown when he directed Indian Affairs; "penicillin," like "genocide," became a widely used term only toward the end of the Second World War. "Medicines that get rid of the infection, assuming it's caught in time. These days nobody should suffer from TB for long. But on the reserves, and in the inner cities, people still do."

"All in all, then, the Indians must still be shrinking in number. Or failing to show much increase. I remember—"

"On the contrary," I interrupted. "They're the fastest-growing part of the Canadian population. Why in Saskatchewan, where I went to high school and university, they account for nearly a fifth of all residents, and half of them are under twenty years of age."

Scott wore an expression on his long, lined face that I can only describe as one of bemusement.

"The total number of Aboriginal people in Canada," I said, "is about 1.4 million. Of course it's hard to know for sure, and it depends on the definition of 'Aboriginal.' Then you have groups like the Mohawks, most of whom never fill out a census form. They see it as a violation of their sovereignty…"

I drifted off into silence, unsure of his reaction.

"One million, four hundred thousand," he finally said. "And that figure would not include all those Canadians who have a mixture of blood, some of it Indian? All those people, I mean, with a grandparent or great-grand-parent who silently and successfully assimilated?"

"That's right. It would include the Inuit and those who choose to iden-tify themselves as Métis, but not all the rest."

"One million, four hundred thousand." I had the impression he was fix-ing the number in his mind, making sure he would remember it forever—whatever "forever" might mean in the shadowlands. "How can the reserves cope with such massive numbers of people?"

"Less than half of them live on reserves," I said. "I've told you I was in Winnipeg a few months ago—well, about 10 percent of the city's popula-tion is now classified as First Nations or Métis. The total was nearly 70,000 in a census several years ago, and I'm sure it has grown since."

"Seventy thousand? In Winnipeg alone?"

"That's right."

"And the majority of Aboriginal people now live in the cities?"

"They do."

He shook his head. "I don't care for the term 'incredible'—a much overused expression—but I can't think of a better word for what you have told me."

"But why?" I said.

He stood up. "We will have to discuss this when I return," he said. "In the meantime, may I set you a little homework, Mr. Abley? Read your Dia-mond Jenness. Read *The Indians of Canada*. You know he was one of my adversaries, to an extent. But he was a decent stylist. And if you read that book, you will grasp my astonishment."

With that, he was gone.

So we beat on, boats against the current, borne back ceaselessly into the past.

I noticed to my surprise that it was drizzling outside. So much for my intention to mow the lawn. How much time had passed since his arrival? When I took a long breath, I realized my shoulders and back were a knot of tension. I found myself longing for a cigarette, and I don't even smoke.

5

The Crushed Essence

ABORIGINALS WERE A DECLINING race—at the start of the twentieth century, nearly everyone agreed about this. Scott had inside knowledge on the matter.

In 1879, the year he began working for Indian Affairs, the census returns in the department's annual report listed the total number of "resident and nomadic Indians" as 103,367, or roughly 2.5 percent of the country's total population. This was a drastic underestimate—in most of the northern and western regions, Indian Affairs had no idea of the actual figures. The Inuit were a remote mystery; sometimes the annual listings included a wild guess of their numbers, sometimes not. The Métis never appeared in these charts. By 1886 the population total in the annual report had risen to 128,761. The figure sounds far more exact than it should, for in some parts of Canada the report relied on pure guesswork: 4,000 Eskimos on the Arctic coast, 8,000 Indians in the Athabasca district, and so on. But then the numbers fell. Fifty years after Scott joined the department, when he was starting to think about retirement, Indian Affairs could be more confident in the accuracy of its statistics. In 1929 it gave the Aboriginal population as 108,012, excluding the Inuit: just 1 percent of all Canadians.

Aboriginal populations were much larger before European settlers arrived, bringing their freight of guns and alcohol, Bibles and infectious diseases. The *Historical Atlas of Canada* gives a conservative estimate of 300,000, though some authors argue for a total well into the millions. Even those who prefer a smaller number would hesitate to adopt the extreme stance taken by Stephen Leacock in his 1914 book *The Dawn of Canadian*

History: "The explorer might wander for days in the depths of the American forest without encountering any trace of human life. The continent was, in truth, one vast silence, broken only by the roar of the waterfall or the cry of the beasts and birds of the forest…There is no evidence to show that the population was ever more than a thin scattering of wanderers over the face of a vast country." While very few Canadians now read Leacock's non-fiction, many are familiar with Gordon Lightfoot's stirring song "Canadian Railroad Trilogy," which sketches a similar picture. Lightfoot says that until the arrival of the white man, "wild majestic mountains stood alone against the sun" and "the green dark forest was too silent to be real." His beautiful images erase indigenous people.

Indian Affairs statistics for certain parts of the country are telling. Nova Scotia and Prince Edward Island, unlike most other provinces, had the same boundaries in 1879 as they did in 1929 (and as they still do today); and after their long histories of British and French colonization, expulsion, settlement and surveying, the numbers given for Indian residents were likely to be fairly accurate. The department's figures showed that in 1879, Nova Scotia's Indian population came to 12,054. Half a century later, it was down to 1,929. The total in PEI had stood at 1,433 when Scott entered Indian Affairs. As he began to prepare for departure, it was a mere 295. The numbers for New Brunswick reveal a similar decline. Tuberculosis, influenza and other sicknesses had taken a devastating toll. This is, Scott may have expected, how the Indian problem would end: not with a bang but a whimper.

Of course, the sharp drop in numbers was only partially the result of disease. It was also a consequence of people leaving the reserves, drifting or purposefully merging into the mainstream of society, and being seen as Indians no longer. Acadians, in particular, often have a high proportion of Indian blood, to use an old metaphor; the Maritime provinces contain only a small number of people who identify themselves as Métis. There, as in every other region of the country, an Indian woman who married a white man would automatically lose her Indian status. From Scott's standpoint, Indians who married outside their community or who moved off the reserve counted as success stories. Every tale of assimilation meant a smaller "Indian problem" and less time and expense for his department.

Even so, the official reduction in living Indians is striking. It was also, according to the accepted wisdom of the day, natural and predictable. Such is the tenor of *The Indians of Canada,* a major study by Diamond Jenness, the chief of anthropology at Ottawa's National Museum. Jenness began writing the book in the late 1920s, and it was published in 1932, the year of Scott's retirement. In those days anthropologists would never have dreamed of studying white Canadians. Their fieldwork in Canada required them to live near—or preferably among—Aboriginal communities so as to record beliefs, spiritual practices and cultural traditions that had survived from the distant past. The more assimilation took hold, the less there would be for anthropologists to observe.

Small wonder anthropologists often had a fraught relationship with the civil servants who oversaw their subject matter. Each group distrusted the motives and behaviour of the other. In 1920 Edward Sapir, Jenness's eminent predecessor at the National Museum, urged one of his staff not to report anything to Scott if he could help it. "I hate to have to make this rule so explicit," Sapir wrote, "but I am afraid...we will find ourselves drifting into the position of genteel spies for the Department of Indian Affairs." A decade later, when a Russian ethnographer asked Jenness about the lives of Indians in the subarctic region, he advised her to consult the relevant chapter in his forthcoming *Indians of Canada.* But, he went on to say, "this book will be a Government publication...as a Government official I cannot express my opinion on the policy adopted by the department which administers all Indian Affairs."

In truth Jenness did precisely this, though in a subtle and discreet manner. "It is important to remember"—for readers in that period, "discover" would be a more accurate verb—"...that the Europeans who came to colonize [the continent] were usurpers in the eyes of the aborigines, except so far as they received rights to their land from the aborigines themselves." The vast majority of his readers would have believed that the peoples who lived in North America prior to 1492 did not own the land: the papal doctrine of *terra nullius* had granted Europeans the right to claim and occupy

land in all non-Christian territories, and although Protestants would challenge many Catholic beliefs, *terra nullius* was not one of them.

The Iroquoian peoples, Jenness noted with admiration, "permitted no
social grading in their communities, no inequalities of rank, no inheritance
of superior status." Thanks to their "keen sense of democracy" and their
"equally keen political sense," they had turned their villages and clans not
only into tribes but into "federated...nations." When he described the sun
dance festival of the prairies, Jenness used the adjectives "outstanding" and
"great"; Indian Affairs had outlawed the ritual while Scott was still a clerk.
As for the west coast potlatch, a criminal practice in the mind of Scott,
Jenness called it "not an entirely harmful institution. It consolidated all the
members of the clan...it was a powerful spur to ambition." He would have
spoken more plainly if he had not been forced to bite his tongue. "In spite
of all its abuses," he dared to say, "its prohibition by the government probably contributed not a little to that decline in the morale of the west coast
tribes which, even more than the ravages of European diseases, is gradually
bringing about their extinction."

Extinction. Jenness had little doubt that *The Indians of Canada* would be
a memorial volume. He had carried out fieldwork in Newfoundland, exam-
ining the artifacts and probing the origins of the Beothuk, the last survivor
of whom died in 1829. The extinction of the Beothuk offered a foretaste of
what, he believed, other peoples would soon experience. While Jenness
disagreed with many of the policies and methods of Indian Affairs, and
while he understood Aboriginal cultures far more deeply than Scott ever
did, he shared the pervasive belief that these cultures were doomed.

What could the future hold, for example, for the peoples of the Pacific
coast? Their intricate social organization had collapsed, leaving them outcasts in their own land. "Economically they are inefficient and an encum-
brance," Jenness wrote. "Their old world has fallen in ruins and, helpless in
the face of a catastrophe they cannot understand, they vainly seek refuge in
its shattered foundations. The end of this century, it seems safe to predict,
will see very few survivors." Likewise in the BC interior, the Carrier "do
not understand the complex civilization that has broken like a cataract over
their heads, and they can neither ride the current nor escape it. The white

settlers around them treat them with contempt, and begrudge them even the narrow lands the government has set aside for them. So they will share the fate of all, or nearly all, the tribes in British Columbia and disappear unnoticed within three or four generations."

Today the determinism of all this is hard to fathom. We are used to living in uncertainty; we know that even the safest-sounding predictions can prove utterly wrong. Thirty years ago, who would have been crazy enough to forecast the collapse of the Soviet Union, the rise of China as a capitalist superpower, the American occupations of Iraq and Afghanistan, or (most significant of all) the birth, rapid growth and dominance of the Internet and mobile electronic devices in our everyday life? Jenness and Scott carried out their work in a time of huge political uncertainty. Fascism, communism, capitalism: who in the 1920s knew what the future would embrace? Yet the broad social patterns seemed obvious—at least for Canada. And until the Second World War, one of those patterns appeared to be the disappearance of Aboriginal people.

This belief had a long history. Scott and Jenness had read the best-selling American historian Francis Parkman, whose writings enjoyed a huge influence; an incident described in one of his works gave Scott the basis for a poem. As a young man Parkman spent a few weeks travelling with a nomadic group of Sioux (to use the old term), prior to writing his 1847 book *The Oregon Trail*. After explaining how the Sioux used the buffalo not just for food and clothing but to make glue, rope, fuel, bedding and much else, Parkman declared: "When the buffalo are extinct, they too must dwindle away." The verbs allow no chance of an alternative future. He admired the warrior spirit of the Sioux: "War is the breath of their nostrils...It is chiefly this that saves them from lethargy and utter abasement. Without its powerful stimulus they would be like the unwarlike tribes beyond the mountains, scattered among the caves and rocks like beasts, and living on roots and reptiles. These latter have little of humanity except the form." The man who would soon be America's most famous historian was describing an entire group of people as subhuman. This was not a rhetorical attitude unique to the United States: in 1896 the *Manitoba Free Press* declared that Clifford Sifton, Canada's new minister for Indian Affairs, faced "the problem of teaching the Northwest Indians to live like human beings."

Scott entered the civil service just when the buffalo had, as John MacLean phrased it, "left the country." The Sioux were still fighting a rearguard battle to maintain their old way of life, but a few years later, after they were massacred by American soldiers at Wounded Knee, it was easy to believe they too were dwindling away. And not them alone. In 1906, *Scribner's* magazine in New York featured a pair of lavishly illustrated articles by the photographer Edward Curtis on Indians of the American Southwest and the Northwest Plains. The overall title was "Vanishing Indian Types." Curtis accompanied his pictures with a text full of angry passion: "We will be found guilty, as a nation, under the manipulations of crafty, unscrupulous politicians, of having committed more than 'the crime of a century.'"

Strong words. Yet Curtis began that passage in a very different spirit: "It is true that advancement demands the extermination of these wild, carefree, picturesque Indians, and, in the language of our President, we cannot keep them or their lands for bric-a-brac."

Intellectuals in Canada seldom if ever wrote about the extermination of Indians—members of the Alberta legislature, of course, are another matter—but they shared Curtis's belief that, one way or another, the advance of civilization would entail the disappearance of the uncivilized. Such was the climate of opinion in which Scott did his work—both the literary and the administrative kind. His poems first appeared in book form in *Songs of the Great Dominion,* an anthology edited by the Montreal lawyer and author W.D. Lighthall and published in London in 1889. Introducing Canadian authors to British readers, Lighthall promised that among the types of poetry they would find would be "the lament of vanishing races singing their death-song as they are swept on to the cataract of oblivion." More than four decades later, Marius Barbeau, a Quebec anthropologist and folklorist of high repute, wrote in an article that would be widely reprinted: "The Eskimos who are still left on the Arctic coast of Canada are likely soon to disappear…The Canadian Indian is now a creature of the past, who can be studied mostly in books and museums." Readers showed an appetite for romantic tales about vanishing Indians, although realistic stories on the same theme were harder to sell. In 1939 a reader for the Ryerson Press in Toronto, evaluating a book of stories by Emily Carr, wrote that "the MS. as a whole leaves one rather depressed—possibly a tribute to the author's skill but rather, I think, to the vision called up of a dying race living in squalor."

That vision applies equally well to Diamond Jenness's account of the Cree, then as now the most numerous and widespread of all the indigenous nations in Canada. The Cree, he wrote in *The Indians of Canada*, have "witnessed a ceaseless encroachment on their hunting grounds and a steady diminution in the supply of game and of fur-bearing animals. Semi-starvation and disease have lowered their physique, and the pitying scorn of the white man destroys their morale and robs them of self-respect and pride of race." Jenness was a great believer in the power of "morale," and in that last sentence he shrewdly imagines his own people from a distance. But elsewhere in the book his phrase "our Saxon forefathers" gives a clear picture of his presumed audience. As a proud New Zealander, he was an outsider in Ottawa; knowing that Maoris were accepted as full citizens in his homeland—they had held reserved seats in the New Zealand parliament since 1868—he could never regard Canada's system of Indian reserves as natural and inevitable. (A statement he delivered to a House of Commons committee in 1947, urging an end to reserves, was read into the official record under the title "A Plan for Liquidating Canada's Indian Problem Within 25 Years.") Yet he remained a son of the British Empire, a subject of the king, aspiring to inform and enlighten some of his fellow subjects. Aboriginal people, the objects of his scrutiny, were not expected to see his words.

Much of *The Indians of Canada* reads like a fact-filled elegy in prose. In the second part of the book, Jenness goes through a list of peoples one by one, giving rough population figures for when they first made sustained contact with white people and again for about 1930. These numbers reflected the knowledge of Scott's Indian Affairs agents, who were far more common on the ground than anthropologists. Time after time, the figures show a precipitous fall. The numbers of Sarcee had dropped from about 700 in the mid-nineteenth century to 160 on their "small and rather infertile tract of land" near Calgary. Within living memory the Bella Coola had consisted of between 2,000 and 3,000 people; a couple of generations later, only 300 survived in a single village. As for the Haida, smallpox and venereal disease had slashed their numbers from 8,400 in 1800 all the way down to 650. Their collapse was both demographic and spiritual. "Whole villages," Jenness wrote, "flocked to Victoria to gain quick wealth by lending their women to immoral white men." The fate of all three groups, and many others, seemed obvious.

Not so. By the twenty-first century they had learned to ride the current. Their prospects had altered, their numbers had grown, and some of the identities by which Jenness and Scott knew them had passed into history. Indeed, Canada now recognizes these and many other Aboriginal peoples by their own names. The Tsuu T'ina are no longer called the Sarcee; the Nuxalk no longer go by the name Bella Coola; and the Haida no longer live on the Queen Charlotte Islands. Those islands, which for more than two centuries honoured the German wife of a mentally ill British king, are now officially known as Haida Gwaii. The renaming took place in June 2010 as part of a "reconciliation protocol" between British Columbia and the Haida nation. That protocol also enshrined BC's commitment that in the future, on issues affecting Haida Gwaii, the province and the Haida nation would make decisions jointly.

~

POETRY IS AN ELEGIAC art. Scott was a master of it: loss could be relied upon to spur him into song. He wrote elegies for, among other people, his daughter and his father, his friends Edmund Morris and William McLennan, and the composer Claude Debussy. (Not, however, for his mother or his first wife.) Inspired by his day job, he even composed an elegy for the inhabitants of an entire continent. Yet the subjects of this particular elegy were still alive:

> The race has waned and left but tales of ghosts,
> That hover in the world like fading smoke
> About the lodges: gone are the dusky folk
> That once were cunning with the thong and snare

And mighty with the paddle and the bow;
They lured the silver salmon from his lair,
They drove the buffalo in trampling hosts,
And gambled in the tepees until dawn,
But now their vaunted prowess all is gone,
Gone like a moose-track in the April snow...

All that remains, Scott concludes, are the "wild names" the Indians left behind. This is a forcefully romantic elegy, but its subject matter is living people who had not accepted their own extinction. Call it a case of premature nostalgia. Or of vast presumption.

It wasn't the only such example. In an essay he wrote for *Scribner's* in December 1906, Scott recycled a line he had used in his recent biography of John Graves Simcoe: "The Indian nature now seems like a fire that is waning, that is smouldering and dying away in ashes; then it was full of force and heat." His sonnet "Watkwenies" describes a very old woman who once took bloody part in the wars "of the triumphant Iroquois"; now, "wrinkled like an apple kept till May," she obeys the instructions of an Indian agent and can do no more than imagine "the war-whoops of her perished day." She is, at least, still alive; in several of Scott's other poems, Indians die at the end. It's as if his consciousness of mortality and of Aboriginal people was closely intertwined.

Whites also die in his work, of course—but "the dusky folk" do little else. In death his Aboriginal characters, often seen by moonlight, prove to have "ivory features" or to be covered by "a beautiful crystal shroud." The transfiguration they undergo is akin to that of Kateri Tekakwitha, the seventeenth-century Mohawk convert who died in Kahnawake at the age of twenty-four after suffering a variety of illnesses and torments. "This face, so marked and swarthy," wrote the Jesuit priest who gave Kateri the last rites, "suddenly changed about a quarter of an hour after her death, and became in a moment so beautiful and so white that I observed it immediately." Likewise the full moon at the end of "At Gull Lake: August, 1810" loses "her dusky shade" as she rises over Keejigo's ruin, "till free of all blemish of colour" she attains "a lovely perfection, snow-pure in the heaven of midnight." The death of colour is the birth of beauty.

Perhaps Scott had his literary self in mind when, in one of his annual reports to the minister of Indian Affairs, he stated that "census statistics over a long period show a slight increase from year to year, dispelling the popular misconception that the race is dying out." With its emphasis on death and its repeated use of the word "waning," his literary work could only have encouraged the mistake. Yet the misconception was useful to the government. Declines in population were to be expected; if census records happened to show a modest increase, the department could pat itself on the back.

In "Indian Place-Names" Scott compares the prowess of "the race" to a snowy moose track melting away in the warmth of spring. The figures of speech that are central to his literary writing suggest much about how he imagined Aboriginal people. A small but telling example can be found in his story "The Winning of Marie-Louise," set in the lumber camps of western Quebec in the nineteenth century. The main characters are French Canadian: the heart of the young hero "thumped his ribs like a woodpecker;" the older man he must somehow defeat "was as sharp as a weasel." But near the beginning of the story, the narrator says that the Algonquins and Ottawas who used to travel and trade through the region no longer appear in their "ancient, savage pageant"; no longer do they paddle up the Rivière du Lièvre in canoes "like a cloud of dragon-flies." Scott likens white men to birds and predatory mammals. He likens Indians to insects.

His poem "The Half-Breed Girl" is written in the style of a Scottish ballad, an apt form given that the father of the girl in question comes from a land of "rock-built cities" and misty moors infused by "the gleam of loch and shealing" ("shieling" being a Scots word for a grazing pasture or a shepherd's hut). But the girl knows nothing of all this. At night she watches the stars "through the smoke of the dying embers, / Like the eyes of dead souls." The girl is caught between two irreconcilable worlds: "something behind her savage life / Shines like a fragile veil." Scott evokes her plight with a distant sympathy but also with the all-knowing conviction that there is, in the end, no hope for her: "she cannot learn the meaning / Of the shadows in her soul." The poet never gives the girl a name or a chance. Yet he has the power to measure the scale of her future dying: the mysterious voice that calls to her from the rapids "is larger than her life / Or than her death shall be." Her mixed blood has sealed her fate.

An objectionable idea today, this was a very common one in the past. The first major study of the Métis in the Canadian West, published in 1945 by the French historian Marcel Giraud, characterizes "the Indian" as lazy, calculating, obstinate, promiscuous, superstitious, incapable of regular work and "always the victim of his natural indolence." These qualities, in Giraud's view, were transferred to the Métis. Despite their good French blood, they were destined to become an impoverished and primitive people. The girl in Scott's ballad, unlike most Métis, lives in a "stifling wigwam." No wonder her "fierce soul hates her breath."

Better the stifling wigwam, however, than how the Iroquois appear in the work of Archibald Lampman. His poem "At the Long Sault: May, 1660," describes the deaths of Dollard des Ormeaux and his comrades at the hands of the Iroquois—an event that in Lampman's day was seen as a heroic sacrifice that had saved New France. (Historians would become a lot more skeptical in the twentieth century, many of them looking on Dollard as a reckless adventurer.) Lampman likens "the red men" to "scores of sleepless wolves, a ravening pack." Dollard holds them at bay for as long as he can, "though each setting sun / Brings from the pitiless wild new hands to the Iroquois horde." The Frenchmen fight long enough to "beat back the gathering horror" of "ruin and murder impending": thanks to their courage, New France will survive. In the end they succumb to the overwhelming force of the Iroquois enemy. Is this enemy human? Is it even animal? The Dollard of Lampman's feverish imagining is a civilized man who stands no chance against "the rush and skulk and cry / Of foes, not men but devils, panting for prey."

"Not men but devils." Lampman's main source for "At the Long Sault: May, 1660" was the historian Francis Parkman. Scott knew the Dollard story was almost certainly a gross distortion—in a newspaper column of 1892 he wrote that "there is probably as much foundation for it as there is for the majority of the romances of history, and these are amongst the dearest possessions of the race." He admired his friend's poem, calling it "a beautiful thing."

~

IT WAS ONE OF those warm June evenings when light never wants to leave the sky. My wife was away in Wales, visiting her sister, and my daughter had gone out with friends. I came in from the garden clutching an empty beer bottle and a muddy trowel. Duncan Campbell Scott was the last thing on my mind. When I heard a slight noise from the living room, I thought one of the cats must have jumped off a chair. I turned on the tap in the kitchen and began to clean up.

"Your poppies are magnificent," a voice said from behind my back.

I gave a jump and turned around, my hands still dripping.

"My apologies for taking you by surprise."

As always he had appeared in a dark suit, black shoes, a striped tie. Such was the ghostly uniform of his visits, winter or summer. In a stained T-shirt, shorts and sandals, I felt at a certain disadvantage.

"I wasn't expecting you so late," I said.

"No. I realize my previous visits have taken place in the daytime. Of course day and night mean nothing to me. I hope this is not too inconvenient a moment."

"Can you give me two minutes to make myself ready?" I didn't just want to wash my hands and face; I needed to prepare my mind.

"Of course. I will wait for you in the living room as usual."

When I reappeared, some photocopied pages in my hand, I was better dressed. Scott gave an approving nod. I suddenly recalled the image of him that Lampman offered in his long poem "An Athenian Reverie." Scott is the likely model for the narrator's friend Euktemon, a man "with clouded brow, " "gloomy and austere," whose smiles "were rare and sudden as the autumn sun." Euktemon did have a sense of humour—his laughter could occasionally roll out "in shaken peals on the delighted ear." But such moments were rare. "How strange, how bleak and unapproachable" the man generally seemed. Indeed, "how self-immured he was."

"Would you like me to put on some music?" I asked before I sat down. "A little Mozart, perhaps?"

The approval in Scott's lined face disappeared at once. "You mean music playing softly in the background? What a dreadful idea! Mr. Abley, if I were to hear the Requiem or the Great G Minor Symphony, I most assuredly would not want to listen to you."

"That's fine," I said. "So. Let's begin. I did indeed read *The Indians of Canada*."

"And?"

"I understand why you're surprised by the population totals now. Diamond Jenness expected most of the Indians to die out."

"So did we all," he replied. "At least, we expected them to vanish as a distinct race. Individual Indians would naturally be absorbed into the main body of the Canadian population—although this would take a certain length of time. I imagine this process has occurred?"

"It has, to an extent. But not only on a physical level—on a psychological one, too. One of our more famous public intellectuals, John Ralston Saul, has made the argument that Canada is a Métis civilization."

"What on earth could he mean? Does this man wear a porcupine quill in his fedora? Does he stroll around in buckskins and a sash?"

"I don't believe so, and he certainly didn't in the years when he lived at Rideau Hall and his wife was the governor general." I paused to let that idea sink in. "His Chinese-Canadian wife."

I paused again. Scott passed a hand across his forehead as though the notion were too absurd for him to contemplate. His life had encompassed seventeen governors general, all of them British, all of them male; when he died in 1947, Rideau Hall was in the grip of an aristocratic field marshal who boasted the title Viscount Alexander of Tunis.

"What he means," I said, "is that the roots of who Canadians are as a people don't come merely from Britain and France and the United States. They're Aboriginal, too. Instead of relying on a racially based concept of citizenship, for example, we have a more inclusive sense of belonging that involves circles of family and community."

"Hmm. It sounds like a nightmare for the poor souls who have to work in the Department of Immigration and Colonization."

"The *what*? I didn't know we ever had such a department."

"You should read a good Canadian history," he said in a tetchy voice. "How can one arrive at a fair understanding of the past if he doesn't know the essential facts?"

"John Ralston Saul would agree with you," I said evenly. "Though I don't suppose you and he would have the same definition of 'a good Canadian history.' He writes about the absurdity of our celebrating the Franklin expedition, for instance. If Franklin hadn't been such a blithering imperial idiot, he would have learned from the Inuit how to survive in the north, and most of his crew would have made it back to England."

Scott looked as though he wanted to argue with me, then thought better of it. "I once wrote a book of popular history," he remarked. "Not that it contains my finest writing."

"I've read it. Parts of it, anyway. To be honest I skipped the political manoeuvrings of Simcoe and the Loyalists. But I was struck by what you said about the indigenous people."

"The Iroquois, I suppose you mean."

I reached for the photocopies I had carried downstairs. "Statements like this: 'The savage nature was hardly hidden under the first, thinnest film of European customs. Scalps were hung up in their log huts, and arms that had brained children upon their parents' doorstones were yet nervous with power.'"

"And is a word of this untrue? Or is it an aspect of history you prefer to forget?"

"I think the Iroquois had a remarkable culture—still do, in fact—and I also think your phrase 'savage nature' is inexcusable." I was trying to keep my voice from rising. "Besides, Mr. Scott, have you forgotten that one of the early British governors of Nova Scotia issued a bounty for Mi'kmaq scalps? Massachusetts, New York, New Jersey, Pennsylvania—all of them had already done the same for Indians in their territory. So it's not only that your wording is aggressive and polemical. I also find it unbalanced."

"And I suppose you think the Iroquois were renowned for kindness and balance?" he said sarcastically. "I do not find my language extreme. What would you say about Stephen Leacock, I wonder?"

"I would say his Mariposa stories are quite amusing. They seem dated now, but—"

"No, no. Leacock taught political science at McGill, and he wrote a lively book entitled *The Dawn of Canadian History*. He had an intense dislike of the Huron—he called them 'despicable' and 'hideous gluttons' and said they gorged themselves 'with the rapacity of vultures.' He even used the expression 'the unhallowed fiendishness of the withered squaw…shrieking her toothless exultation.' I happen to recall those words because as the Deputy Superintendent-General of Indian Affairs, I was deeply struck by them. Yes, the gentlemanly Professor Leacock. As for the Iroquois, who all but wiped the Huron out, when he turned his attention to them he used the phrase 'diabolical cruelty.' If you're going to accuse me of writing aggressively, Mr. Abley, I think you ought to read my peers."

I shook my head. "And I think if you or Stephen Leacock or anyone else is going to talk about diabolical cruelty, you should turn your thoughts to Jeffery Amherst."

"A British commander, if I remember right, during the Seven Years War."

"The man himself. He led the successful attacks on Louisbourg and Montreal. In his old age the king granted him the title Baron Amherst of Montreal."

"A very distinguished military career," Scott said. "I thought he was also known for treating the defeated French with respect."

"He was. That's why Montreal has an Amherst Street to this very day. Personally I believe it's a disgrace."

Scott's lips were pursed. "You must enlighten me."

"A British officer was killed near Detroit in 1763," I said, peering at a second photocopied article on the coffee table. "I'm not sure which Indian nation was responsible, but the man's heart was torn out and rubbed across the faces of British prisoners. When Amherst learned the news, he wrote to a subordinate and said, 'Their total extirpation is scarce sufficient atonement for the bloody and inhuman deeds they have committed.' Total extirpation."

"Surely you can understand his fury," Scott said.

"What I can't understand, or forgive, is what he did next: he told one of his colonels to spread smallpox-infected blankets among the Indians. In fact he urged the officer not only to do this, but 'to try every other method, that can serve to extirpate this execrable race.' A leading historian of the period—a Scot, incidentally—has called Amherst not just 'rampantly racist' but 'openly genocidal.' In your book on Simcoe you praised European customs. I wonder if this was the type of custom you had in mind."

He sidestepped the question. "This spreading of smallpox that you mentioned. Did it succeed?"

"It's hard to be sure, but we know that tens of thousands of Indians soon died of the disease. Today we might call it government-sponsored terrorism."

"I see." Scott was silent for a moment, gathering his thoughts. "And do you think it's fair and appropriate to judge a military leader of the eighteenth century, fighting for the life of his people, by the standards of the twenty-first?"

"You thought it was fair to condemn the Iroquois. When you wrote about them, you threw around phrases like their 'savage nature.'"

"Yes, but I had the weight of science behind me. You seem to have merely a few letters and the odd conjecture."

I couldn't believe what I'd just heard. *The weight of science?*

"Besides, Mr. Abley, it seems a sad activity for you to forage through the distant past seeking out reasons for shame. I can't be certain from your surname, but are you of British stock?"

"I am."

"So is it your perverse desire to make yourself ashamed of your ancestors?"

"Not at all," I said. "Although I have to say my ancestors were humble people, not military officers and aristocrats. But I think your own work—I mean your literary writings, not the stuff you did at the office—could have the effect of making Aboriginal people feel ashamed of *their* ancestors. If there's such a thing as a right to collective pride, they deserve it as much as

I do. Why should I want to celebrate the colonial masters any more than the people they subjugated?"

"You speak their language. You read their literature. You share their heritage. You belong to their race."

"No," I replied quickly. "I refuse to accept that term. I prefer to follow your namesake, Frank Scott: 'The world is my country / The human race is my race.' I'll stand by that. You knew his work, I imagine?"

He wore a heavy frown. I had forgotten that in a mocking poem entitled "The Canadian Authors Meet," the young Frank Scott had satirized the worthy generation above him:

> The air is heavy with Canadian topics,
> And Carman, Lampman, Roberts, Campbell, Scott
> Are measured for their faith and philanthropics,
> Their zeal for God and King, their earnest thought.

"A facile sentiment," he said. "The world was never my country. Am I to suppose that when the Olympic Games are taking place, you gain as much pleasure in a medal won by Hungary or Japan as you do in a medal won by Canada?"

He saw me hesitate. "Let us move on," he said. "We are engaged in a futile debate. It smacks of precisely what I've been hoping to overcome."

"Meaning?"

"A wallowing in useless remorse. A quest to identify the worst in history. You will remember this is what brought me here in the first place."

I nodded, caught by a sudden memory of his first visit in midwinter. How strange it had seemed in January to converse with a ghost. Now it felt alarmingly natural.

"Mr. Abley, I have been wondering, before I leave this evening, if there is anything in particular you want to ask me. Anything that would help you in your researches."

The summer light had finally weakened in the garden. We were sitting in semi-darkness inside. No matter how many visits he paid me, I wondered if I would ever learn the meaning of the shadows in his soul.

"There is one thing," I said. In fact there were many, but this was the most delicate. "It won't be an easy question for you to answer, but I'll ask it anyway. I've been thinking about the terrible death rate in the residential schools. Did you not have any doubts about it? Did you not feel any qualms? After what happened to your daughter, I mean."

I can hardly write that he stiffened. Nonetheless, that was the impression he gave.

"Mr. Abley, I am not here to discuss—that."

"What you have to realize," I said as gently as I could, "is that if you still want me to write something that will make people understand you— something that will help them to realize you were not just a cold-hearted, thin-blooded Ottawa bureaucrat—I'll have to mention your daughter. How could I not?"

"Elizabeth's death has nothing to do with my work, either as a poet or as a public servant. Those are the areas I presume you are investigating. It should not matter to you whether I preferred to wear black socks or brown. Neither should it matter what…"

He didn't finish his sentence. Where an angel might have feared to tread, I rushed in.

"But it does. It matters because you still had twenty-five years of a distinguished career ahead of you in the civil service."

Silence. I waited, not knowing if he would choose to leave.

"This goes entirely against the grain," he said.

"I know. I'm sorry."

"Next I suppose you'll want to pry into the romantic details of my second marriage."

"No," I said, "I won't do any such thing. You married Elise a year before your retirement, so your relationship with her scarcely overlapped your job at Indian Affairs. Whereas the death of Elizabeth occurred when you were still a rising man in the department. The poems you wrote about her are very beautiful."

"Thank you," he said softly.

"But what I can't understand, and I say it not as an attack but out of real bewilderment, is this: you sent your only child off to a foreign school.

Far away—to France. She died in a convent school in the most exclusive *arrondissement* in Paris. In that same year, P.H. Bryce issued his devastating report on residential schools. And two years later, you were put in charge of the entire system. So after your own daughter had died alone in a distant boarding school, how could you ask Indian mothers and fathers to let themselves be separated from their own flesh and blood? You knew the conditions were so miserable in the schools that many of the children would die there."

"It was for the good of their people as a whole," he said, so quietly I had to strain to hear him. "They were supposed to go back home and work diligently on behalf of civilization. But not many lived up to our hopes."

I waited in case he had something else to add. He didn't.

"Could you tell me about her?" I said. I kept my own voice low. If I'd been clutching a radio or TV microphone, my producer would doubtless have expected me to ask, "And how did you *feel* when you saw her body?"

"She was a remarkable child. So gifted and quick-witted. So passionate in spirit—a redhead, like my wife. Such a lovely sense of humour. She lifted my spirits and the spirits of everyone around her."

"When she was four years old and you were travelling in northern Ontario, I know you sent her an Ojibwa cradle. And you wrote her a limerick about a bear."

"More than one limerick, if I remember right. Elizabeth loved the idea of my encountering a bear. I wish she'd had the chance to see one. But how do you know about the cradle?"

"I found a letter you sent from Sault Ste. Marie in 1899—it's been preserved with some of your other papers. A beautiful letter, I have to say, speaking as a father myself. You said of the Ojibwa children, 'They very rarely cry and look out upon you with very contented eyes. The mothers are very good to them and scratch their eyebrows and behind their ears to keep them in good humour. I bought a good many candies and gave them to the boys and girls and they liked them very much.' You sound so happy in that letter! But did you never take Elizabeth out into the wilds?"

"Not my wife's cup of tea." His face had twisted into a slight grimace. "It was Belle's desire to have Elizabeth educated in a more cultured fashion than our local schools could provide. You must remember, Ottawa in that day and age was still a rough town in some respects. It had a veneer of civilization, of course."

He paused, as though lost in memory.

"A thin veneer," I prompted him.

"Indeed. And my wife adored Paris—she had enrolled at the Conservatoire at the age of thirteen. She studied the violin there, of course, whereas our daughter concentrated on the piano. Elizabeth would rise to a greater destiny—Belle was convinced of this—if she were trained in the Old World."

"So when your daughter was eleven, you shipped her off to a convent school in a foreign language."

"When she first went, she was only nine. Does that shock you? Belle accompanied her on the voyage across the Atlantic, of course. Elizabeth came back home for a time, and then returned to Paris when she was ten. She even made a little will, leaving her dollhouse to her mother and what she called her museum to me. She had a premonition, you see. Just as I did."

"You must have missed her terribly."

"More than I can say. She sent regular letters, but still. When I sailed across the Atlantic in the spring of 1907, I could hardly contain myself. Not the calmest of seas, but I suppose it mirrored my feelings. We saw Elizabeth for a few days in Paris, so we did have the pleasure of a last reunion. The time abroad had brought a great change in her. I felt that. Yet she was overjoyed to see us. She was sorry we wouldn't be spending the whole summer together. And when we kissed goodbye, she seemed quite well. Later we could never forgive ourselves…"

"You travelled on to Spain."

"Yes. I had worked so hard for the department—the treaty negotiations and all—they gave me some extra time off. And Spain was a country we had always wanted to visit. Belle and I both took an interest in Spanish music and painting. Bullfighting, too—is that so surprising?" I must have raised my eyebrows. "We arrived at the hotel in Madrid and found a telegram awaiting us: it said Elizabeth had a worrying illness, probably scarlet fever, and we should return to Paris. We changed our plans, but before we could board the train a second telegram arrived: *Élizabeth Morte.* Those words—a knife in our hearts. It felt like the end of our lives. Of course I had imagined it all before."

"I don't understand."

"In my poem 'Death and the Young Girl.' 'The low-draped couch before the window, where / The mute blue gentian dropped and pined away...' I wrote that poem years before Elizabeth was born. How could I have known? 'See the fair threshold of eternity...' Words. Mere words."

I let a few seconds pass before I spoke again.

"So your heart broke. And your wife's. But I still don't understand, after this had happened, how could you go back to Indian Affairs and oversee the residential schools?"

"By keeping my heart in cold storage, of course."

I let out a slow sigh.

"It was helpful for me to return to the office. Looking back, I suspect Belle might not have been so high-strung if a position had been available for her. But in those days, that was out of the question—I mean, for a woman who enjoyed hosting euchre parties and sipping tea at Rideau Hall. I was the lucky one. If I'd been confined to the house, I would have gone mad."

"Still, to be in charge of the residential schools..."

"There was a long period, I admit, when everything called Elizabeth to mind. At home we tried not to speak her name. I read the agents' reports from the schools, and her picture sprang to mind. But would it have been any different if I'd supervised the Department of Railways? I might have thought continually of those train journeys to and from Madrid. Soon the government decided to create a Department of Health—would my life have been easier if duty had made me responsible for the fight against scarlet fever? No. I had to turn away from my heart—I do not care for such language, but I will use it for now—and immerse myself in work. Its demands were soothing because I felt nothing."

"Nothing?" I said. "That was unfortunate. I mean, for the children in the residential schools."

"Oh, I don't know. Our budget was always a tight one. And as I've told you already, the powers of the department were limited. Not in theory, perhaps, but certainly in practice. We respected the authority of the churches just as they respected the authority of the government."

"Maybe you shouldn't have done."

"The public wouldn't have stood for anything else. You know how they look up to men of the cloth. Besides, there was the medical context. Often, as I drank my morning coffee, I would notice in the *Citizen* or the *Globe* an article about some new epidemic. You might be unaware of this, Mr. Abley, but every year in Canada thousands of children used to die of diphtheria. Simply of diphtheria! You remember Francis Bacon's words: 'He that hath wife and children hath given hostages to fortune.' I'm sure that will always be true."

"Yes, but we need to make sure the hostages survive."

He looked at me hard. I realized my mistake.

"I'm sorry, I shouldn't have said that. Forgive me."

"Tears are the crushed essence of this world," he replied in a low tone.

"Another line of your poetry."

"Yes. From my elegy for Eddie Morris. I'm glad you recognize it. Someone else who died before his time—I wonder if he jumped to his death or if it really was an accidental fall. But life is always a risk. Always. Admittedly the Indian schools took a heavy toll. But was the toll much worse than what you'd find if you examined the deaths that occurred in orphanages and mental asylums and schools for the handicapped?"

"I don't suppose we'll ever know," I said. "Not many of those institutions kept proper records, and I'm sure the death rates were sometimes terrible. But it was only the residential schools that set out to destroy entire cultures. It was only the residential schools whose staff were paid to extinguish other languages and beliefs. It was only the residential schools where the teachers looked down on the children as members of an inferior race. I'm sure some of the cruelty was casual and thoughtless. But much of it was deliberate."

Scott carried on as though I hadn't spoken. "I recall a feeling of drift. But I had to believe I was working for the public good. How else could I keep going?"

"I couldn't say," I replied. "But thank you for sharing all this with me. It can't have been easy." Even as I spoke, my words sounded stupid in my ears. "I remember reading that when Rupert Brooke stopped off in Ottawa in 1913, he could see the lingering effect of Elizabeth's death on both you and your wife. It had happened six years earlier, but he felt you were still dazed by it."

"Yes. He was a keen observer as well as a good poet. We were in each other's company for a full week. He loved the wildflowers in the Gatineau. But do you know what I did when he was about to leave?"

"I have no idea."

"I gave him an open letter to all the Indian agents in the West. I also handed him a private letter addressed to the principal of the Indian school at Brandon, and another to the agent for the Stoney tribe off the road between Calgary and Banff. I hoped he might have time to visit the Blood reserve in southern Alberta, too. Now tell me, would I have done all this if I'd felt ashamed of the department's efforts? Brooke was a writer, and I knew his trip across Canada would set his pen hurrying to the ink bottle. Would I have invited him to visit reserves and Indian schools if I'd thought he would denounce our work?"

His voice had recovered its firmness, his eyes their steely glint.

"Did Brooke ever follow up on your invitations?"

"He wrote an essay about the Stoney reserve for the *Westminster Gazette*."

"And what did he say?"

"He called the Indians picturesque and praised the men for their dignity. And he also wrote"—Scott cleared his throat—"'The Government, extraordinarily painstaking and well-intentioned, has established Indian schools, and trains some of them to take their places in the civilisation we have built.' You see my point?"

"Is that all he said?"

"No, it isn't. But I'm sure if you took the trouble, you could find out the rest for yourself."

I was feeling a little jangled. The evening had become a warm blur. Somewhere a cat was meowing at a door.

"I remember," Scott said, "Brooke was very fond of my cat. Skookum greatly appreciated his willingness to be playful. I'm afraid that Belle and I had lost the habit."

"You gave your cat an Indian name?"

"Indeed. Skookum means 'strong' or 'brave' in the Chinook that people speak up and down the west coast. Or merely 'good.' I think our cat lived up to all three possibilities."

I stood up to let one of my own cats in, and Scott took the hint.

"That's enough for a single evening," he said. "The slender moon and one pale star."

"I beg your pardon?"

"I was quoting myself again. A bad habit. Not one of my best poems, I suppose, though it does express the sentiment 'Tis sometimes better not to know.' Perhaps in the afterlife I should have followed my own advice."

His thoughts were coming so thick and fast I had trouble following him.

"You mean ignorance is bliss?" I said. Another cat was demanding my attention.

"Nothing is pure bliss," he said. "And nothing will come of nothing. But thank you for your attention tonight. I shall return."

"Wait!" I called from the back door. "Come and look at this!"

The garden was alive with fireflies. No sooner did my eyes catch a shimmering flash than it vanished and another flickered into life elsewhere. They spangled the night air like stars. Everywhere I looked—beside the white pine, beyond the rows of chard and spinach, in front of the apple tree—points of light were dancing in the darkness.

But the visitor had gone.

6

The Sacredness of Treaty Promises

DUNCAN CAMPBELL SCOTT DID not lead a thrilling life. He had no record-ed love affairs. He never went bankrupt and was never arrested. He lived in a single city and worked for a single employer. Even his friend Madge Mac-beth admitted he had "a rather aloof and forbidding exterior." Year after year he strolled from Lisgar Street to Sparks Street in the morning, and in the late afternoon he strolled from Sparks Street back to Lisgar Street. Hayter Reed, one of his predecessors as Deputy Superintendent-General of Indian Affairs, was keen to dress up as the St. Lawrence Iroquoian chief Donnacona at a "historical ball" in the Senate chamber, which he entered in dark makeup, wearing a long wig and carrying a raised tomahawk; Reed uttered war whoops before making a few remarks in Cree to the governor general and his wife. This was, to say the least, not Scott's style. His delight was classical music: as well as listening avidly to the latest recordings in his home, he kept a muted piano in his office and could, on occasion, be found silently practising a sonata or a rhapsody at the keyboard instead of poring over departmental papers. He served for many years as president of the Ot-tawa Little Theatre, seeing it through the worst of the Depression; he was a patron of the National Gallery. (When you walk up the colonnade in the present gallery from the entrance to the main hall, you pass a long engraved list of donors to the collection; the name Duncan Campbell Scott is there.) His truest life was a life of the mind.

As his career flourished, it gave him more and more chances to length-en his horizons and nourish his mind far from the confines of Ottawa. The summer of 1899, for example, found him travelling by railway and canoe through northwestern Ontario. In 1910 he visited Indian schools and reserves in Western Canada. The following year he toured the Maritimes. And so on. In later years a warm-weather trip to inspect far-off reserves became a regular event. But the longest and most significant of these expeditions took place in the summers of 1905 and 1906, when he journeyed by canoe through the far reaches of northern Ontario (at the time, much of it still qualified as the North-West Territories) as one of three treaty commissioners. He was representing the government of Canada.

The commissioners' job was to persuade the Ojibwa and Cree who roamed the region to sign the recently agreed-upon Treaty Nine. Its provisions had been agreed upon, that is, by the governments of Ontario and Canada, after delicate and quiet negotiations in which Scott played a pivotal role. The ensuing trips were among the great experiences of his life, the catalyst for some of his finest poems. Conditions were often rough—hard rain and heat, mosquitoes and vicious blackflies—but the trips allowed him to spend many weeks amid forests and waterways untouched by industrial development and inhabited by Aboriginal peoples who were not yet under the full control of Indian Affairs. They fished, hunted, trapped and gathered wild plants freely throughout the region. Few of their children were enrolled in a residential or any other kind of school.

Treaty Nine meant a relinquishment of their title to a vast territory. Henceforth there could be no annoying disputes about ownership of the lands and waters: about 90,000 square miles of what Scott and his fellow commissioners saw as untamed wilderness. Both levels of government were eager to win formal approval of the treaty, thereby ensuring that railway building, mining, forestry, hydro-electric development and other sorts of bustling enterprise could go ahead without any risk of lawsuits or confrontation. Ottawa's position—as expressed today on the website of Aboriginal Affairs and Northern Development Canada—is that "in response to continuous petitions from the Cree and Ojibwa people of northern Ontario, and in keeping with its policy of paving the way for settlement and development, the federal government in 1905–1906 negotiated Treaty 9, also known as the James Bay Treaty." This statement implies that the Cree and Ojibwa played an active role in working out the terms of the deal.

Nothing could be further from the truth. Aboriginal people were offered no chance to amend the treaty; in the scattered trading posts, forts and villages where they gathered, Scott and his fellow commissioners presented the deal to them on a take-it-or-leave-it basis. In return for their signatures, or a cross beside their names, the Ojibwa and Cree received eight dollars per person, the pledge of four dollars a person each year in the future, and a small amount of land reserved for their communities, places where outsiders would be forbidden to trespass. Signing was generally followed by a feast and, to Scott's regret, a dance. Along with the gifts went a promise that indigenous children would be educated and an assurance that indigenous families could hunt and fish throughout their traditional lands—in principle, that is. The commissioners did not explain the ruinous impact that roads, mines, logging camps and a new transcontinental railway were likely to have on the populations of beaver and other fur-bearing mammals. Many of the grim effects that Scott described in his final report to the minister in 1931 were a legacy of Treaty Nine. It had indeed "paved the way."

Scott was the senior government official on the trips. He made speeches, showed the flag, collected signatures and kept a scanty journal. From time to time, especially in the summer of 1906, he also wrote poems. He had the leisure to do so, because the white men in the party—three commissioners, a doctor, a Hudson's Bay Company official and a pair of Mounties—left the paddling and pack-bearing to their Métis and Indian crew. Not that Scott was always averse to canoeing or portaging. He had gone on some arduous canoe trips with Archibald Lampman, introducing his friend to the rivers and lakes of the Gatineau and the Lower St. Lawrence. But on those occasions, pitching their tents in clearings bright with wildflowers, listening to the elusive thrushes and warblers overhead, he and his friend were young writers free of obligations. Now Lampman was dead, and a middle-aged Scott shouldered the government's duty.

On the 1905 trip he was struck by "the landscape for the most part desolate beyond compare, loneliness seven times distilled." In 1906, to reduce his loneliness, he invited Pelham Edgar, a professor of French and English literature at the University of Toronto, to accompany the party. It was a productive decision. As Edgar later recalled, "A stanza or two would be jotted down as he sat beside me in the canoe. Lunch was always a risky meal, for I would find the poet a hundred yards off the trail scribbling another stanza." I suspect that at such moments Scott didn't want to be found, even by his genteel, moustachioed friend. The poems he drafted on the canoe or off the trail are alive with emotion and vibrant imagery. They evoke a "land of quintessential passion / Where in a wild throb Spring wells up with power." They describe "the partridge drumming in the distance, / Rolling out his mimic thunder in the sultry noons." They recount how "like fireflies the stars alight and spangle / All the heaven meadows thick with growing dusk." In northern Ontario the natural world came alive for Scott, and his imagination flared up in joyful response.

Such poems have a very different tone than the essay he published about these journeys in the New York magazine *Scribner's*. "The Last of the Indian Treaties" appeared in print in December 1906, while memories of the trips were still keen in his mind. For the most part the essay is a loose travelogue, though it includes a brief account of the intricate political manoeuvring that led up to his northern experiences. Scott also gives a casual justification for policies that decades later would come under sustained attack.

His approach to the Aboriginal people of northern Ontario was paternalistic. Scott would not have seen that as a criticism; a century ago, "paternalistic" was not a bad word. What could the Indians grasp, he asked rhetorically, "of the pronouncement on the Indian tenure which had been delivered by the law lords of the Crown," or of the "elaborate negotiations" between Ontario and the federal government that produced the treaty agreement? "Nothing. So there was no basis for argument. The simpler facts had to be stated, and the parental idea developed that the King is the great father of the Indians, watchful over their interests, and ever compassionate." This was a metaphor, of course, but as a poet more than anyone else should know, a metaphor can have tremendous power—especially if a listener encountering it for the first time hears it as fact.

In Ottawa, a very different sense of metaphor prevailed. In 1899, with Queen Victoria still on the throne, a dispute had arisen between the Mohawks of the Bay of Quinte and the Department of Indian Affairs. The Mohawks trusted and respected a physician who worked on their reserve, a man the department chose to dismiss. Unhappy at his firing, the Mohawks protested to the queen. The governor general of the day, Lord Minto, sympathized and tried to intervene on their behalf. He was coolly brushed off by the minister responsible for Indian Affairs, Clifford Sifton: "It is as Your Excellency remarks quite correct that the Indians have always looked upon Her Majesty as a final Court of appeal for any complaint which they may wish to make. As a matter of practice however the actual discharge of such functions has for many years been confined to recommending the representations which may be made by the Indians, to the careful attention of the advisers of the Crown." Even in the late nineteenth century, then, Ottawa was insisting that the Crown has no power regarding Aboriginal people except to pass their concerns to the government of Canada.

This is not the belief that many Aboriginal people—including Chief Theresa Spence of Attawapiskat—retain to this day. She repeatedly asked to meet the governor general, as well as the prime minister, while conducting a six-week hunger strike in 2012–13. Canadians who are puzzled by the continuing demands of Aboriginal people that the Crown should be involved in political talks would do well to consider how matters were construed to them when the relevant treaties were signed.

In their official 1905 report, for instance, Scott and the other two commissioners described a meeting with the Ojibwa of Fort Hope, near the headwaters of the Attawapiskat River. They quoted Moonias, "one of the most influential chiefs," as saying, "Now, you gentlemen come to us from the King offering to give us benefits for which we can make no return. How is this?" An Oblate priest, François-Xavier Fafard, stepped in and explained that by signing the treaty, "the Indians were giving their faith and allegiance to the King and for giving up their title to a large area of land of which they could make no use, they received benefits that served to balance anything which they were giving." In his private journal the Ontario commissioner,

George MacMartin, revealed more: "Mr. Scott thro' an Interpreter stated to them that the King had sent the Commission to see how his people were and to enter into a Treaty with them, and that the King wished to help his subjects and see they were happy and comfortable." Their annual payment, Scott told the gathering, was a gift from the king.

Scott mentioned the Fort Hope payment in his *Scribner's* essay, recalling that "Chief Moonias was perplexed by the fact that he seemed to be getting something for nothing... He was mightily pleased when he understood that he was giving something that his great father the King would value highly." The phrasing suggests a sort of complicity between Scott and his audience, a wink of mutual irony: the author and his readers realize that Edward VII had never heard of Moonias and would have been flabbergasted to think of himself as the chief's father.

But in Aboriginal culture, as the historian J.R. Miller puts it, "relationships were established with strangers through the making of ascribed or fictive kinship. A series of ceremonies—speeches, gift exchanges and the smoking of the pipe—was the protocol by which European strangers were converted into kin and their leader, the monarch, into a parental figure." Moreover, among people with an oral culture, "the treaty consisted of everything that was said, and not just things that the government of Canada's representatives chose to write down."

Near the start of his essay, Scott characterized the first treaties between the British Crown and Aboriginal people in what would soon become Upper Canada as "these puerile negotiations...this alliance that was based on a childish system of presents." Even so, at the heart of the treaties was an agreement of great importance: "Whatever has been written down and signed by king and chief both will be bound by so long as 'the sun shines and the water runs.'" Scott was using a metaphor again, but this time taking it seriously. Small wonder, then, that to this day (in J.R. Miller's words) "the Crown is the symbol of their relationship to the rest of society as First Nations conceive it to be. They insist on the eternal nature of the treaties they made, and choose not to recognize that the rest of Canada has evolved a different relationship to the Queen." To generalize broadly, Aboriginal people look on a treaty as the acknowledgment of a relationship; non-

Aboriginal people look on a treaty as the acknowledgment of a transfer of power.

⁓

SCOTT WAS NEVER A man for loose talk; he kept a close watch on his emotions. So did most of the indigenous people he met along the way. Recalling how impassive the Ojibwa had appeared to be when his party's canoes reached Osnaburgh, a trading post and Anglican mission in northwestern Ontario, he wrote: "Nothing else is so characteristic of the Indian, because this mental constitution is rooted in physical conditions. A rude patience has been developed through long ages of his contact with nature which respects him no more than it does the beaver." Somewhere beneath the surface of his prose, a compliment may be struggling to get through.

His encounters with Aboriginal people in northern Ontario might have been more rewarding if Scott had been less of an introvert. Many years later William Arthur Deacon, the literary editor of the *Globe and Mail,* urged him "to be more aggressive. You have always been so shy as to appear aloof and haughty—even disdainful. I know you are none of these terrible things." Scott's friend Edmund Morris—a painter who came along for part of the 1906 trip—learned a song in the Ojibwa language and would later amaze the residents of an Alberta reserve by singing it to them. Such antics were not for the head commissioner. He was a proud man, more than a little afraid of the wilderness. When he wasn't conducting business on the journey, or drafting fresh stanzas of poetry, he preferred to spend his time reading Victorian poets like Meredith and Swinburne. The contrast between the low, dark conifers all around him and Swinburne's "bloomless buds of poppies, / Green grapes of Proserpine" was acute; the contrast, too, between the hunters and trappers in his face-to-face meetings and the classical gods in his books. As Stan Dragland points out in *Floating Voice,* Scott noticed cultural difference but read it as cultural inferiority. "It's easy to wish," Dragland writes, "that he had been vouchsafed the internal distance that time has granted us, but he can't be plucked out of this...encounter, like an Ebenezer Scrooge by some consciousness-raising ghost, and retroactively granted the power to understand before it's too late."

"The Last of the Indian Treaties" shows compassion, now and then, peering shyly through a thick forest of words. It soon escapes, chased away by Scott's absolute refusal to countenance any sort of protest or rebellion. "He—" the generic Indian, that is—"enriches the fur-traders and incidentally gains a bare sustenance by his cunning and a few gins and pitfalls for wild animals." ("Gins" are leghold traps, not alcoholic drinks.) "When all the arguments against this view are exhausted it is still evident that he is but a slave, used by all traders alike as a tool to provide wealth, and therefore to be kept in good condition as cheaply as possible." *But a slave?* This was a bitter and dangerous perception. Scott pursued it no further.

When he republished "The Last of the Indian Treaties" forty years later in his final book, *The Circle of Affection,* he did not reprint any of the photographs he took on the journeys. A large camera had been a constant accessory. Some pictures had appeared in *Scribner's* with succinct captions: "An Indian family, travelling" or "Poling up rapids, Abitibi River." One of the best pictures, taken at Osnaburgh, showed "the blind chief Missabay making a speech"—a man in a dark hat, a white shirt, a vest and heavy pants, a sash wrapped around his waist, a tall stick in his left hand. His listeners sat on the ground near the palisaded walls of a fort. In the photograph Missabay's sightless eyes were cast down toward the sunlit earth. This was the trusting leader who, as Scott reported in his essay, told the commissioners, "We know now that you are good men sent by our great father the King to bring us help and strength in our weakness. All that we have comes from the white man and we are willing to join with you and make promises which will last as long as the air is above the water, as long as our children remain who come after us."

Missabay was speaking in Ojibwa, a language Scott appreciated on an aesthetic level but could not understand. How much, I wonder, do those English sentences reflect the speaker's actual images and thoughts? How much do they reflect the perceptions of the translator, a hulking Métis boatman named Jimmy Swain? And how much do they reflect Scott's own purposes in writing the essay? I suspect that the words he quoted Missabay as saying were configured, in part, as a riposte to Edward Curtis, whose illustrated essays about "vanishing Indians" had appeared in *Scribner's* earlier in the year. Scott had published many poems and short stories in the magazine; he was a regular reader.

Curtis is often condemned today. Academics steeped in postcolonial theory look on his photographs with scorn, finding them naive and patronizing; he stands accused of exploiting his subjects on the one hand and of romanticizing them on the other. Such critics underestimate the man even as they oversimplify his work. To read his essays is to glimpse how deeply he sensed the suffering of the people on the far side of his lens— even though, or perhaps because, he couldn't bring himself to view them as adults. "In many despondent hours of pondering over the fate of these native children," he wrote in *Scribner's* in 1906, "I have felt that perhaps if they, too, could have perished with the buffalo herd it would have been vastly better for them." He attacked the Indian office in Washington: "The continual changes of the department's so-called policies have been one of the Indians' greatest curses." And he quoted a series of accusations he had repeatedly heard from the Plains Indians: "that the management of the reservation affairs is dishonest and corrupt; that the principal effort the employees are making is to keep their positions; that the returned students are given no opportunity to advance, but, on the contrary, are kept down; and that the Government at Washington is not keeping the promises of the past, nor those of today." Curtis professed to find these accusations "extreme," though he said nothing to refute the charges.

"The relationship of the Indians and people of this country is that of a child and parent," Curtis wrote. (Notice how he defined the American people so as to exclude Indians.) "We will stand convicted for all time as a parent who failed in his duty." Months later, to readers of the same magazine, Scott set out to reveal how much better Canada treated its own "wards." It's always a delicate task to tell Americans that they could learn from another country's experience, but Scott wanted them to grasp the ways in which Ottawa's approach was wiser than Washington's. Curtis, for example, had confessed to his readers: "In all our years of handling the Indians we have taught them one thing—the white man seldom told the truth." Intending to show those same readers how different things are in Canada, Scott declared that the Indian diplomacy in this country—carried out first by the British, then by the authorities in Ottawa—had always relied on "the principle of the sacredness of treaty promises." And that principle remained valid. The government had not altered its policies; the government had kept its promises. Missabay's speech demonstrated the result: Canada was a good parent whose Indian children were humbly thankful.

That's what Scott wanted his readers to believe, in any event. He was neither the first nor the last Canadian to distort the truth for an American audience. It was in Pittsburgh in 2009 that Prime Minister Stephen Harper made the astonishing statement, "We also have no history of colonialism. So we have all of the things that many people admire about the great powers, but none of the things that threaten or bother them." Did he really believe what was coming out of his lips? Three years later, with the Idle No More movement gaining strength, a former prime minister, Paul Martin, stated: "We have never admitted to ourselves that we were, and still are, a colonial power."

When his essay finally appeared in book form, Scott retained its misleading title, although two more treaties had been signed since, in northern Saskatchewan and the Northwest Territories. But he or his publisher decided not to reprint a document that had appeared in *Scribner's* under the heading "Part of the Albany address in Cree syllabics." The commissioners had heard this letter read aloud—Scott doesn't identify the author, whose name was William Goodwin—once they had emerged from the apparently endless forests of northern Ontario, the intertwining rivers and lakes, and had reached the shallow coast of James Bay. In the rare villages along the almost featureless shore, "a few of the better elements of our civilization were noticeable." (Scott meant, I imagine, that the people appeared to be clean, suitably dressed and reasonably fed.) Transliterated into a style of English reminiscent of the King James Bible, Goodwin's letter reads: "From our hearts we thank thee, O Great Chief, as thou hast pitied us and given us temporal help. We are very poor and weak ... and we pray for thee to our Father in Heaven. Thou hast helped us in our poverty ... And we trust that it may ever be with us as it is now; we and our children will in the Church of God now and ever thank Jesus." This was how Scott liked his Indians: tame, humble, unthreatening.

Perhaps that's a cheap shot. After all, he chose to conclude "The Last of the Indian Treaties" with a portrait of a young Indian man named Charles Wabinoo, a "wild fellow" who appeared in Fort Albany just as the commissioners were about to leave. "He did not ask for anything"—this was guaranteed to raise him in Scott's opinion—"he stood, smiling slightly. He seemed about twenty years of age, with a face of great beauty and intelligence, and eyes that were wild with a sort of surprise—shy at his novel position and proud that he was of some importance." The commissioners found his name on the recipients' list and gave him the eight dollars he was entitled to. He kept a crucifix in his clothing, and after receiving the money he took it out, kissed it and thanked the commissioners from his heart. "There was the Indian at the best point of a transitional state," Scott writes, "still wild as a lynx, with all the lore and instinct of his race undimmed." To meet the commissioners, Charles Wabinoo had travelled down the James Bay coast from the village of Attawapiskat.

A residential school had opened in Fort Albany a few years before Scott's arrival. No doubt that's why he was impressed by the clothing and appearance of the Cree people he met—according to a saying popular in his era, "cleanliness is next to godliness." He encountered plenty of godliness too: the welcome his party received at Fort Albany "was literally with prayer and songs of praise and sounds of thanksgiving." Anglicans and Catholics each had a mission in the little settlement, the competitive faiths separated from each other by the busy and neutral space of a Hudson's Bay Company post. The imposing three-storey school was in the hands of the Oblates of Mary Immaculate.

From time to time children ran away from it; from time to time children died. Yet St. Anne's School remained open until 1973, housing students from the local area as well as from Attawapiskat and other James Bay settlements. Perhaps some of them benefited from the experience. But when the journalist Peter Moon visited Fort Albany in 1996, he found dozens of former students who had vivid, disturbing memories of the school.

They spoke of sexual attacks on both girls and boys; they spoke of repeated violence and humiliation; they spoke of confinement in darkness. In particular, they recalled a homemade electric chair in which unruly or rebellious children were confined. "The nuns used it as a weapon," Mary-Anne Nakogee-Davis said. "They would strap your arms to the metal arm rests, and it would jolt you and go through your system. I don't know what I did that was bad enough to have that done to me." The following year, seven men and women who had worked at St. Anne's were charged with a variety of offences including assault, assault causing bodily harm, administering a noxious substance, gross indecency, and indecent assault. The noxious substance was the children's own vomit, which they had been forced to eat.

"It was a really traumatizing experience," Leo Loone would tell a Toronto gathering in 2012 organized in support of the Truth and Reconciliation Commission. "It was like being in a hard-time prison." The trials of former staff had dragged on for years. Decades after the residential school in Fort Albany closed its doors, the damage persists.

⟜

IN HIS MAGISTERIAL BOOK *Treaty No. 9,* John Long of Nipissing University gathered together as much historical memory of the 1905 trip as he could unearth a century later: not only Scott's published essay and the commissioners' final report, but also each commissioner's private journal, the doctor's report, payment records, photographs, Aboriginal oral histories and so on. These items reveal some striking discrepancies in the accepted version of events.

Scott was not much of a diarist. His entry for August 1 reads, in its entirety: "Up at 4:30. Left 6:10. Sailed with a light wind. Paid Inds at Cheepy River. Camped at 6." Luckily the two other commissioners were more loquacious. George MacMartin, representing the province of Ontario, noted that as the boats sailed down the Albany River that morning they passed an abandoned Hudson's Bay Company post; he remarked on the "excessively hot" weather and described an Indian burial ground by the riverbank. Samuel Stewart, a colleague of Scott in Indian Affairs, mentioned the "grand display of Northern Lights" that evening and told of a Cree boy the party had taken downriver to rejoin his parents at Fort Albany. Stewart also commented on the mingled emotions of hope and fear the commissioners found among a group of Indians who had camped on a beautiful spot of land "at the foot of the Chepai Seepee or Ghost River, or River of the dead." Anxious to receive their treaty money, they were terrified of the two policemen travelling with the commissioners. "One of the Indians, an old man, fairly shook all over with fear, and I think one of the happiest moments of his life was when, after paying him their money, we sailed away." Thanks to Stewart, we know the party later watched a school of belugas sporting in the salt waters beyond Moose Factory.

Such details, which could well have been useful to the only poet in the canoes, were almost never recorded by the only poet in the canoes. Scott's journals grew more and more succinct as the journey unfolded. On the first day of camping he made an entry in a disapproving tone—"Inds here had shot 2 moose. Were lazing about gorging themselves on it"—and noted his own consumption of a snack. But soon he was limiting his entries to dates, times and places. The much fuller journals of Stewart and (especially) MacMartin not only provide a better record of events and places along the way; they also reveal that the official record is not always in line with what the commissioners actually said.

What would be the true purpose, for example, of the reserves? Some Ojibwa, in particular, were suspicious that they might be confined in their new homes—the government was promising them one square mile per family. At Marten Falls, MacMartin's journal shows that both before and after the feast, local people expressed doubts about the offer. When the meal was over, "the chief and his councillors came to our quarters saying that they wanted both banks for 50 miles down river as a hunting reserve." This was unacceptable. MacMartin says "it was forcibly put before them"—by Scott, presumably—"that it was a home for them that was being provided & not a hunting preserve and that they could hunt wherever they pleased." Only on that basis did they sign the treaty. It seems a far cry from Scott's published description of the Ojibwa as "stoical, even taciturn."

This and several of MacMartin's other journal entries suggest that the commissioners neglected to tell their Aboriginal listeners about the underlying motive of the trip: to ensure that what Scott in his *Scribner's* essay called "many million feet of pulpwood, untold wealth of minerals, and unharnessed water-powers sufficient to do the work of half the continent" would be procured for future development at minimal expense. In that light, the trip was an extraordinary success. "The silver mines at Cobalt," Brian Titley writes in *A Narrow Vision,* "which had started all the excitement, produced in excess of $206,000,000 of the precious metal during their first eighteen years of operation. Knowing that the budget for the first round of treaty negotiations was less than $40,000 makes the magnitude of the 'bargain' clear." Today, about 90 kilometres west of Attawapiskat, the largest diamond company in the world, De Beers, operates a massive open-pit mine with its own townsite and airstrip. The mine is intended to process more than 7,000 tons of rock per day, and to produce 600,000 carats worth of diamonds each year.

John Long asserts in *Treaty No. 9* that "traditional territories…were not mapped or surveyed—or even inquired about—at treaty time. And, by MacMartin's account, the Ojibwa and Cree of northern Ontario were never asked to surrender them." By contrast, the commissioners' official report says that "the terms of the treaty having been fully explained, the Indians stated that they were willing to come under its provisions." What they signed was a parchment document whose provisions allowed Aboriginal people to hunt, trap and fish throughout their traditional lands, "subject to such regulations as may from time to time be made by the Government… and saving and excepting such tracts as may be required or taken up from time to time for settlement, mining, lumbering, trading or other purposes." In short, governments and private companies would now have the power to evict Indians as and when they wished. If the commissioners failed to explain this crucial point to the people affected, is the treaty valid?

The forests chopped down or broken up; the waterways polluted; all that was eventually left to the Aboriginal people were their scattered reserves: dots on a map, homes secured by the sacredness of a treaty promise. Yet as the decades passed, more and more people in the cities of southern

Canada began to see these reserves as backward remnants of a bygone age. Who in their right mind would want to live in Attawapiskat if they could move to Toronto, or even Sudbury? Such a question usually leads to another: And why should we pay for them anyway? "There are no economic reasons for Attawapiskat to exist," wrote a columnist in the *National Post* in 2011, "and it does so only because it is underwritten by the Canadian taxpayer." He condemned the reserve's leaders for financial mismanagement but added, "The real killer is remoteness."

The best short response I've found is an article by the novelist and journalist Richard Wagamese, who was born in northwestern Ontario on what is now the Ojibway Wabasseemoong First Nation. "When you're down to the last thing that represents a connection to who you are," Wagamese writes, "when you've watched everything that was part and parcel of the story of your people get torn away, and you're left to stand with only one thing to hold onto, you will cling to that last thing with everything you have in order to not disappear. Any human being would. That's why native people won't leave reserves despite the dire circumstances—because they're the last thing they have."

Outsiders often look on such places as isolated enclaves, cut off from the modern world, disconnected from everything that matters. To Wagamese, that view is radically mistaken. In the minds of many Aboriginal people, their reserves "represent the tie to cultural ways, traditional teachings, spirituality, language, history, world view and self-identity. They are roots and they are a reminder that a people's sovereignty was never, and is not, for sale, barter or surrender." A reserve is a place of kinship, not of rupture. Its land is sacred. A reserve is also, from an Aboriginal standpoint, the result of a nation-to-nation agreement—a notion that would have baffled Scott. You can't measure its success in purely economic terms: as Wagamese puts it, a reserve is "the essence of community."

One day in 2012 I attended a talk in suburban Montreal by Ellen Gabriel, a Mohawk activist from the community of Kanesatake. (If William Scott had had his way, of course, there would be no Kanesatake.) Much of her speech dealt with the Oka crisis of 1990, in which as a young woman she had acted as a leading spokesperson and negotiator. Her PowerPoint slides were projected from a computer operated by a hefty young man, Clifton Nicholas, whose black T-shirt featured an image of Aboriginal warriors and the slogan "Homeland Security: Fighting Terrorism Since 1492." Land was the underlying focus of Gabriel's talk. "This is the land of our ancestors," she said, looking at Nicholas. "At least we have some of it left." She turned to face the audience. "Having access to our lands—it's about taking care of all our relations, including the four-legged ones. It's about having access to our medicines." Twice she said, "There has to be a better way."

Gabriel spoke with a sort of fragile hope about the United Nations Declaration on the Rights of Indigenous Peoples, adopted by the General Assembly in 2007. Canada at first rejected the document, Indian Affairs minister Chuck Strahl calling it "unworkable in a Western democracy." Three years later, the government changed its tune and quietly endorsed the declaration. But it's easy to see why Ottawa would find it threatening. Among its many provisions is this: "Indigenous peoples have the right to own, use, develop and control the lands, territories and resources that they possess by reason of traditional ownership or other traditional occupation or use." The entire purpose of Duncan Campbell Scott's work on Treaty Nine had been to extinguish that right.

〜

MY GARDEN NEEDED SERIOUS care. Rain had not fallen for nearly a month, and in its absence, the vegetables were suffering. The lilies had finished blooming early, the marigolds were wilting and even the prickly blue scabious could have used a good drink. I was about to mow the front lawn, where the height of the yellowing grass had begun to attract reproving looks from my neighbours. But when I looked into the dining room and saw him standing beside the window, I knew the lawn would have to wait.

"Greetings, Mr. Abley. I imagine the weather will be hot today."

"As you see by my clothes. Would you like to come into the garden? It seems a shame to stay inside on a beautiful morning like this. We could sit at the table on the back deck."

"No, thank you." His expression gave nothing away. I recalled a reporter's description of him: "Duncan Campbell Scott, with his pale, deeply furrowed face, his pointed features and spare figure, seemed to have much of the greyhound in his make-up, and might have been mistaken for a keen, alert, and watchful Yankee."

"You prefer to stay indoors then," I said.

"Without going into further details about my—situation, I can say that in the open air it would become harder for you to retain a coherent vision of me. There might be some dissipation, as it were."

"And we wouldn't want any dissipation."

He did not reply. I gestured toward the heavy armchair, and after a final glance at the riot of yellow and blue in the nearest flowerbed, he sat down as before. Clearing away some newspapers and magazines from the sofa, I found a place for myself. For a few moments I waited in silence for him to begin the conversation; then I realized that on this occasion he was waiting for me.

"Last week I saw a documentary about you."

"Ah. That seems most unlikely. Will you describe it for me?"

"It was made by the National Film Board back in 1995. I watched it in downtown Montreal, at the NFB's film library. I was quite impressed. The actor who played you is one of the best in the country. R.H. Thomson— you wouldn't know his name, of course. You died shortly after he was born."

"Did he do a good job?"

"Absolutely. He looked very austere. But to my surprise, he also made you appear downright handsome."

Scott and I shared a laugh. I was reminded of a line by the literary scholar Robert McDougall: "His eyes, behind rimless glasses, may seem cold, but they can light up quickly with a twinkle that is both impish and warm."

The laugh didn't last for long. "What was the name of this documentary?"

"*The Poet and the Indians*," I said.

"I see. And did it repeat the usual libel?"

I wasn't sure how to answer. "It quoted from your work. Your poetry, I mean—'The Onondaga Madonna' and so on—but it also quoted material you produced as a civil servant. And there were interviews with experts who have written about you."

"What kind of experts?"

"A literary critic—a very good one, Stan Dragland. And a couple of historians. One of them is Cree herself, Winona Stevenson."

"A historian who's a Cree woman…" Scott's voice trailed off as though in disbelief.

"Well, times have changed. She talked about the legacy of your work— First Nations families who don't know how to raise their children, because the three previous generations weren't allowed to." I paused, in case he wanted to reply. He did not. "Another of the talking heads—the people who were interviewed, that is—was national chief of the Assembly of First Nations at the time: Ovide Mercredi, a very articulate man. He made a fascinating point: cultural oppression can turn into its own worst enemy. Oppression can actually become the driving force in maintaining a people's identity. 'You can't get rid of a culture by edicts of Indian Affairs,' that's how he put it."

"Perhaps not," said Scott. "But neither can you maintain a culture by an act of will, if all the weight of history opposes it."

I needed to think about that one. So I carried on as if he had not spoken. "James Cullingham, who was the filmmaker, included lots of old black-and-white photographs. You took many of them yourself. And a film crew went out to Osnaburgh. They—"

"To Osnaburgh. Really!" His eyes were bright with interest. "How does it look now?"

I felt a curious reluctance to speak openly. Over the previous months I had come to realize that for Scott's ghost, plain speech was often hurtful. It was also necessary, of course. But I wanted to choose my moments.

"I can't honestly say. The film was shot nearly twenty years ago. I remember a big lake in the background—Lake St. Joseph, I guess…"

Scott gazed at me in silence for a few seconds. Silence, and disappointment. I suddenly grasped another of the reasons he had enjoyed so much success as a bureaucrat: he could tell when somebody was giving him less than the full story.

"The truth is," I said, "the village had to be moved to a different location. I believe there's only a fishing lodge at the old site now."

"*Had* to be moved? Why?"

"Soon after you retired as deputy minister, white men pushed into the area and built a few dams. Then they put a road through the reserve. Gold had been discovered north of Osnaburgh. Eventually they reversed the flow of Lake St. Joseph so the water drains west now, all the way to Manitoba. But the water level fluctuated wildly, and one year it rose so much that the burial grounds were flooded and people found their ancestors' remains washed up along the shore. You can understand how difficult that was for them."

"Yes, I can. I suppose progress always comes at a price."

"I'm not sure I believe in progress," I said. "Or at least, here's an example of the kind of progress I believe in: the community has dropped the name Osnaburgh. It was felt to be colonial. Today it's called the Mishkeegogamang Ojibway Nation."

"Colonial," Scott repeated slowly, drawing out the syllables. "Tell me, are the names of Halifax and Calgary under threat as well? Or Vancouver? Or Montreal, come to think of it? Aren't they all 'colonial'? I trust Regina and Victoria still enjoy their proper names." I nodded at this. "As for 'Ojibway Nation,' that's quite a mouthful for a village in the middle of nowhere."

"Nowhere to you," I said. "It's not nowhere to the people who live there."

"And what do they have to say for themselves?"

"I haven't been there, remember. But the filmmakers interviewed a man named Ray Jacobs. He talked about how his people walk softly on Mother Earth. Then he added, 'Our way will not disappear.'"

"Do you believe him?"

"Frankly, I'd like to," I said. "But I don't know if I can. After the mines were established and Lake St. Joseph was flooded, they say the fishing got worse. The hunting too. Logging companies are active all over the region. It's the usual story: the wealth from resource development almost never stays in the north. What gets left behind is the waste."

Apart from its footage of Mishkeegogamang in the 1990s, *The Poet and the Indians* showed a number of striking black-and-white pictures Scott had taken in Osnaburgh, notably of the tense, unsmiling faces of Ojibwa girls and boys. Of course nobody smiled at a camera a century ago, least of all Duncan Campbell Scott; but a knowledge of what the future held for such children, soon to be hauled away to a residential school, makes it easy to read fear and foreboding in their downturned mouths and eyes.

"Most of the Indians have left, I suppose. For Kenora or the Lakehead."

"No, apparently more than nine hundred people still live in the community."

"Do they, indeed! Surrounded by roads and logging camps and mines and hydro-electric dams. I wonder how they spend their days."

I wasn't sure of Scott's tone. If there was anger in it, where was the anger directed?

"Going back to R.H. Thomson," I said, "I was interested to see him—I mean you—walking through the Parliament Buildings. There were other shots of him sitting at a typewriter, lighting a pipe, gazing out the window, doing all the usual solitary poetic things. But in Canada we don't think of poets being close to the centre of power."

"Hmm," he said. I was beginning to find his steadfast gaze unnerving. "When I was in charge of the department, my office was located on Sparks Street. Rather less photogenic."

"And the Champlain Monument," I added, flailing about. "They showed an image of that as well. The one in Ottawa, I mean, out on Nepean Point."

"I suppose you're about to tell me it's no longer acceptable."

"Now why would you think that?" I said innocently.

"Perhaps because Champlain is standing in too heroic a posture for your unheroic age. Or perhaps because the base of the monument depicts an Indian scout."

"Right second time. The Assembly of First Nations complained about how the Ojibwa scout appeared eternally inferior to the Frenchman. He was kneeling down in a subservient posture, with a European high above him. Soon after the film's release, the scout was taken down and became a statue of his own. Today the base of the Champlain Monument is bare."

"*Became a statue of his own?*" Scott was giving me his most severe look. "What kind of weasel talk is this? Mr. Abley, metal statues do not get up and move."

"Right...But will you allow me to say the Ojibwa statue now enjoys a new home? Still near the Ottawa River, but open to view from all sides. Especially being so close to Parliament Hill, the original monument sent the wrong message."

I remembered a trip I made in 2011 to San Francisco, one of the most liberal cities in the United States. It has been willing to commemorate the suffering endured there in the past by Japanese, Chinese, Mexicans, gays and lesbians. The exception are the Ohlone, the indigenous people of the region, who were imprisoned in compounds by Spanish Franciscans until most of them had died of disease. In San Francisco I was surprised to find their memory all but obliterated. The city's oldest graveyard, Mission Dolores, holds a statue in honour of Kateri Tekakwitha, who had died at Kahnawake long before the first missionaries reached California; the statue rests atop a column inscribed "In prayerful memory of our faithful Indians." None of those Indians are named. Very few local people see that statue, whereas tens of thousands pass through United Nations Plaza every day. Among the most striking objects in the plaza is the huge Pioneers Monument, a collection of statues adding up to 820 tons of bronze. One grouping features a missionary and a cowboy, both of them standing with an arm raised, an Indian cowering below them on the ground. So much for commemorating the Ohlone.

"So the—what's the name you're using—the Assembly of First Nations believes that monuments send messages, do they?" Scott said. The sarcasm in his voice felt razor-sharp. "Are these messages directed to the moon and the stars?"

"No, to the general public. Just like your poems, in fact."

"I hope you have not detected any objectionable messages in my poetry. I did not seek to change the world with my writing—I merely did my best to add to its stock of beauty. Throughout my career I sought to follow Coleridge's dictum: that perfection can be found in the blending of passion with order."

Something about the abstract high-mindedness of this statement annoyed me. "There are lots of messages in your poems," I replied. "Coded ones, of course. You might think you were a disciple of Coleridge, but you were also a follower of Francis Parkman. As well as attempting to maintain an imperial culture by an act of will, you were sinking under what you call the weight of history."

Scott stared my way for several moments before he said, "If you're not making a clumsy attempt to insult me, you'd better explain."

I swallowed hard. "You knew the work of Rudyard Kipling, I assume?"

"Of course. I admired some of it."

"So will you not admit that his poem 'The White Man's Burden' sends out a clear message? He wrote it in response to the American seizure of the Philippines in 1899. 'Go bind your sons in exile / To serve your captives' need'—those lines are polemical, surely. What sticks in the craw of readers now is his description of what the American empire was about to face: 'Your new-caught, sullen peoples, / Half-devil and half-child.'"

Scott shifted a little on his chair. "I won't argue about Kipling," he said, "but you will concede that my poems were never so strident in their political sentiment."

"All right, then, let's talk about 'The Half-Breed Girl.' You might want to think it represents a blend of passion and order. And maybe it does. But in another sense, it's all about a particular time in Canadian history, when the children of European fur-traders and Aboriginal women were struggling to find their place in a fast-changing world. Same goes for 'The Onondaga Madonna.' 'At Gull Lake: August, 1810' looks at the issue again, though the subject matter is an earlier generation. Even before you joined Indian Affairs, reading Parkman had given you a sense of what the past meant to Aboriginal people and what the future might have in store for them. That's why those poems are full of phrases like 'dead souls' and 'nation's doom' and 'dying embers,' and even, I suspect, 'the beauty of terror.'"

To my surprise, he was slowly nodding his head.

"What your poems show," I went on, "is how difficult it is for two cultures to meet, especially when there's such a mismatch of power between the two. I think it's fair to say you consistently sent out this message. You didn't write any poems about the ease and comfort of assimilation. As a poet, your sympathies were with the victims of change. But as a civil servant, you looked forward to assimilation. That was the goal you were striving to achieve. That was the policy you were paid to promote. So you had to keep your sympathy under strict control. Maybe you'll still argue that assimilation was necessary for Indians in the long term, but in the short term you knew the steep price its victims had to pay."

"I did."

I waited. He said nothing more. I decided to take a risk.

"And perhaps all this helps to explain why you were subject to nightmares and visions of horror—why you were racked by guilt in the small hours of the night. You were such a good poet, and such a superb civil servant, that in the daytime it didn't seem to matter if different parts of your mind contradicted each other. But in the darkness, when you couldn't sleep…"

I trailed off, uncertain if I'd gone too far.

"How do you know about my nightmares?" To my relief, his voice was calm. The mockery had gone.

"After your death, E.K. Brown wrote a long introduction to a book of your selected poems. He mentioned the vengeance and terror in your dreams—I imagine you confided in him at some point."

He nodded slowly. I wondered if he took these remarks as a betrayal by his friend. If so, he disguised his feelings with a thin-lipped smile: "I can't help wishing you'd said 'such a good civil servant' and 'such a superb poet.'"

Silence seemed the wisest option. The morning sun came streaming through a slightly open window, but Scott had chosen a chair where he would not be touched by it. Outside a house a few doors down, a dog kept barking.

"Well then," he said, "if you have reached this point of understanding— and I admit there is a certain shrewdness in what you say—then you must answer the question: how can I not be forgiven? I was a creature of my age, just as you are, Mr. Abley. Just as we all are. How will men and women in the future look back on your generation, I wonder?" He leaned toward the coffee table and gestured at the latest issue of the *Guardian Weekly*. "Every time I visit you, I notice how sombre is the news in this publication. It seems clear from the headlines alone that the natural world is in a state of absolute crisis. If you are fortunate enough to have grandchildren and great-grandchildren, will they hold you accountable for the failings of your time?"

"I fear they might."

"What will seem obvious to them may be entirely opaque to you. They may be stunned at your obtuseness. "

"Yes," I said, "I agree."

"And yet I am held personally accountable for actions that made perfect sense at the time, not just to me but to nearly everyone else in Ottawa."

"Did they really?" I asked. "There were always some dissenting voices, weren't there? Peter Bryce. Diamond Jenness. I imagine there were others too..."

He cleared his throat. "I remember a letter I wrote to Pelham Edgar. It was several months after Elizabeth's death, and my office duties gave me no joy. Christmas was coming—our first Christmas without her. A dreary festival. I suppose I envied Pelham's university job—the chance it gave him to engage the minds of students and to work with ideas, real ideas. I had a moment of inner revolt. Looking around me, I told Pelham the Indian department should be full of idealists and enthusiasts and philanthropists. That was what we needed. You see, I harboured no illusions about my colleagues. Dogged time-servers, most of them."

I sympathized—a little. "But you stayed there for another twenty-five years. When you wrote that letter to Pelham Edgar, you weren't in charge of the department. A few years later a new government made you Deputy Superintendent-General, and did you get rid of the time-servers then? Did you announce any significant changes? Did you bring fresh enthusiasm to Indian Affairs?"

"Up to a point." His voice was low, almost tentative. "I always tried to maintain my ideals."

I remembered E.K. Brown's summation of his friend's work: "It was to the end of bringing the Indians into the national society that he strove with that mixture of guile and idealism that is the mark of the highest sort of civil servant."

"And what happens when you hold the wrong ideals?" It was on the tip of my tongue to add that both Hitler and Stalin started off as idealists of a particularly warped kind.

He stirred in his chair.

"I wonder where your easy certainty comes from, Mr. Abley. Can you be sure that everything we did in the Indian department, in the best of faith, was wrong? Has society tested the wisdom of your own ideals? Are you confident they could be put into practical effect?"

"Not as confident as you always were," I said. "But if I saw a child eating something poisonous, I'd have a responsibility to stop it. It wouldn't matter if I didn't know the antidote."

Scott closed his eyes for a long moment.

"I have not found this an easy conversation," he replied, "and I don't know how many more of them we shall have. But may I suggest you conduct more research into the prevailing ideas of my time? I think you presume to judge me from an unfair vantage. Dante was a man of the Middle Ages—he believed in the fires of hell. And the ice. Should we neglect his poetry on the grounds that he lacked compassion? In his later years, Tolstoy became a sort of pacifist anarchist—he managed to convince himself that wars and private property were morally indefensible. He had a great aversion to meat-eating, too. Should we avoid reading his novels because of his eccentric beliefs?"

"They're not all eccentric," I said. "But yes, of course we should continue to read him."

"I'm glad you agree. So please, in the next few weeks, look into the beliefs that prevailed among my contemporaries. Find out what people thought and said about the aboriginal races. Will you do that for me?"

It was almost a plea. I could have pointed out to him that Aboriginals are people too, but instead I merely said, "Yes, I will."

And now the chair was empty again, the room silent. I remained on the sofa for a few more minutes, thinking about Scott's words. Somewhere in the bright heat outside, the neighbour's dog continued to bark. I heard the noise of footsteps coming up the driveway until the mailbox creaked open and shut. Then the footsteps dwindled away. A distant child gave a happy shout. Had Scott really used the word "forgiven?"

7

A Glimpse of Real Savages

OTTAWA WAS HUMMING IN the fall of 1920. A 2,530-seat movie palace opened on the corner of Queen and Bank with a dozen silent-film stars in attendance. The Ottawa Hunt Club hired a leading Scottish architect to design a new eighteen-hole golf course. And the Stanley Cup champion Senators were so dominant that the National Hockey League stepped in and transferred two of their players to other Canadian teams. Engrossing though these matters were to many local residents, they were not the concerns that delayed Duncan Campbell Scott's annual report to the minister. Preparing changes to the Indian Act and shepherding them through Parliament had taken up much of his time and energy. In several provinces, veterans of the Great War had obtained title to "unused" Indian land. By contrast, Indian soldiers returning from Europe were facing widespread racism.

That fall, when Scott closed the green baize door of his office and turned away from the muted piano to the papers on his heavy desk, he could look back with satisfaction on what he had achieved. Parliament's amendments to the rules, he remarked, "give the department control and remove from the Indian parent the responsibility for the care and education of his child, and the best interests of Indians are protected and fully promoted." (Nearly a century later, the astonishing thing about that sentence is that it didn't seem astonishing at all in 1920.) Moreover, the department now enjoyed much greater power to enfranchise adults by removing their Indian status, whether or not they agreed. Scott kept a distance from the day-to-day business of his department—the repair of bridges, the construction of drains, the sale of Douglas fir and so on—but he was deeply attentive to "the ultimate object of our Indian policy…to merge the natives in the citizenship of the country."

In his belated annual summing-up, he seized the chance to reflect on the government's tireless efforts. "After a hundred years of civilization," he began, "the Canadian Indian is a difficult subject to treat within the limit of a brief report." He went on to do so, nonetheless. "Asked to describe a Canadian Indian, one might choose between a medical graduate of McGill University, practising his profession with all the authority of the faculty, or a solitary hunter." The graduate he had in mind, Joseph Jacobs, was a Kahnawake Mohawk who had earned a B.A. from McGill in 1911 and an M.D. four years later. (He had attended l'Institut Feller, a Protestant boarding school near Montreal that functioned mainly in French; few if any of the other students were Indians.) As the department's accountant in 1908, Scott had backed Jacobs' request that Indian Affairs should pay his university fees and buy his textbooks, though he scribbled a skeptical note on the file: "This young man may be over-estimating his ability: but if this is so we will find it out before long." As it turned out, Jacobs would succeed in his university studies and go on to spend more than twenty years as a doctor in Kahnawake. Above the entry in his college yearbook appears a line that Shakespeare's Cleopatra utters in her final hour: "I have immortal longings in me."

The reference to Jacobs appears in the opening paragraph of Scott's 1920 report. He began the third paragraph in a tone of mingled pride and praise: "Confidently it may be said that the Indian has justified the trust that the early missionaries placed in him, his mentality and temperament and constitution fitted him for progress, and he has valiantly borne the ordeal of contact with our boasted civilization. Although he has been wasted in the struggle, he has not been worsted." The linguistic play in the last line reveals a rare flash of Scott the poet in a document written by Scott the civil servant, though exactly what he meant by those two verbs is an open question. To Aboriginal people, as he well knew, contact with settlers had proved to be a constant ordeal. Survival demanded courage. And because a great many Aboriginal people were not just brave but intelligent, cool-headed and physically strong—at least, this is what I take from "his mentality and temperament and constitution"—their future could be happy.

The second paragraph of the report tells a different story. It plunges off in another direction, as if Scott were having an inconclusive argument with himself. "It may be conceded," he writes, "that the typical Canadian Indian is the hunter and trapper, and, when one thinks of him, buckskins and beadwork and feathers are still cloaking him with a sort of romance." (Romance had wandered in from Scott's other life, his inner life—not the world of memoranda and legislation but the realm of fiction and poetry, where he tried to sustain his own immortal longings.) "But these are rarely seen, except in pageants and on holidays when the superior race must be amused by a glimpse of real savages in warpaint."

The superior race? He would later republish this part of the report in two very similar versions, without bothering to change the phrase. Yet he seems to have used it nowhere else. Was he in earnest? Is that what he truly believed? Or was this simply a weary moment where a shot of irony misfired?

~

THE YEAR BEFORE SCOTT travelled by canoe to Osnaburgh and Fort Albany, Charles Nowell and Bob Harris travelled by train from Vancouver to St. Louis. Despite their English-sounding names, Nowell and Harris were leading members and clan brothers of a people then referred to as Kwakiutl and now usually known as Kwakwaka'wakw; they lived on the northeast shore of Vancouver Island. The Kwakwaka'wakw, like nearly all the Pacific Coast nations, were in numerical decline, and both art collectors and anthropologists had begun to take a keen interest in them. W.J. McGee, for one, was fascinated by how their clan houses gave elaborate visual and tactile form to a society with a complex lineage system—and by what were said to be their unusually long heads, light skin, and facial scars symbolic of cannibalism. He arranged for the two Kwakwaka'wakw men, as well as a pair of families of the neighbouring Nuu-chah-nulth (Nootka) people, to journey to Missouri.

McGee—first a land surveyor, then a self-taught geologist—had switched disciplines again in middle age and had risen to preside over both the National Geographic Society and the American Anthropological Association. By 1904 he was the anthropological director of the Louisiana Purchase Exposition, better known as the St. Louis World's Fair. He had the desire, and the fair had the means, to bring in people from all over the globe—not just as visitors but as living exhibits. As a late Victorian definition had it, one of the central aims of anthropology was "to discover a natural classification of man." McGee wanted to test and flaunt this young "science," tracing the course of human progress from the most primitive society to the most advanced: the United States. One St. Louis newspaper called him the "Overlord of the Savage World." He aspired to place the racial divisions of the human species at the heart of the fair. Its organizers hoped that by adding "the world's first assemblage of the world's peoples" to their other attractions, they would draw large numbers of tourists, thereby making the whole event profitable as well as educational. Classification went hand-in-hand with showmanship.

And so Geronimo—the elderly Apache leader who had languished for the previous seventeen years as a prisoner-of-war in Alabama and Oklahoma—was put on display, selling souvenir photos of himself and taking part in roping contests at the Wild West Show. Boer and British soldiers, who two years earlier had been trying to kill each other in South Africa, staged battles where they pretended to kill each other. At a Model Indian School, which the fair's president called "a representation of actual human development from savagery and barbarism toward enlightenment," a kindergarten class learned to speak English in public, girls demonstrated how to launder starched shirts, and a band of children played "The Star-Spangled Banner," "Indian Maiden" and "I Love Thee, Columbia." Meanwhile, in the fair's "anthropology colonies," Congolese pygmies danced, Japanese Ainu carved knives, Mexican Cocopas wove baskets, and Charles Nowell and Bob Harris staged Kwakwaka'wakw rituals. They made friends with one of the pygmies and caused a sensation one day by pretending to kill and cannibalize him during a performance. The press loved it, though other indigenous people on the fairgrounds did not.

The St. Louis World's Fair exhibited humans more lavishly—Mc-Gee would have said "comprehensively"—than had ever been done before. But the idea of putting "savage races" on display was nothing new. In 1891 Buffalo Bill's Wild West Show had toured Europe, twenty-three of its performers being Ghost Dancers of the Lakota nation whom the U.S. Army had kept as prisoners prior to their release into the tender care of Bill Cody. The Greater Britain Exhibition, held in London in 1899, had promised "A Vivid Representation of Life in the Wilds of the Dark Continent," its baboons, wildebeests and elephants sharing the spotlight with 174 black Africans, including Swazis "magnificent of physique" and "howling Matabeles." And for decades Carl Hagenbeck, the founder of a private zoo in Hamburg, had been displaying wild animals beside human beings. The people enclosed in his zoo were ones that German crowds were sure to find exotic: Tierra del Fuegans, Somalis, Samis, Aboriginal Australians and so on, including two Inuit families from Labrador. "Who knows what these children of the roughest North may be thinking about their highly educated European fellow humans?" a German journalist asked in 1880. Who indeed? The Inuit made a popular exhibit, but not for long; all eight of them contracted smallpox and died.

In 1904, had it been up to Duncan Campbell Scott, the Kwakwaka'wakw and Nuu-chah-nulth participants, as well as some Onondaga and Oneida lacrosse players, might never have won approval from the government of Canada to meet each other in St. Louis. But at the time Scott was merely the department's chief clerk and accountant. The world's fair gained wide attention outside as well as inside the United States—the Canadian Pacific Railway, for instance, paid for sixteen women journalists to make the trip, trusting that their articles and columns would create an urge among Canadians to attend. As it turned out, the fair would sell nearly 20 million tickets, giving undreamt-of exposure to the beliefs of W.J. McGee. His Model Indian School was meant to show that "one of the gravest tasks of any progressive nation is that of caring for alien wards, i.e. bearing the 'White Man's Burden,' as told by Kipling." And the breathing, walking exhibits in his Anthropology Building were supposed to prove that "living savages and barbarians" were culturally on a par with "the prehistoric ancestors of more advanced peoples."

In 1904, this was not the fringe. This was the mainstream. This was what North Americans saw, heard, read. This was what North Americans thought. The distinction between savagery and civilization had the weight of science behind it. Race was not a discredited concept; race was an inescapable concept. Racism was not even a word at the time, although society was shot through with it.

That was the year, for example, in which the Laurier government in Ottawa increased the head tax on Chinese immigrants from $100 to $500—the equivalent of roughly two years' wages. Richard McBride, the young premier of British Columbia, was so distressed at the prospect of "Asiatic hordes" entering his province, he called for "Mongolian exclusion." In 1909 Mackenzie King, Canada's new minister of Labour, received a Harvard doctorate on the strength of a thesis about Oriental immigration to Canada. To restrict immigrants from Asia "is regarded as natural," he wrote, and "that Canada should remain a white man's country is believed to be not only desirable for economic and social reasons but highly necessary on political and national grounds." (Perhaps he saw women as further cargo in the white man's burden.) In 1938, with war on the horizon, Prime Minister King noted in his diary: "We must seek to keep this part of the continent free from unrest and from too much intermixture of foreign strains of blood."

King was no friend of the Indians, either. During his final months as prime minister in 1948, when he was negotiating the terms of Newfoundland's entry into Confederation, he is said to have asked, "What about the Beothuk you have in Newfoundland?" A Newfoundland delegate replied, "We don't have any, sir. We shot them all." Laughter filled the room. King said, "I suppose that's one way of dealing with a problem of that kind." Perhaps it's unfair to judge a politician by such offhand remarks. Yet can they simply be overlooked?

In other countries too, leading figures held views that today—if expressed publicly—would be denounced at once. Scott was still alive at the end of the Second World War, when British subjects made up a quarter of the world's population. The political hero of that war, Winston Churchill, was even more of an outright racist than Mackenzie King. "I hate people with slit eyes and pig-tails," he once remarked. While serving as Britain's War Secretary in 1919, he wrote in a memo: "I am strongly in favour of using poisoned gas against uncivilised tribes…It would spread a lively terror." Churchill was foreshadowing Saddam Hussein, as the "uncivilised tribes" in question were the Kurds. He had a fierce aversion to Hindus—"a beastly people with a beastly religion"—and when British officials in 1943 pleaded with him to send food to the starving people of Bengal, he refused, saying they had provoked the famine by "breeding like rabbits." Six years earlier he had said: "I do not agree that the dog in a manger has the final right to the manger even though he may have lain there for a very long time. I do not admit that right. I do not admit, for instance, that a great wrong has been done to the Red Indians of America or the black people of Australia. I do not admit that a wrong has been done to these people by the fact that a stronger race, a higher-grade race, a more worldly-wise race, to put it that way, has come in and taken their place."

Racism was, in short, stitched deep into the fabric of Western society. Men and women in Scott's era turned to the notion of race casually, carelessly, unthinkingly, as though it were a natural way of thinking about human beings. In his biography of Simcoe, he referred to the Scots as a race. His uncle, Duncan MacCallum, once said: "The French-Canadian is a Celt, and, like other members of the Celtic race, is keenly sensitive to abuse and insult." Henry James would have done well to pay attention. James was the most scrupulous of writers, and the grandson of an Irishman. But he complained to a Boston friend that the Irish are "an inferior and 3rd rate race, whose virtues are of the cheapest and shallowest order, while their vices are peculiarly cowardly and ferocious." That was not James's last or only word on a complex subject—his views of the Irish were entangled with his feelings about Catholicism, poverty and the working class—yet it's significant that in his scornful letter, he resorted to the word "race."

Insulting other peoples is an age-old habit. In Shakespeare's *Henry VI* trilogy, for instance, the French are called "a fickle, wavering nation" and "the false revolting Normans," French women being "shrewd tempters with their tongues." Yet none of Shakespeare's characters speaks of the French as a race, for in the sixteenth century the concept hadn't been invented. It rose to prominence at the exact moment its services were needed: when Europeans were dividing up the portions of the globe inhabited by people with dark skins. A French count named Arthur de Gobineau developed the theory of the master race in his 1855 *Essay on the Inequality of the Human Races,* and the idea became disastrously fashionable. By the early twentieth century, when Quebec's most influential historian, Lionel Groulx, took pen in hand to write a novel that would double as a nationalist tract, he could entitle the result *L'Appel de la race.* French Canadians were no longer just a people; they had become a race. Such was the language of the time.

～

ONE OF THE MAIN sources of racial doctrine was the greatest scientist of the nineteenth century: Charles Darwin. His studies of the animal realm convinced him that no fixed, irrevocable division cut other creatures off from humans. This and many of his ideas took shape in the early 1830s, when he sailed around the world as a young naturalist on the *Beagle.* The ship stopped in the Galapagos, where the diverging types of finches and giant tortoises provided key evidence for the concept of evolution, and in Tierra del Fuego, at the tip of South America, where what Darwin saw of the indigenous people made an indelible impression on him. They did not wear clothes; they slept on wet ground exposed to wind and rain; they spoke with what he heard as hoarse, guttural, clicking sounds. He called them "miserable degraded savages."

They were close, he thought, to some of the lower primates. Not that Darwin had anything against lower primates. Decades later, in his book *The Descent of Man,* he rose to memorable and disturbing heights of rhetoric: "I would as soon be descended from that heroic little monkey, who braved his dreaded enemy in order to save the life of his keeper, or from that old baboon, who descending from the mountains, carried away in triumph his young comrade from a crowd of astonished dogs—as from a savage who delights to torture his enemies, offers up bloody sacrifices, practices infanticide without remorse, treats his wives like slaves, knows no decency, and is haunted by the grossest superstitions." Darwin was superb at noticing behaviours in animals that resemble those of human beings. He could imagine the lives of monkeys and tortoises, finches and pigeons. What he was not so good at imagining were the lives of people and societies unlike his own.

"At some future period," he wrote, "not very distant as measured by centuries, the civilized races of man will almost certainly exterminate and replace throughout the world the savage races." He assumed the great apes would be exterminated too. "The break will then be rendered wider, for it will intervene between man in a more civilized state, as we may hope, than the Caucasian, and some ape as low as a baboon, instead of as at present between the negro or Australian and the gorilla." Darwin did much to break the ancient spiritual hierarchy that tied human beings to God. But he set a biological hierarchy in its place. Christians were still able to take comfort from the belief that God was responsible, as a Victorian hymn put it, for installing and maintaining "the rich man in his castle, / The poor man at his gate." Now atheists and agnostics could find solace in the idea that evolution was doing the same. When Rupert Brooke, fresh from his visit with Duncan Campbell Scott, passed through Saskatoon in 1913, an American businessman told him, "We must be a morally higher race than the Indians, because we have survived them. The great Darwin has proved it."

It's often said that Darwin was not a Social Darwinist. Herbert Spencer, who invented the phrase "survival of the fittest," led the way in applying biological theories to political and social issues. But Darwin's writings, like it or not, provided plenty of fodder on which Spencer and many others avidly dined. Spencer popularized the notion of progress in many of its forms—geological, biological, economic, linguistic—and he claimed to have found a "parallel developmental process" by which "traits of the barbarous races have been turned into those of the civilized races." In the 1860s he tried to assess racial progress by measuring brain size and leg length. Spencer found, not surprisingly, that "the civilized divisions of the species" had made greater progress than "the lower human races," who reminded him of chimpanzees and gorillas. Decades later in St. Louis, the technicians in W.J. McGee's "laboratories" set out to calculate the racial differences of physique and intelligence in the fair's anthropological colonies. In general, the darker a people's skin, the lower the ranking.

Such assertions gave the British and other European empires a pseudo-scientific rationale. Until well into the nineteenth century, the idea of civilization had remained distinct from that of race. But in the heyday of political imperialism, when Duncan Campbell Scott was young, Social Darwinism emerged as a popular and apparently scientific doctrine. The result was that race and civilization became dangerously blurred. Such was the fertile soil from which Nazism sprang, and it would be grossly unfair to see Germany as the only source. In the wake of Darwin, "savages" were no longer men, women and children with darker skin and fewer clothes than those who claimed to be civilized; "savages" were biological links to other mammals. As a young lawyer in British-ruled South Africa, Mohandas Gandhi (not yet known as a mahatma) described black convicts as "only a degree removed from the animal." The racial rhetoric was appallingly infectious.

Members of oppressed and powerless minorities were more than willing to adopt race-based language when it served their own interests. One of the leading black intellectuals in the United States early in the twentieth century was W.E.B. Du Bois, a co-founder of the National Association for the Advancement of Colored People and a prolific author who had earned a Harvard doctorate some years before Mackenzie King. "The Negro is primarily an artist," Du Bois wrote in 1913. "This means that the only race which has held at bay the life destroying forces of the tropics, has gained therefrom in some slight compensation a sense of beauty, particularly for sound and color, which characterizes the race." He ascribed many of the achievements of ancient Egyptian art and civilization to "the Negro blood which flowed in the veins...of the Pharaohs." Du Bois was countering previous American authors like the sociologist William Wilson Elwang, in whose eyes "Negroes cannot create civilization...theirs is a child race, left behind in the struggle for existence." He made his powerful assertions, however, on Elwang's terms.

THROUGHOUT SCOTT'S LONG CAREER, such issues were alive in the public consciousness. We have already seen how in 1883 Sir John A. Macdonald rose in the House of Commons to justify the growth of the residential school system. Macdonald contrasted the experience of an Indian girl or boy who attends school on a reserve ("the child lives with his parents who are savages") with the experience of such children at a boarding school ("they will acquire the habits and modes of thought of white men"). When his speech was over, an Opposition member took the floor: "The evolution, I understand, is a very gradual one. Has the Honorable Gentleman any information as to the number of generations it will take?" Macdonald replied, "I am not sufficiently Darwinian to tell that." Darwin had been dead for only a year, but already he had become an adjective.

Macdonald was a far-sighted, strong and sometimes progressive leader. He fought to safeguard the rights of French-speakers in Canada, and as early as 1885 he suggested that women should have the vote. (His party refused to go along with him.) That year, however, he also proposed an amendment to the Electoral Franchise Act, denying the vote to anybody "of Mongolian or Chinese race." He wanted to preserve "the Aryan character of the future of British America." The violence of Macdonald's rhetoric surprised even members of his own party. He declared in the House of Commons that "the Aryan races will not wholesomely amalgamate with the Africans or the Asiatics," and he claimed that "the cross of those races, like the cross of the dog and the fox, is not successful; it cannot be, and never will be." It's symptomatic of such feverish discourse that Macdonald was talking about sex. Over many countries and centuries, few topics have aroused such morbid, lethal eloquence as intermarriage.

Australia, even more than Canada, would turn theories about racial mixing into national policy. Whereas white Canadians and Americans often expressed a grudging or nostalgic respect for the Indians whose lands they had seized, white Australians showed no such respect for the Aboriginal peoples of their country. Black-skinned, naked, nomadic, they were widely seen as the quintessence of savagery—so primitive, indeed, they might well be Darwin's "missing link." "We cannot fail to recognise in their extinction a decided widening of the chasm by which mankind is now cut off from its animal progenitors," the *Melbourne Review* announced in 1878. Many Australians believed that if "pure-blooded" Aboriginal people were confined to their small and remote reserves, they would die out; but mixed-race Aboriginals were another matter.

Of all the nations colonized by the British, Canada is unusual in recognizing a group with mixed heritage as a distinct people. "Half-breeds" in the United States, unlike the Métis in this country, have never enjoyed official status. In New Zealand, a person with some Maori heritage can choose whether or not to identify as Maori—the country has no official category for people of multiple origins. Australia follows the same model. There, well into the twentieth century, only those Aboriginal people with paler skin and European "blood" were thought to be salvageable for civilization. "Generally by the fifth and invariably by the sixth generation," declared the Northern Territory's Chief Protector of Aborigines (this was an official title), "all native characteristics of the Australian Aborigine are eradicated. The problem of our half-castes will quickly be eliminated by the complete disappearance of the black race, and the swift submergence of their progeny in the white." Cecil Cook was a medical doctor; he made these remarks in 1934.

And so a policy emerged: removing paler-skinned Aboriginal children from their families and raising them somewhere else—permanently. Children who were kidnapped by the government and brought up far from their families would not return home for holidays and were not expected to find their way back as adults. The government believed it owed a duty to children who had white "blood": to save them from growing up amid the backwardness, squalor and immorality that most white Australians saw as typical of Aboriginal homes. Boys and girls continued to be seized and raised apart from their culture and families until the late 1960s, victims of a policy that was no more successful than its Canadian counterpart. The injustices done to these "Stolen Generations" would finally prompt Kevin Rudd, the prime minister of Australia in 2008, to issue a much broader apology to the Aboriginal people of his country than Stephen Harper made in his equivalent statement four months later.

Policies based on racial doctrine lasted in Australia for many decades. Unabashed popular racism also had a long life—the original version of Rolf Harris's famous song "Tie Me Kangaroo Down, Sport" includes a verse with the refrain "Let me Abos go loose, Lew." The speaker is a jaunty old stockman issuing his last instructions to his mates, who have gathered to share his final hours. Most of the requests involve wildlife: a kangaroo, a koala, a cockatoo, a platypus. But not all. As well as telling his friends what to do with his animals, the stockman says his "Abos" are of "no further use" and can therefore be set free. The song was written in 1957.

In Australia and North America alike, private biases and public discrimination against indigenous people far outlasted the pretext for racial doctrine. That justification had eroded quickly in the early decades of the twentieth century. At the vanguard of the movement against it stood Franz Boas, an anthropologist with a very different vision of his field than W.J. McGee. Thanks to Boas, cultures rather than races became the main topic of anthropological study. In his most important book, *The Mind of Primitive Man* (1911), he showed that the mental abilities of "civilized" and "savage" people are almost identical. Aspects of history and culture, not of race, account for the remarkable social diversity of human beings. "What then is the difference between the civilization of the Old World and that of the New World?" Boas asked in an early essay. A rhetorical question, which he answered by saying: "It is only a difference in time. One reached a certain stage three thousand or four thousand years sooner than the other…Certainly the difference of a few thousand years is insignificant as compared to the age of the human race." Notice how Boas refers to the cultures of North and South America as "civilization." This alone was a radical departure. *The Mind of Primitive Man* showed the folly of racial thinking. Its influence was both broad and immediate.

It came, however, a little late for Duncan Campbell Scott. He had mastered the old rhetoric; he accepted the old divisions. By the early 1920s Boas had won the battle among North American scholars: no longer did anthropologists see it as their job to establish and justify a hierarchy of races. McGee's beliefs had been consigned to the intellectual scrapheap in a single generation. But the top floor of the Booth Building in Ottawa was hardly a haven for new ideas. And Scott, in the course of a 1923 essay entitled "The Aboriginal Races," showed that he continued to mix up the notions of race and civilization.

His essay appeared in the *Annals of the American Academy of Political and Social Science,* and to a scholarly readership Scott now admitted (in contrast to what he had written for *Scribner's* in 1906) that the Aboriginal peoples of Canada were not faring well. The "Eskimos," for instance, suffered because "the quality of such smattering of our civilization as has reached them has been inferior and has been detrimental." Scott was making a more honest admission of failure than senior bureaucrats in Australia, South Africa and the United States would probably have done. But he added: "The rude whaler first, and afterward the casual fur-hunter have not been worthy specimens of our race and the adoption of such habits as they could acquire from such associates and the unfortunate dissemination of some of our most deadly diseases have been all against the permanence of the race." The Inuit, in short, were doomed. Scott was wrong again—and his insistence on framing the issue in racial terms made it hard for him to realize his mistake.

∼

HE MUST HAVE BEEN watching, biding his time. No sooner had my wife gone out on her bicycle than he was standing in the sun-dappled living room. I was getting used to his sudden arrivals—they no longer held any shock value. I suppose he was getting used to me as well.

"I was wondering when you'd come back," I said.

"Were you, Mr. Abley? I'm not sure if you enjoy my spectral visits."

"Enjoy is hardly the word. But they've become important to me. You remember what Canadians are like—it's only by our lack of ghosts we're haunted."

Scott stared out of the window, his eyes roaming the greenery. Behind the brown-eyed Susans and the purple echinacea, goldenrod was starting to bloom—a sign that summer had already begun to turn toward fall. The outer branches of the pine, where they stretched beyond the shade cast by the big maple, were glowing a soft grey-green in the sun.

"We had an unpleasant experience in the garden a little while ago," I remarked.

He turned toward me, his eyebrows raised.

"Annie and I were sitting on the deck, eating supper. Over the past few weeks we'd noticed a pair of starlings making themselves busy around the maple. They built a nest in a hole, high above the fork in the trunk. And lately we'd heard the cheeping of baby birds coming from the hole. The parents were tireless, flying back and forth to feed them. But as we sat there with our meal, we saw a big raccoon walking along the back edge of the lawn. It had a purposeful air—it knew exactly where it was going."

"Ah," said Scott. "And couldn't you do anything about it?"

"I tried. I shouted at it, I threw a few stones—but at first I don't think I really intended to hit the raccoon. Then I did, but it was too late. The raccoon climbed straight up the trunk and reached into the hole. Somehow what made it worse was how human its hand looked. We had a perfect view and we were utterly helpless. When it had got hold of the first baby, it climbed down a little way and sat in the fork of the tree to eat the bird alive. Then it—"

"Enough," said Scott. "If you don't mind." He passed a hand over his forehead. "I have seen a similar incident myself."

"I'm sorry, I didn't mean to distress you." I felt suddenly weary and sank onto the sofa. The noise of a lawn mower seemed to push through the window. Scott sat down too.

"You didn't distress me. This is how the world works, after all. You know your Tennyson, I imagine. At least I hope you do. What you have raised is the question he wrestled with in his greatest poem—*In Memoriam* struggles to answer why Nature is 'so careless of the single life.' We imagine God is love: that's what I was brought up to believe, against a great deal of evidence I observed even as a boy. We imagine—how does Tennyson put it?—we imagine that love is 'Creation's final law.' A few of my verses express that very hope. But as the poet says, Nature 'shrieked against his creed.' Perhaps the universe is moving towards an eventual God of love, but for the moment the claims of love are denied by 'Nature, red in tooth and claw.' I'm sure that when your raccoon had finished his meal of starlings, it was indeed red in tooth and claw."

"And I know the natural world needs predators," I said. "But this doesn't reduce my sense of pity when I see a young bird being ripped apart."

Scott looked at me thoughtfully. "Your mention of pity brings up a point. Nothing to do with raccoons, I hasten to say. I've been meaning to talk to you about my uncle."

"The professor of medicine?"

"Indeed. Duncan MacCallum was a significant influence on my family, though I saw little of him in his later years. He loathed indecisiveness, and when I was still a young man he delivered a lecture before one of the first classes to study nursing at McGill. It was printed a few years later in a small book. He warned the future nurses not to let their natural kindness go too far. I recall his words: 'Kindness must be governed by judgment and tempered by firmness. To allow a feeling of pity to influence you...would be a serious error on your part.' I believe I've quoted that accurately. Those remarks were a useful guide in my own work."

"Useful in preventing you from feeling too much sympathy for the Indians, you mean."

"Useful in reminding me that policy should not be based on sentiment. I was not a monster, Mr. Abley! I had feelings. But I had a mind as well."

It occurred to me that I was wearing him down. The haughty figure who had stood before me in January, so convinced that posterity had wronged his name, so confident I would uphold his claims of innocence, had been reduced to a shadow in a chair, protesting that he was not a monster. I wasn't sure if I should be proud of my accomplishment.

"I know you did," I said, "and I have to thank you for pointing me to the writings of some of your contemporaries. Shocking stuff. It's amazing to think how much Western society has been transformed since the 1940s."

"You mentioned that a woman of Chinese origin has served as the governor general of Canada. That alone is an extraordinary statement, and I suspect there's much more you could tell me."

"There is. Did you know the United States now has a black president?"

He gave a start of surprise. "I'd heard a rumour to that effect, but I didn't believe it could be true."

"Yes, he was elected in 2008 and re-elected four years later. And when he was first seeking the Democratic nomination, he received the support of an elderly West Virginia senator named Robert Byrd." I pulled out a sheet of paper from the coffee-table folder. "Byrd was also a Democrat. But as a young man, while you were still alive, he was a proud member of the Ku Klux Klan. In 1944 he wrote a letter saying, 'Rather I should die a thousand times, and see Old Glory trampled in the dirt never to rise again, than to see this beloved land of ours become degraded by race mongrels, a throwback to the blackest specimen from the wilds.' Ugly stuff. Yet in his last years Byrd was happy to endorse a candidate with a white mother and a black father. That's an example of how one man's views of race changed after the Second World War. Things that had been widely said became almost unsayable, at least in public."

"And did the attitude to Indians in North America undergo a similar change?"

"Not as dramatically. But a couple of years ago, when a broadcaster named Kevin O'Leary called his fellow host 'an Indian giver with a forked tongue,' he was reprimanded by the CBC and forced to apologize. 'Squaw' is another term that's no longer acceptable anywhere. If you look at Hollywood, too, you find a major change of attitude. Do you recall a 1940 movie by Cecil B. DeMille, *North West Mounted Police*?"

Scott frowned slightly. "I remember reading something about it. But Elise and I didn't go out to movies very often."

"It starred Gary Cooper," I told him, "as a Texas Ranger who rides north across the 49th parallel to get his man. Except that he ends up in the middle of the Riel Rebellion. Or as the publicity for the movie put it, he finds 'a little squad of Mounted Police, ambushed by thousands of war-maddened half-breeds and Indians.'"

"Historically absurd," Scott said, "but what can you expect of Hollywood? I'm not sure I see your point."

"I mean that, in your lifetime, Indians were nearly always the bad guys. The good guys were cowboys. The good guys were white. But in the last few decades, all that has changed. Successful Westerns have been made from the Indian point of view. Here in Canada, no one would use the term 'half-breeds' any more. But even in the States, I don't think mainstream advertising copy could get away with 'war-maddened half-breeds.'"

"So the Indian can now be seen as a heroic figure."

"Indeed."

"I'm pleased to hear it."

Now I was the one to be startled.

"I thought you'd be upset," I said. "I thought you might say this was modern society going to the dogs."

"Am I so predictable? Mr. Abley, what do you find if you look at my Gull Lake poem? Or my story 'Labrie's Wife'? Or my story 'Expiation'? Who are the most sympathetic characters?"

"The Indians," I said. "Although a lot of them are actually Métis. They tend to be the victims, too."

"Well yes, I wasn't attempting to write comedy."

Irreverent thoughts raced through my head: *Maybe you should have. Maybe your work would be the richer for it. It would certainly be more fun to read…* I remembered something the Cree playwright and novelist Tomson Highway once said to me: "Cree is the funniest language on the face of the earth."

But Scott had carried on. "And, in general, who are the foolish characters in my works? Who are the failures and the villains?"

"White men," I said.

"I rest my case."

I thought quickly about the works he'd mentioned. "Expiation" describes the folly of Forbes Macrimmon, a Hudson's Bay Company trader whose prosperity depends on the work of his faithful servant, Daniel Wascowin. A brilliant hunter, Daniel "was almost a pure Indian, but there was a little white blood in him." A cunning French Canadian working for the rival North West Company succeeds in turning the trader against Daniel. Maddened by what he thinks is his servant's betrayal, Macrimmon attacks the man, branding him in the forehead and leaving him deaf. After nearly a year's exile, Daniel returns to the fort, a broken man, and dies. "Labrie's

Wife" is also about a Scottish trader who fails to understand matters of the heart, this time involving his young white assistant and a Métis woman named Madaline Lesage. As for "At Gull Lake: August, 1810," the poetry and pathos belong to Keejigo, an indigenous woman who falls for an Orkney trader; the consequences are ruinous.

"And," he added, "you might want to consider 'On the Way to the Mission.'"

I nodded mutely. In this poem Scott excoriates "two whitemen servants of greed" who follow an Indian trapper through a wintry forest; they believe the heavy toboggan he's pulling is loaded with the pelts of fox, otter and mink. At night they murder the man—only to discover that the weight on his toboggan is the corpse of his dead wife, a Montagnais woman with a crucifix under her fingers. The trapper had been hauling her body to a Catholic mission for burial in the spring. In a poem of less than sixty lines, Scott uses the phrase "servants of greed" three times.

"So," he said, "suppose you were a segregationist, like the American senator you were telling me about. Or suppose, indeed, you were Charles Dickens. Would you not see me as a traitor?"

"Dickens?" I replied. "What do you mean? I know Jewish people who object to the character of Fagin in *Oliver Twist,* but—"

"The Jews got off lightly. You should read his essay on 'The Noble Savage.' If memory serves, Dickens spoke of the savage as 'cruel, false, thievish, murderous; addicted more or less to grease, entrails, and beastly customs; a wild animal with the questionable gift of boasting.' There was more, too, which I can't recall offhand. I'm sure he used the word 'diabolical.'"

Scott must have seen my shocked expression, but he didn't stop. "Dickens wrote that 'the savage has no moral feelings of any kind, sort, or description.' He would have thought my writing terribly soft-hearted."

"Because the Aboriginal people in your stories and poems *do* have moral feelings?"

"Not just that," he said. "On various occasions I wrote about the clash of races—about the impact of the white man on the Indian, to be precise. The loyalty and valour are generally on one side of the equation. The evil is mostly on the other."

"But you set these works in the past."

"Of course I did," he said with a touch of impatience. "Given my job, I could hardly have described in realistic fiction the tribes of my own day. Admittedly my story 'Charcoal' was set in the present—what was then the present, I mean. The Indian agent is a minor character, unable to exert much authority as the sad events unfold. But that was a single story, an experiment I didn't repeat."

Something was worrying me. I struggled to articulate it. "But look. You oversaw a department in which the Indians were a subject people. They were under your thumb, to be blunt. You made innumerable decisions on their behalf. Yet in your writing, as you've just showed me, you often paint white men in a bad light. They degrade and corrupt the Aboriginal people they come into contact with. Isn't there a contradiction?"

"Not at all," he replied. "The offending characters in my stories and poems are low white men. A constant aim of my department was to protect the Indians from low white men."

"You mean—" I wasn't sure I understood.

"I mean if we succeeded, they would be safe on their reserves from the worst elements of our civilization. They had already suffered grievously from the fur trade—I used the word 'slave' in print, and I stand by it. Do you remember why the North West Mounted Police were created? It was in response to the Cypress Hills Massacre—a disgraceful episode when American riffraff rode across the border and slaughtered dozens of Assiniboine. I remember hearing of it as a boy—my father was shocked, though he wasn't surprised to learn the massacre took place near a whisky post. By then I suppose most of the Assiniboine were in thrall to the traders. The worst of those men would debase the alcohol they sold with pepper, soap, red ink, even strychnine."

"Yes." I could think of nothing else to say. Scott peered at me over his glasses and carried on.

"Or among the Indians of British Columbia, think of how the Haida and Kwakiutl were ready to prostitute themselves for money. Obviously these were intelligent people: their carvings were quite remarkable. They also kept slaves of their own, of course, and practised some degrading customs. I regret to say that men from these tribes would go down to Victoria and sell their wives and young daughters to sailors, gold miners, adventurers. It may be conceded you find debauched, licentious white men on every frontier, contemptuous of the most basic tenets of morality. And so the government of Canada, working together with the churches and police, devised ways to shelter the Indians, and to ensure they would gradually develop to a point where they could find a place in the respectable body of society. Mr. Abley, the people for whom I had the greatest scorn were not the Indians but the dregs of our own race."

I was shocked. But now I felt I also grasped a phrase that had puzzled me when I came across it. In 1909 Scott wrote an introduction to *People of the Plains,* a loving account of Plains Indian life by a woman who had known it well. Amelia Paget was the daughter of a Hudson's Bay Company trader in what is now Saskatchewan; as a teenage girl she had been captured by Big Bear's forces during the 1885 uprising. For more than two months she lived among the Cree, who did not mistreat her. She already spoke their language and, as her book makes clear, she deeply admired them. In his introduction Scott called the Cree "these proud, shy people," using adjectives that also applied to himself, and he praised the Cree and Ojibwa languages as "highly expressive" (adding that Ojibwa was "eminently flexible and poetic"). He undercut Amelia Paget's work a little by commenting on its "tone of championship for all Indians" and its "idealistic tendency which places everything in a high and favorable aspect." But, he added, "This animating spirit is pleasant; there is no reason why the arrogance of our so-called civilization should everywhere prevail." For a man who praised the traditions of civilization in his other writings, the last sentence is astounding. Unlike his official reports, it suggests he entertained serious doubts about the worth of what he upheld.

Scott and I looked at each other in silence for a long few seconds. He was the one to break it. "Have you never witnessed the actions of these, these dregs?"

A succession of images flitted through my head, things I'd heard and seen in several provinces. But one image would not go away: a round-faced girl in a junior-high classroom, speaking only rarely, her voice little more than a whisper. Her family came from the Blood reserve south of Leth-bridge. It was her first year in a city school, and I sat behind her. "Hey, Rosie! Squaw!" The insults, day after day; the shunning in the schoolyard; the acts of violence in a hallway; the invitations to perform obscene acts. "Come on, squaw, you wanna…" None of my classmates dared to befriend her. The next year she was gone.

"Yes, I have."

"If by now you've read what Rupert Brooke wrote after visiting the Stoney reserve in Alberta, you'll recall what the Indian agent told him: every white man 'thinks an Indian legitimate prey for all forms of cheating and robbery.' We knew that, Mr. Abley. We were not innocents in Ottawa; we were men of the wider world. So do you not understand why keeping the Indians on reserves was something we did for their own good?"

"No, I don't. Nor do I see how it was supposed to work, bearing in mind another of your ideals: wanting Aboriginal society to vanish by intermarriage. If Indians were confined to their reserves—in parts of the West, they were supposed to get government permission just to set foot elsewhere—how did you expect them to assimilate? Because that was your goal: assimilation. You wanted to guard their identity at the same time as you wanted to destroy their identity."

Scott looked unruffled.

"The process will take generations," he said. "Centuries, even. And in my day the vast majority of Indians were not confined, as you put it. They would leave their reserves for a time, then come back, and when they returned they would bring outside influences with them. Outside blood, indeed, for a young woman would often be carrying a white man's child. I am not saying this is a simple process or a straightforward one. But assimilation must happen in the end. It *will* happen in the end. As it must be happening now in Winnipeg and other Canadian cities. Will you concede the point?"

"It's not for me to say," I replied.

Again we sat in silence. Again it was Scott who broke it. "You're evading my question. Answer it, if you please."

"But I can't answer it! How could I? You're asking me to predict something that more than a million indigenous people will decide for themselves. Each of them is an individual, each of them belongs to a family, and they'll make their own choices based on what's right for themselves. And on who they love—yes, love. We haven't spoken much about love in these conversations, have we? I wonder why. I talked a little while ago to a Cree writer named Tomson Highway, and he said to me: 'The English language is terrified of pleasure.' Anyway, most—"

"Nonsense," said Scott.

"As I was saying, most Aboriginal people have stopped obeying the churches and the government—thank goodness. Nobody has the right to tell them what they should or should not do. It's not the 1920s now."

A slow anger had unfurled inside me. My voice was rising. My own words were taking me by surprise.

"Back then you had all the power, Mr. Scott. And you enjoyed it. You liked it, didn't you, sitting over a bottle of wine in the country club, chatting with senior lawyers and deputy ministers, perhaps a member of Parliament or two, smoking a handmade cigar as you settled the fate of the less fortunate. A high-minded little company, full of Chablis and goodwill. I'm sure you all told yourselves you were acting in the highest interests of the nation. But were you? Wouldn't—?"

His chair was empty.

It was my sudden memory of Rosie Gladstone that had made me drive him away. In my mind I saw her face again, fighting to remain impassive. I don't know how she made it through the year. I never heard her answer the tormentors. I never stood up for her.

I never saw her cry.

173

8

I Have Done So Little

AS THE YEARS WENT by, Scott—a very private man—became increasingly well known. No one in Canada has spanned the realms of literature and public service with such nonchalant ease. He was better acquainted with prime ministers, book publishers and newspaper editors than with Aboriginal leaders. But his eminence set him apart from his fellow writers. In his day, as in ours, poets tended to make wild suggestions, play with possibilities, toss out ideas, knowing full well that their ideas would never be acted on. Not Duncan Campbell Scott. He didn't make suggestions; he gave orders. He spent much of his life being obeyed.

After he took over the department, he grew accustomed to deference not just from his underlings in Indian Affairs but also from the men and women of the press. In December 1915 the *Boston Evening Transcript* published an article full of praise for the man: "He is far and away the best honorary secretary who ever managed the Royal Society of Canada, wherefore writing folk can't but rejoice to celebrate his proven skill as Administrator of the intricate Indian Service." The reporter applauded the work of Indian Affairs, while also clenching a fist inside the velvet glove: "Old fashioned Indians, those who cannot be broken of the filthy residential ways they acquired as nomads—who move camp instead of cleaning camp—are doomed." Earlier that year F.H. Abbott, secretary of the U.S. Board of Indian Commissioners, had issued a report based on a trip to Canada and a study of the Canadian system. His findings, declared the *Evening Transcript,* cited Canada's administration of Indians as a model the United States should try to adopt.

"Poet Is In Big Demand While Visiting Toronto," read a cutline under Scott's photograph in the *Globe* in 1925. The next year his collected poems would appear: a 341-page hardcover edition complete with an embossed cover and a frontispiece of the frowning author wearing a bow tie. When he made a western tour in August 1928, the reporters were almost reverential. The *Calgary Herald*: "Good progress in education and health work is being made among the aborigines of Canada, according to Dr. Duncan Campbell Scott." The *Ottawa Citizen*: "Edmonton Will Honor Distinguished Poet." That was the headline, which was followed by "Dr. Duncan Campbell Scott To Be Entertained." When he returned from an inspection tour of reserves, the article promised, "he will be entertained by the Northern Alberta Pioneers' and Old Timers' Association at an old-fashioned tea party in the log cabin on the fair grounds." He was expected to sing for his supper, or rather his tea. "Doubtless amid such surroundings…he will find inspiration for a souvenir poem that will become the Old Timers' 'national air or slogan.'" Such were the genteel hazards of Scott's modest fame. He was a sixty-six-year-old unsmiling public man.

The early spring of 1929 found him in Victoria on government business. British Columbia had been battling to retain rights over Indian land that no other province claimed, and for once Scott could be seen as acting not only on the federal government's behalf but also to secure the interests of Aboriginal people. Yet his mind wasn't entirely on the complex negotiations at hand.

He had for some time been exchanging candid letters with Elise Aylen, an aspiring writer in Ottawa who had been born two years before his daughter Elizabeth. She showed him her poems, on which he made encouraging comments. Her Christmas present in 1928 had provoked him to write, "I prize your gift above all others." Coming into Banff on a CPR train at the beginning of March, he wrote: "How I wish you could see it all with your clear eyes & your sensitiveness to beauty." On March 16, from the Empress Hotel in Victoria, he sent her one of his most revealing letters. Evidently she had challenged him to explain himself. "My philosophy after a life of drift," he wrote, "is no consolation to one who is young & who wants sweetness & activity. I know now that I have never fought against anything nor worked for anything but just accepted & drifted from point to point—I have dimly felt that if I worked & protested & resisted I should be wrecked—So maybe you will understand why with some gifts I have done so little." (In the minds of many Aboriginal people, of course, Scott had done far too much.) This was not quite a love letter. But it was an admission, an appeal, and an almost unprecedented exposure of his heart—an organ that was, much to his own surprise, coming alive again. To no one else would he confess a fear of being wrecked.

He returned to Ottawa on March 30, looking forward to seeing Elise as soon as possible. Two weeks later his wife was dead.

Belle received a discreet obituary in the *Citizen,* its anonymous author using the phrase "a comparatively short illness" and observing that "the late Mrs. Scott had a fine personality." The obituary stated that "she was constantly engaged in various phases of social activity," and emphasized that "widespread sympathy is felt with Dr. Scott in his bereavement." What mattered for newspaper readers in Ottawa was that a "Wife of Distinguished Canadian" had died—Belle's career as a musician lay far in the past. The funeral was a private one, held at 108 Lisgar Street, the only home she had known during her thirty-five years in Canada.

Three months after her death, Scott took a train to Boston and visited Belle's family. By then he was again exchanging intimate letters with Elise. "I would love you to understand me better," he wrote, "if there be anything to understand. I find it most difficult to say anything about myself. Whenever I begin, something stops me, some ancestral emotion I suppose— afraid to give anyone power over me? is that it?" He quoted a line from John Donne—"Love's mystery in souls do grow"—without reminding her of what follows: "But yet the body is his book." His grief, and perhaps his guilt, were balanced by shy exhilaration.

Elise Aylen had a small book of her poems published in 1930, the foreword being written by Duncan Campbell Scott. "Mastery is to be gained by severe discipline," he wrote there, "rather than through easy liberty." He may not have been thinking of poetry alone. "Melancholy," he added, "is a luxury of youth." Scott mentioned nine of Elise's poems in his foreword, though not the two on Indian themes ("Rent is the tepee of my heart, that sheltered you…I will sing your death song in the forest"). His life of drift was changing its course: in March 1931, the couple were quietly married at 108 Lisgar Street.

News of the wedding caused a stir in Ottawa. Two days after the event, Mackenzie King wrote in his diary: "Heard tonight Duncan Campbell Scott remarried on Friday Miss Aylen—he is over 60." In fact he was in his sixty-ninth year. The marriage showed no signs of public stress: Elise remained by her husband's side until December 1947 when, after repeated attacks of angina, his heart gave out.

During the last two years of his life, he and Elise became close friends with John Watkins, a diplomat who shared their love of literature and music. A scholar of Scandinavian literature at the University of Manitoba, he had joined External Affairs in the postwar glory days of that department. If Scott realized that Watkins was a homosexual ("gay" seems the wrong word), he was evidently unperturbed—Scott called him "a familiar of the house" and "a great addition to our inner circle." In 1954, at the height of the Cold War, Watkins was posted to Moscow as Canada's ambassador to the Soviet Union. A couple of indiscreet sexual encounters left him open to blackmail, which he resisted. But the RCMP learned of the blackmail attempts and began to question him. He died in a Montreal hotel room in 1964 while being, as they say, "forcibly interrogated" by the police.

Elise's fate was equally surprising. Within a few months of Scott's death she packed some belongings and sailed across the Atlantic, never to return to Canada, never to remarry. After a short spell in England she moved on to Ceylon and India. There she would spend the remainder of her life: some of it near Lama Anagarika Govinda; most of it as a disciple of Swami Yogeshwarananda. The widow of a man born before Confederation, she survived long enough to see her elderly gurus swarmed by acid-dropping freaks. In a letter to her uncle, Arthur Bourinot, she said, "I have written a series of poems on the Hindu gods, which Hindus seem to like very much. They all tell me I must have had many incarnations in India, and always ask, 'However did you come to be born in Canada this time?' Sometimes I wonder myself." She completed five novels, none of which has ever been published. Their protagonists, wrote the critic Robert McDougall (perhaps the only person to have read all her books), are "a sorrowful lot who pursue their spiritual quests weighed down by doubt and, ultimately, despair." Elise died of cancer in a hill station in Tamil Nadu on December 19, 1972—the twenty-fifth anniversary of her husband's death.

For some years the Finnish Embassy occupied Scott's house on Lisgar Street. In 1958 it was demolished in favour of an office building that displayed a plaque in his memory. Later the office building, in turn, was demolished and the site became a parking lot. A twenty-two-storey luxury condominium project called The Merit now fills the space. The whereabouts of the plaque are unknown.

Duncan Campbell Scott was buried in a prominent spot in Beechwood Cemetery in Ottawa. A flat stone slab gives his name at the top, and those of his first wife and daughter below. Dates of birth and death are inscribed for Belle and Elizabeth. No dates follow his name. It's as though he continues to wait.

⁓

SCOTT HANDLED MEN WITH composure and cunning. Politicians, lawyers, poets, journalists, subordinates in his department, victims of his department: with all of them, he could assume a tone of cool authority. He rarely needed to speak to them about himself. Personal reticence did not interfere with his air of impersonal command.

Women were another matter. Women could sense a vulnerability he did not reveal to men. His daughter stole his heart away and died. The diplomatic skills he displayed at work were never enough to bridge the chasm between his strong-minded mother and his equally strong-minded first wife. Though Elise was easier to live with than Belle had been, the surviving letters show the degree to which Scott put himself, in writing, at her mercy. (She would eventually destroy much of their correspondence.) In his late sixties, composing what he admitted was almost the first love letter of his life, he compared his love for Elise to "a flower that grows out of the rock— the granite is proud of it and you, even you, who pluck it may find some greater beauty in it because it found difficulty in blooming." He scribbled a line from Balzac's story *La Recherche de l'absolu* into one of his last note-books: "Blessed are the imperfect for theirs is the Kingdom of Love."

Professionally, as well as personally, women could draw Scott to a point of fleeting disclosure. It was Amelia Paget, the author of *People of the Plains,* who provoked him in 1909 into letting slip the words "our so-called civilization." He would repeat the phrase decades later, again while introducing a book by a woman. In 1944 the author was Mildred Valley Thornton, a BC painter who had put together a collection of *Indian Lives and Legends.* "She has produced enough evidence," Scott wrote, "that the Indian is gradually coming to enjoy any progress our complex life may be making and she has given proof…that he has been able to survive the contact with our so-called civilization." Not exactly a ringing endorsement of mainstream society. After Scott's death one of his long-time friends, Madge Macbeth, produced a shrewd two-line analysis of him: "He never sought an argument and never took part in one if he could help it. A genu-ine humanitarian, he loved his fellow man in small doses." As a friend and family member, as president of the Royal Society of Canada and the Can-adian Authors' Association, sometimes as a poet too, he could look on individuals with warmth and empathy. As a government official control-ling the daily lives of more than 100,000 people, he found warmth and empathy impossible.

What moved him about Aboriginal women—to judge from his literary writing—was a combination of strength and extreme vulnerability. Few of the Aboriginal women in his poems have long to live. What moved him about Aboriginal men was loyalty, reliability and the willingness some of them showed to move forward into a new life. Charles Wabinoo, the young Cree man from Attawapiskat whom he met in 1905, was "still wild as a lynx" yet "possessed wholly by the simplest rule of the Christian life." For the time being, he remained "unspoiled by the arts of sly lying, paltry cunning, and the lower vices which come from contact with such of our debased manners and customs as come to him in the wilderness." Guided by mis-sionaries along a trail of righteousness, this was a man Scott could respect.

Thirteen years later, he wrote to the prime minister urging the govern-ment to grant full Canadian citizenship to Aboriginal soldiers. Manhood was much of his reason: "The fact that they have had the manhood, the sense of duty and responsibility to come to the assistance of their country in the hour of need and the discipline and experience which they have had as soldiers would indicate that they are…qualified to take care of themselves and to exercise the franchise." The reward for proving their manhood amid bullets and poison gas would be the loss of their Indian identity. By then Scott had spent nearly four decades in Indian Affairs, and he still knew Aboriginal people so little.

Among all his literary peers, it was an Aboriginal woman who almost certainly gave him the most unease. Pauline Johnson—Tekahionwake, or "double life," to use her adopted Mohawk name—was born in 1861, a year before Scott. Her mother was English, her father a Mohawk chief respected and prominent enough that two governors general visited their home. She grew up amid Victorian comfort on the Six Nations reserve in southern Ontario. Its residents—especially those who were Mohawk—tended to regard themselves as a kind of aristocracy among the Aboriginal people of North America. Her first publication in book form was also Scott's: they each had a few poems in the 1889 collection *Songs of the Great Dominion.*

By then he had made a careful decision to remain in the civil service and "not to depend for one's livelihood upon one's imagination and fancy." As an unmarried Indian woman, Pauline Johnson had fewer choices. She opted for an arduous life of freelance glamour, supporting herself by writing essays, stories and poems, and by performing her work onstage before admiring crowds—a spoken word artist, if you like, before the art of spoken word existed. Beginning each performance in an evening gown, ending it in a wildly untraditional Indian costume, she toured the continent many times. But the travel, the pressure and the financial insecurity took a toll on her health. After years of sickness she died of breast cancer in 1913.

Scott had witnessed the rhetorical force of her work in Toronto in 1892, when the Young Men's Liberal Club of the city sponsored "An Evening With Canadian Authors." The evening proved to be a lengthy one, and the prose sketch that Scott read failed to stir the crowd. Other speakers were equally dull, long-winded or both. But then Pauline Johnson walked onto the stage and recited from memory "A Cry From an Indian Wife":

Curse to the fate that brought them from the East
To be our chiefs [...]
They never think how they would feel to-day,
If some great nation came from far away,
Wresting the country from their hapless braves,
Giving what they gave us—but war and graves [...]
By right, by birth we Indians own these lands,
Though starved, crushed, plundered, lies our nation low...
Perhaps the white man's God has willed it so.

The young Indian Affairs official listening to the rapturous applause would have gained a sharp insight into poetry's subversive potential. All the more so because "A Cry From an Indian Wife" is set during the Northwest Uprising of 1885. The conflicted narrator evokes and, to an extent, justifies the armed resistance waged by the wards of Scott's department. The young Liberals and others in the Toronto crowd cheered for so long that Pauline Johnson had to come back onstage and deliver an encore.

Soon she was famous, and therefore free to say things no other Aboriginal person could get away with. Being a woman was both a shield and a handicap. By never challenging the stereotypes of gender, she made it hard for men to attack her. Yet by accepting those conventions, she made it easy for men to ignore her. Scott was tireless in promoting the work of Archibald Lampman and a few of his other male friends; he wrote almost nothing about Pauline Johnson. Once, in an overview of a decade of Canadian poetry, he briefly praised her "virile touch"—an odd and revealing phrase. Otherwise he kept silent. On a visit to England in 1906 she mixed with the likes of Lord Strathcona, Lady Blake, Lady Ripon and Sir Gilbert Parker; but Belle Scott, who was in London at the time, shunned her.

That year Pauline Johnson published a short article in *The Boy's World* entitled "Sons of Savages." "The Redskin boy-child," she wrote, "is but an atom in the most renowned of the savage races known to history, a people that, according to the white man's standard, is uncivilized, uneducated, illiterate, and barbarous." The white man's standard, of course, was exemplified by the Department of Indian Affairs in general, and by Duncan Campbell Scott in particular. His poem "Watkwenies," describing an aged Iroquois woman, had begun: "Vengeance was once her nation's lore and law." Pauline Johnson went on to explain how manners and learning were understood in Iroquois society: "The Redskin races hold that staring marks the lowest level of ill-breeding ... No Indian talks of food, or discusses it while taking it." This was a plea for the awareness of cultural difference—a celebration of it, even—aimed at a young readership being trained to believe that only white people have a culture worth the name. The ending is both affirmative and bitter: "When, finally, he goes forth to face his forest world he is equipped to obtain his own living with wisdom and skill, and starts life like a brave, capable, well-educated gentleman, though some yet call him an uncivilized savage."

~

FIVE WEEKS BEFORE PAULINE Johnson's birth, a Redskin boy-child named Frederick Loft was born at Six Nations. He too was a Mohawk from a respected Anglican family; he too attended a high school off the reserve; he too would see his writings published in *Saturday Night,* the *Toronto Globe,* the *Brantford Expositor.* In a series of four articles that appeared in *Saturday Night* in 1909, he called for the closure of Indian residential schools as "veritable death-traps." But unlike Pauline Johnson, he did not earn his living by his pen. Fred Loft settled in Toronto, married and had children, and worked for many years as an accounting clerk in the city's insane asylum. His talents entitled him to a much higher position. On two occasions, each time with the hereditary council's endorsement, he applied to be named the superintendent of Six Nations; but the Department of Indian Affairs had the final say in the matter, and each time it refused.

Loft lied about his age in 1917 when, with a world war in bloody progress, Britain was desperate for recruits and Canada was keen to oblige. He was fifty-six, a year older than Duncan Campbell Scott, but to enlist in the Canadian Forestry Corps he claimed to be forty-five. Loft spent several months with the troops in France and, before returning home, visited King

George V at Buckingham Palace. (Mohawks often found a way to meet the British nobility on equal terms; their skill at this was not appreciated by Indian Affairs.) When Loft got back home, his awareness of the injustices done to Aboriginal people grew—or perhaps it would be more accurate to say that his willingness to tolerate those injustices vanished. In December 1918 he organized a meeting at the Council House in Ohsweken, the main town on the Six Nations reserve. That gathering saw the creation of the League of Indians of Canada. Provincial Indian bodies had already been formed in BC and Ontario, but this was the first serious attempt to found a national Aboriginal organization.

Scott disliked it from the start. Small wonder, because in one of the first circulars Loft sent out, he called for Aboriginal people across Canada to "free themselves from the domination of officialdom" and to assert their rights "as free men under the British flag." The League had more immediate aims, too. It called for more and better schools to be built on Indian reserves, so that fewer children would have to endure the residential system far from home. And it wanted a 1911 amendment to the Indian Act to be overturned. That amendment gave the government the power to move any reserve away from a nearby municipality, and to expropriate any land on an existing reserve for the sake of a road, a railway or other public works. Even the small tracts of land Indians still owned—in the case of Six Nations, a mere 5 percent of Britain's initial land grant, "which them and their posterity are to enjoy for ever"—were at risk of further depletion. It wasn't just railways and roads that posed a threat. Many Canadian soldiers coming home after service in the Great War coveted land of their own and saw the uncultivated fields and woodlands on Indian reserves as ripe for the taking.

The delegates to the Ohsweken meeting elected Fred Loft president and secretary-treasurer of the League. Annual congresses in the next few years took place in Alberta, Saskatchewan, Manitoba and northern Ontario. Some of the press reports were enthusiastic: the *Toronto Sunday World* praised Loft for "putting up a determined fight against the disintegration of Indian lands under the plea of enfranchisement and soldier settlement." Scott thought that "the end of the war should mark the beginning of a new era" for Indians, but the new era he foresaw was one of speeded-up assimilation, not Indian resistance. Loft was exactly what he didn't expect or want: a returned veteran who, even while holding down a job in Toronto, worked devotedly to oppose the government.

"What he ought to get is a good snub," Scott told his minister. "He has some education, has rather an attractive personal appearance, but he is a shallow, talkative individual. He is one of the few Indians who are endeavouring to live off their brethren by organizing an Indian society, and collecting fees from them." It was 1921, and Scott's latest and most controversial amendment to the Indian Act had recently passed into law; Ottawa now had the power to enfranchise any Indian in the country. Fred Loft was an ideal candidate. If he lost his Indian status, he would also lose his legitimacy as head of the League of Indians of Canada. Scott began the process. Loft objected.

The battle ended when the Conservative government fell, a Liberal regime took its place, and that particular amendment to the Indian Act was quickly repealed. Henceforth, Scott would be unable to dismiss Loft as a non-Indian. But he could, and did, make the man's life difficult. On his instructions, agents across Canada told Aboriginal people to have nothing to do with the League. Indian Affairs led the way by refusing to accept Loft as an intermediary between the government and any local band. In the wake of the Russian Revolution and the Winnipeg general strike, nervous officials perceived him as an agitator, a threat to harmony, a possible Communist. "A vast network of spies," Brian Titley writes, "which included missionaries, police, and subservient Indians, kept the department's agents informed of the agitator's every move." Against such well-funded and well-organized hostility in Ottawa, the League had little chance of success.

Loft retired from his accounting job in 1926 and, mindful of his wife's poor health, spent the next four years in her hometown, Chicago. The League of Indians of Canada sputtered on during his absence, but eventually petered out as a national body (branches did survive in Saskatchewan and Alberta). He died in 1934, perhaps believing his efforts had been a sorry failure compared to the terrible success of Duncan Campbell Scott.

IN THE EARLY 1920S, Fred Loft was not the only leader from Six Nations to arouse Scott's chilly fury. A chief named Deskaheh—he preferred the Cayuga term to his English name, Levi General—became the main spokesman for a movement to have the historic rights and powers of the Iroquois Confederacy affirmed on the international stage. Deskaheh, who adhered to the ceremonies of the traditional Longhouse, was the speaker of the Confederacy Council of the Six Nations. That body asserted that the Six Nations were historic allies of Britain, rather than the dependent subjects of either London or Ottawa (an idea that Scott dismissed as "childish"). It demanded that Six Nations be recognized for its special status, either within the Canadian federation or without. Many people on the reserve endorsed the movement, although Scott called its leaders "fanatical" and claimed that the feud with Ottawa was "carefully fomented by a few reactionaries."

One of those "reactionaries" was Deskaheh, a farmer, a former lumberjack and a middle-aged father of nine. Not the usual profile for a staunch activist of a kind more familiar in our own time than in Scott's. In 1921 he sailed to England, failing to win the support of the British government in the Six Nations dispute but succeeding in his effort to intrigue the British press. The sovereign rights of the Iroquois were the main issue when he spoke in London. At home the dispute with Ottawa encompassed many other things too; conscription, land sales, alcohol and forced enfranchisement had all become topics of dissent. When the RCMP made a sudden raid on Six Nations territory in search of bootleggers, gunfire was exchanged.

Scott had—unusually for him—gone to a public meeting on the reserve so as to explain the department's views. But as the dissent grew, he arranged for a permanent RCMP detachment to be installed at Ohsweken, a stone's throw from the Council House, against the Council's wishes. In 1923 he appointed a new superintendent for the reserve: an army colonel named Cecil Morgan who had fought in the Boer War and served the colonial regime in South Africa. By then Indian Affairs had commissioned an outside report looking into the structure of Six Nations, and the report (written by a second military officer) declared that the traditional Confederacy had "long outlived its usefulness." Scott agreed. After all, hereditary councils did not govern the Mohawk territories anywhere else. Yet Six Nations was a singular case. Its modernizing reformers, who wanted to see a ballot-box system of elections, had always been in the minority. Until the 1920s, Indian Affairs had never tried to dismantle the Confederacy Council, in which chieftainships passed through the female line; in fact women enjoyed significant power, including the right to remove a chief who was failing in his duties. "This obsolete system," in Scott's mind, was "wholly unsuited to modern conditions of life and detrimental to progress and advancement."

The Council at first hired Canadian lawyers to put forward its case in Ottawa, one of them being Scott's old friend and literary colleague W.D. Lighthall. Dissatisfied with the results, it turned to an American, George Decker, who accompanied Deskaheh to Europe in 1923. This infuriated Scott. Having entered Switzerland on a Six Nations passport, Deskaheh spent much of 1923 and 1924 in Geneva, working to have Iroquois claims recognized by the League of Nations (the doomed forerunner of the United Nations). Persia, Ireland, Estonia and Panama were willing to see the case put forward; Britain was not. It warned other nations not to engage in "impertinent interference in internal affairs of the British Empire."

Deskaheh was still in Geneva in the fall of 1924 when Scott decided the moment had come to crush the traditional government. By doing so, he would ensure that the new leadership of Six Nations accepted the control of Indian Affairs—and he would also undercut the embarrassing campaign that Deskaheh was waging in Europe. On October 9, the Confederacy Council began its monthly meeting at an agricultural hall in Ohsweken (the Council House being under repair). Colonel Morgan and some RCMP constables showed up without warning. Morgan read out a federal order-in-council that abolished the hereditary government of Six Nations. One by one, its members walked away in silence. Police broke open a chest and seized artifacts and documents, some of them dating back more than a century. They also raided the homes of a few chiefs.

With a band council in place to match the system in so many other reserves, Scott had won the day. But his victory was partial. The election for the new council had a dismal turnout—most of the electorate showed what they thought of Ottawa's actions by refusing to vote. Scott was undaunted. In 1927 he had the Indian Act amended again, this time to stop anyone from raising or receiving funds to pursue legal claims without the minister's consent. There would be no more crusading outsiders like George Decker, who had declared: "The Canadian government…is trying to imitate the ruthless imperialism of Congress in its treatment of American Indians." Now the only lawyers Aboriginal people could hire would be ones approved by Indian Affairs. Scott justified this move on the grounds that unscrupulous lawyers and agitators were taking advantage of the Indians—a foreshadowing of the claim by Frances Widdowson and Albert Howard that indigenous people in the twenty-first century are being exploited by an "Aboriginal industry."

By then Deskaheh had died, exiled to the Tuscarora reservation in upstate New York, worn out by his struggles. "An enemy's foot is on our country," he said in his final address. He was buried at Six Nations, where his funeral became a political event attended by two thousand people and patrolled by the RCMP. The police were unable to tell Scott what had been said, for the lengthy speeches at the funeral were given in Cayuga and other Iroquois languages.

There was, I suspect, a personal side to Scott's hostility to Deskaheh, Fred Loft and, more generally, the Six Nations. They refused to show a trace of deference to the Deputy Superintendent-General. Their persistent desire to be treated as Canada's equal, and not as members of a subservient race, won them attention and respect of a kind often denied to Aboriginal groups. In 1925 Toronto's *Star Weekly*—a colour magazine distributed by newspapers across the country—mourned the loss of the traditional Council. It spoke warmly of "the great confederacy of the Six Nations… the oldest continued parliamentary body on the American continent." Three years later the *Detroit Free Press* ran a provocative full-page article on the subject of "Six Nations Independence." In 1929, representatives of the Six Nations travelled back to Geneva, hoping for support at the League of Nations, and in 1930 they were in London again, asking Britain to take their side against the government of Canada. These ventures produced no results apart from further publicity, but they showed—to Scott, that is—a stubborn lack of gratitude.

He had expected more of them. Not only was Six Nations the most populous reserve in Canada, it was also the richest. In his *Scribner's* article, written a generation earlier, Scott had celebrated the progress its occupants had made over the course of a century. Assimilation, he believed, would be the next and inevitable step. Unlike the Dene or the Innu, who still survived by hunting and trapping in the snowstruck forests of the north, the Iroquois appeared ripe for the relinquishment of Indian status. Yet nearly all of them, like Fred Loft, spurned the offer. Cherishing their own identity, guarding their own history, the people of Six Nations refused every invitation to become full citizens of Canada. (To this day there are Iroquois people who believe that until Aboriginal leaders at Six Nations formally adopted the Indian Act on June 21, 1880, Canada was not a legal nation.) The Department of Indian Affairs, it turned out, had no control and little influence over the desires and beliefs of most people on the reserve.

In Scott's mind they were behaving like obstinate children who refuse to be thankful for everything their parents have given them. The only way they could mature would be to renounce their identity as Indians. The only power he would allow them was the power to deny who they were. In return they gave him a name in Mohawk, which his friend Arthur Bourinot would eventually disclose and misspell. It was either Tahawennontye or Tehawennontye: "flying (or floating) voice, coming towards us" or perhaps "words flying (or floating) in both directions." What Scott thought of this name is unknown.

While he was engaged in the long Six Nations dispute, one of his supposed wards did express his gratitude. In the late 1920s, Buffalo Child Long Lance ranked among the most famous Indians in North America. He moved smoothly along the shifting borders of journalism, public relations, acting and public speaking. *Long Lance: The Autobiography of a Blackfoot Indian Chief* became a bestseller in both the United States and Canada; it was dedicated to "the two White Men who have guided and encouraged me most since I have taken a place in civilization"—Indian Affairs commissioner Bill Graham in Regina and Canon Samuel Middleton on the Blood reserve in Alberta. Then the author added: "And to a friend of the Indian: Hon. Duncan Campbell Scott, Deputy Superintendent-General of Indian Affairs."

Scott's pleasure must have vanished when news leaked out that Buffalo Child Long Lance was really Sylvester Long, an American of mixed black, white and Cherokee heritage who had grown up not in the sage-scented foothills of Montana and Alberta but in the factory town of Winston-Salem, North Carolina. If few identities seemed more romantic than that of a Blackfoot chief, few could be less romantic than that of a "colored" janitor's son. In 1932, exposed as a fraud, he committed suicide. A few weeks later, the "friend of the Indian" retired.

The brief introduction to Mildred Valley Thornton's book, written when Scott had passed his eightieth birthday, marked the last time he made any public comment about Aboriginal matters. The essay gave him a chance to summarize what he felt he had accomplished during fifty-two years of work with the Indians of Canada: "My lifelong association with them and their affairs, ranging from the custody of their Funds and the protection of their material interest to the amelioration of their social conditions and the promotion of their education was the source of my interest in the sympathetic outlook of the artist-author." No mention of how he had thwarted Fred Loft and Deskaheh, or stripped the Six Nations Confederacy Council of its ancient power. Protection, amelioration, promotion: it's as if Scott hoped the "sympathetic outlook" of Mildred Valley Thornton would cast a warm glow over his own labours. This was how, approaching death, he wanted to remember his career.

Or how he needed to remember it. "It is not your memories which haunt you," the British poet James Fenton wrote in "A German Requiem," his brilliant evocation of post-Nazi amnesia. "It is not what you have written down. It is what you have forgotten, what you must forget. What you must go on forgetting all your life."

RAIN HAD SWEPT THROUGH after midnight, and morning arrived without the benefit of sun. My wife and daughter had left the house early, and as I sipped my coffee and peered out at the garden through the kitchen window, I noticed a watering jug had been blown off the deck onto a lawn strewn with wet leaves. In the dark beds the remaining brown-eyed Susans jostled for space with purple asters, the last flower of the year to emerge. A migrant songbird was pecking away near the base of the maple. Despite a promise I'd made to Scott last winter, the sprawling tree had not been trimmed.

"A white-throated sparrow, I expect," said a baritone voice. There he was, standing in the doorway between the kitchen and the dining room, the light from a pod lamp reflecting off his glasses. One of the cats had been asking for a second breakfast. At the sight of Duncan Campbell Scott, she scurried away.

I decided to play it cool. "No, I think it's a fox sparrow. The tail is reddish."

I felt a strange sense of relief. Six weeks had passed since his abrupt departure. Even if we would never say goodbye on the best of terms, I wanted the chance to bid him a courteous farewell.

"Will you sit down?" he said. He had told me that days and nights meant nothing to him, yet he somehow gave an impression that he hadn't slept all night. His face appeared drawn. His voice too sounded weaker than before, as if his ghostly presence carried less force. I took my coffee and followed him into the living room, turning on a light as I went.

"I wasn't sure I'd see you again," I said.

"And I wasn't sure if I would return. But I am not a man who gives up easily. And it now seems I will be allowed one further visit—after today, I mean."

"Very good. That means you should see the fall colours again. The trees are just beginning to turn. Soon it will be 'October with the rain of ruined leaves.'"

This was the final line of a poem by Archibald Lampman. I knew Scott had loved it and often quoted it to his friends. But instead of responding with the warmth I expected, he looked at me with a stern, unsmiling gaze.

"I have something I particularly want to say, Mr. Abley."

So he wasn't in the mood for preliminaries. Fine. That morning I felt ready to engage with him.

"Go ahead," I said, staring back. By Mohawk standards of politeness, our behaviour was already rude.

"Well. Thinking about everything you have told me in these conversations, I can understand why some Indians may wish that events in the past had taken a different course. Most Indians, perhaps. People are unlikely to find their own conquest easy to accept. I met this sentiment among a few of the French Canadians I knew, and while I thought it was not always healthy, I understood it. I can appreciate, to a great extent, the frustration of the tribes in British Columbia where the provincial government wanted to retain control over even the small areas of land it was willing to grant as reserves. Settlement along the Pacific coast did not proceed in an orderly manner, and the social consequences were appalling, for a time. One might even use the word 'tragic.'"

He paused and leaned toward me, his hand in his chin. I felt a "but" coming on.

"But are this very natural regret and this understandable resentment enough to justify the animosity that, I now realize, is aimed at the Indian department in general and myself in particular? I am a scapegoat, it seems. I served a series of governments whose Indian policies are said to have failed. Yet this was not the judgment of most people in my own time. Newspapers praised me, universities honoured me, governments relied on me. Would I have lasted so long in my post if there had been a clamour for change? Is it not true that posterity will always latch on to certain actions as wrongheaded? Wisdom comes easily to those who enjoy the privilege of hindsight. Wisdom thrives in the past tense. It is harder to discern in the present."

"Of course," I said. "Not that—"

"I will give you an example," he continued as if I had not spoken. Only on his first visit in January had I felt so strongly that I was listening to a prepared speech. "One of my predecessors as Deputy Superintendent-General, Hayter Reed, was convinced that because the Plains Indians were at a lower stage of development than white people, they should be forbidden to use modern machinery in their farming. He thought they needed to pass through the peasant stage of civilization first. So he decreed that the inhabitants of reserves on the prairies had to bind their sheaves with straw rather than rope, even though prairie straw is too short for the job, and he told them to cut their grain with sickles, even if half the crop was lost as a result. Not only that, he insisted that after the grain was harvested, it had to be ground by hand. No wonder the Indians' enthusiasm for farming faded away. But are people familiar with this story now?"

"I've never heard it before. It sounds absurd."

"Exactly. Yet for several years, this was government policy. And is Hayter Reed held responsible for the folly? I expect history has forgotten the man."

"Not entirely," I said. "Some people still remember that before he was forced out of the department, he called Western Indians 'the scum of the plains.' But in later life he changed his tune. By the 1920s he thought that if the Indians were disappearing, it was largely the white man's fault."

"The Indians used to call him 'Iron Heart.'"

"So I've read. But as you say, he's not a well-known figure now."

"Whereas I am still remembered," Scott said with sudden passion, "and evidently I am held to account for the foibles of the residential schools and the unfortunate deaths of children. Not to mention the blame that is attached to my name because of later policies that brought adverse results."

"So you admit the schools were a failure."

"I knew," he said carefully, "they were not succeeding nearly as well as we had hoped. I knew most of the schools fell far short of our ambitions for them."

"Well, that's something. That's more than you were admitting a few months ago. And you had the power to change the system, if only you'd chosen to use it. But the residential schools are only part of the issue. The larger question is why the whole system proved to be so destructive."

"Did it, Mr. Abley? Did it?"

I gaped at him. "Yes, it did."

"I wonder. If you think of the Aborigines of Tasmania, we know that by the middle of the nineteenth century, British convicts and settlers had wiped them out. If you think of the Mission Indians along the coast of California, we know they were decimated—in the true sense of the word. I won't even ask you to imagine the horrors in the Amazon, or the Belgian and German parts of Africa. Before the colonial enterprise made life much better, it often made life much worse. You have told me that in Canada, the Indian population now stands at well over a million people—a far greater number than were alive when French and British explorers arrived on these shores. You have mentioned the successes of Aboriginal people, which I am pleased to hear about. Why then must you continually speak of failure?"

For almost the first time in our conversations, I found myself at a loss for words. Scott sat back in the navy-coloured chair, the creases standing out in his neck and face. For a few seconds he closed his eyes. He looked, in Archibald Lampman's phrase, "self-immured."

"You mean," I said finally, "I'm supposed to praise what happened in Canada merely because things were even worse elsewhere?"

"No. Well, yes, up to a point."

"I find that sad. I won't say more. Just sad."

A telephone rang in the kitchen. I ignored it. Watching Scott now, I had the odd sensation that his face was flickering, as though I were looking at a low-definition image on a screen. The phone fell silent.

"I also find it sad," I said, "to think that a man who was in charge of Indian Affairs for an entire generation could have declared, in cold print, 'Altruism is absent from the Indian character.'"

When Scott spoke, his voice was slightly blurred. "A provocative phrase, in a somewhat tedious essay I had to prepare as part of my job. Had I known it would be held against me in a future century, I might have revised it. Do you remember the context of the phrase, Mr. Abley?"

I shook my head.

"No. I thought not. It seems my enemies have been combing every sentence I wrote in search of all the damage they can find. Well. I don't believe they will find much more. If memory serves, I said the following, with reference to the volatile politics of the late eighteenth century and the Mohawk leader Joseph Brant: 'One must recognize his worth, and record that he worked diligently for his people. Altruism is absent from the Indian character; yet Brant's last words were for his race: "Have pity upon the poor Indians; if you can get any influence with the great, endeavour to do them all the good you can."' This is a rather different tone than Sir John A. Macdonald used with regard to Orientals, wouldn't you agree?"

"I would. But still. You knew there were enormous differences among the Iroquois, the Cree, the Haida and all the other nations—so how could a man in your position generalize about 'the Indian character'? I just don't understand."

"But everybody does this! Or should I say 'did this'? I can only assume from your puzzlement that people don't make such generalizations now."

"We try not to," I said.

"I wrote that essay in 1914. Have you any idea what was said in English Canada—not just then but also in my later years—about the character of the Oriental races, the Italians, the Jews, the French Canadians, the Negroes, the Russians and, above all, the Germans?"

"I do," I replied. "Or at least I can imagine. I'm not sure I want to hear the exact words."

"Precisely. You dredge up a single phrase—not even a complete sentence—from an obscure essay, instead of contemplating what should be as plain as the nose on your face. Rather than applaud the sympathy towards Indians you will find in a number of my poems, you attack me on the basis of a single line of prose." He gave a slow sigh. "I did not want to suffer this kind of conversation again, Mr. Abley. I hoped this would be a civil discussion. But again, I have to remark that not only have you chosen to distort my writing; you have failed to answer one of my questions."

I cast my mind back without success. "You mean ... ?"

"I mean this: I gather from what you've told me on my previous visits that long after I retired from the Indian department, certain things continued to—go wrong, shall we say."

"They did indeed," I said.

"Please give me an example."

I frowned. There were so many possibilities to choose from.

"Well, let's take the Sixties Scoop," I finally said. "It's a light phrase for a heavy chain of events. Starting in the 1960s, child welfare officials across Canada stepped in and grabbed all the Aboriginal kids who might be at risk because of alcoholism or broken homes or teenage mothers—any number of reasons, really. I'm sure the social workers often meant well. This time round, most of the children weren't locked away in residential schools; they were put into foster care or adopted by white parents. Some of the children suffered abuse. But even when they didn't, the government's attempt to make things better just led to further distress. The children were caught between two cultures, two worlds. It was another effort to get rid of the Indian problem, as you once said, and another generation that ended up suffering from disrupted family life and a confused sense of identity."

"The Sixties Scoop, you called it. So this happened thirty years or more after I retired. Yet, and here is my question again, am I now held to blame?" His voice had a slight quaver.

"Not directly, no. But it's part of your legacy, Mr. Scott. The Sixties Scoop occurred as a result of the terrible disarray the residential schools had produced. Most of the parents who lost their children in the '60s were survivors of the residential system. And those damaged children became parents themselves, and the cycle carried on. I'm not saying there are any easy answers. But maybe, just maybe, if Canadians can agree on what went so wrong in your time, we can start to fix the mess in our own."

"I had no idea." A pause. "How could I?"

We sat in silence for a little while. I finished my coffee and wished I'd made more. But somehow the anger I'd felt in earlier conversations had disappeared. In its place was a great sadness. Duncan Campbell Scott had been a gifted and hard-working man, a lover of nature, a champion of the arts. Devoted to his country, loyal to his friends, he was an exemplary figure in many ways. Now his ghost sat in front of me, dispirited, forlorn. Yet I would not, could not, remove the blame.

"I will not stay much longer," he said at last. "So I will make a final request. I would like you to think about it—you should not feel obliged to give me an answer now. It sticks in my throat as I speak, for I was a proud man, and even in the wilderness of the afterlife I have sought to maintain my pride."

He paused for a few seconds. I remained silent.

"I am assuming," he finally said, "that after all my visits, and all the research you have done, you may indeed be inclined to write something about me. When I come back for my final visit, Mr. Abley, will you assure me that, regardless of the errors you have discerned in the past, the wrong turns that you think government policy took over the years, you will not hold me up to personal scorn? The idea that you might think me among the worst Canadians of all time"—his voice shook like a dry leaf—"I would find this hard to bear."

"I can give you that assurance now," I said.

"Really?"

"Absolutely. I won't promise to turn you into a hero, though."

"Quite right," he said. "I wasn't a hero. Who in the world lives up to his own expectations, let alone the expectations of his wife?"

A brief, shared smile.

"But I don't mean to let you off lightly," I said. "There you were, at your desk in the Booth Building, information streaming in from across the country, and yet you never dared to ask what was *really* happening to the Indians. Perhaps in your heart you knew the answer. But you were a proud man, as you say, and you couldn't face the thought of failure, the possibility of disgrace. Not with Belle. Not with your mother, either. So you turned away. You let yourself drift. Of course it was easy to believe the conventional wisdom of the age. You succeeded at so much, but you failed at bravery. You gave in to fear. Perhaps this was your tragic flaw."

He was sitting absolutely still.

"You had the courage of the government's convictions, not the courage of your own doubts. I know, you were a man of your time, just as I am. I'm not saying I have all the answers about Aboriginal issues or anything else. But I *would* say your ideas were far more limited than you ever imagined. You carried your chains within you. You had no clue about the value and resilience of Aboriginal culture, you had little sense of the pain your policies were inflicting, and you believed the lies of the empire you served."

"They weren't all lies." It was a half-hearted response, but the flickering was stronger now.

A wind was worrying the branches outside the window. I said, "I don't like to imagine what my ghost might need to ask a century from now."

"Thank you," a dim voice replied from the blue armchair, although I could no longer discern a body sitting there.

9

The Sin of Blindness

IF DUNCAN CAMPBELL SCOTT had got his wish, the Calgary Stampede would never have included Indians. The first stampede took place in 1912 and caused anxiety in the department. An American cowboy, vaudeville artist and entrepreneur named Guy Weadick announced "the greatest Frontier Days Celebration in any man's country heretofore," named it the Stampede and invited the governor general, the Duke of Connaught, to attend. The daily entertainment featured an "Indian relay race." About two thousand Indians took part in the festivities, dressing in their finest feathered and beaded costumes for the grand parade. Yet their involvement was in doubt until a late stage. Only the pressure applied by such prominent Albertans as Senator James Lougheed and R.B. Bennett, a future prime minister, enabled the minister of Indian Affairs to overrule his department's wishes and allow the Blackfoot, Stoney, Sarcee and other Indians to enter Calgary. Just to be sure, Weadick also brought in about a hundred Indians from the United States—though it was a man from the Blood reserve south of Lethbridge, Tom Three Persons, who won the bronc riding championship on the closing day.

Scott disliked such events for both economic and moral reasons. His agents were trying to turn the Plains Indians into farmers, and they resented the long absences from reserves that dances, fairs and summer entertainments were likely to provoke. "Obviously this plays havoc with summer ploughing," Scott wrote. Crops might fail; cattle might die. Equally important, the Blackfoot sun dance and the Cree thirst dance were seen as morally objectionable. Traditionally the ceremonies had involved an element of self-torture as a man danced round and round in pain, his breast pierced by long sticks, making a sacrifice of his body to the sun. Most of the Protestant missionaries and all the Catholic ones hated the practice. "Christianity and advancement, and paganism and indolence cannot flourish side by side," wrote Father Hugonard, principal of the residential school in Qu'Appelle. "One or the other has to give way; paganism, dancing and indolence are most natural to the Indian, who has no thought for the morrow." Scott agreed.

Within months of his appointment as Deputy Superintendent-General, he wrote to the Indian agents in Western Canada, urging them to prevent dances that might "destroy the civilizing influence of the education imparted to Indian children at the schools." As he well knew, the legal status of these dances was in doubt. An amendment to the Indian Act as far back as 1895 had forbidden all festivals and ceremonies at which "money, goods, or articles of any sort" were given away or at which "the wounding or mutilation of the dead or living body of any human being or animal" took place. The restrictions on giving took aim largely at the elaborate potlatches on the west coast, although Aboriginal dances on the prairies also entailed certain gifts. The restrictions on wounding affected the sun dance, the thirst dance and the potlatch alike. But many policemen and white settlers, some Indian agents and even the occasional Protestant missionary disliked the law. Aboriginal people flouted it with impunity. Scott was determined to tighten the rules.

In 1914 he added new and harsher measures to the Indian Act. From now on, Indians in the four western provinces and the territories would need the department's permission before dancing outside their own reserve or appearing in "aboriginal costume" in any "dance, show, exhibition, performance, stampede or pageant," even at home. (For good measure, the law also made it illegal for anyone else to hire an Indian to perform in such a show.) In practice Scott was prepared to allow small dances limited to a single reserve, his main priority at the time being the enlistment of Aboriginal soldiers. He insisted he was not being puritanical, and in 1915 he sent out a circular to agents saying that "reasonable amusement and recreation should be enjoyed by Indians." Still, "they should not be allowed to dissipate their energies and abandon themselves to demoralizing amusements. By the use of tact and firmness, you can attain control and keep it, and this obstacle to continued progress will then disappear." Exactly how agents could tell a reasonable amusement from a demoralizing one, he did not specify.

For several years after the first stampede, Calgary saw nothing more spectacular than the usual agricultural fairs of summer. Indian participation was small. But in 1919 Guy Weadick returned from Wyoming, this time as the main organizer of a Victory Stampede. He applied to Scott for permission to include Indians, and Scott refused. Weadick defied the law. He invited cowboys from across North America and Indians from across southern Alberta. They would not play an official role in the gathering—or so he told the press in advance—"yet their appearance in the coming celebration is necessary to make the event a complete success, as no showing where the wild life of the west is depicted would be complete unless they were present." In fact the Indians were essential to the success of the Stampede, and in the opening parade Chief Yellow Horse of the Blackfoot rode beside Weadick. The many other Indians who joined the parade preceded the cowboys and the mounted police.

A similar scene played out four years later. No Stampede was held between 1920 and 1922, years in which Calgary's summer exhibition concentrated on farming displays and horse races. Indians were absent. Excitement was minimal. In 1923, when the Stampede became an annual event at last, the organizers again wrote to Scott asking if Indians could take part. Again Scott said no. But the new minister of Indian Affairs, Charles Stewart, was a former premier of Alberta, and Stewart overruled his deputy. Much to the chagrin of the department, Aboriginal people would henceforth play a key role in the Stampede regardless of the Indian Act. Scott had foreseen the problem in 1921, when he told a subordinate, "It has always been clear to me that the Indians must have some sort of recreation." What he had in mind, though, was less clear: "If our agents would endeavour to substitute reasonable amusements for this senseless drumming and dancing, it would be a great assistance." In another memorandum that year, he directed his agents "to use your utmost endeavours to dissuade the Indians from excessive indulgence in the practice of dancing."

But the Calgary Stampede had opened a door, and Aboriginal people on the prairies strode—or danced—through it. In the 1920s some of them were arrested for holding sun and thirst dances, yet the dances did not come to an end and the drums continued to beat. The strands of dissent around recreation, spirituality and politics would often prove hard to disentangle. In November 1924, for example, more than a hundred people from all three of Alberta's Blackfoot reserves met to discuss their grievances in the old North West Mounted Police town of Macleod, where they were warmly greeted by the mayor and the president of the Board of Trade. Scott knew nothing of the gathering and was infuriated when he learned of it the following week. What angered him even more was the participants' resolve to hold a larger meeting the following July, in conjunction with Macleod's three-day rodeo.

This event, again encouraged by the local Board of Trade, acquired the name "Dominion Indian Celebration." Scott and his agents tried to stop it, without success. On Dominion Day of 1925, a parade of about three thousand Indians stretched for two miles down Macleod's straggling main street. Blackfoot people came up from Montana as well as elsewhere in Alberta, and they were joined by Stoneys, Sarcee and Cree. A powwow took place near the rodeo. The political talk achieved no immediate results, but the size of the celebration—and the backing it gained from the people of Macleod—sent a robust message to Ottawa.

What's important about the Macleod event, and the early Calgary Stampedes, is that Aboriginal people chose to take part, even though they were breaking the law. True, their participation depended on the support of powerful members of society who were willing to defy Indian Affairs. But this support would have meant nothing if the Aboriginal people themselves had given up. Such resistance came as an unpleasant surprise to the department. It had grown used to passivity; it expected compliance. After Rupert Brooke had spent a week in Scott's company in 1913, he visited the Stoney reserve and described his experience to the readers of the *Westminster Gazette*. "What will happen?" he asked his London audience. "Shall we preserve these few bands of them, untouched, to succeed us, ultimately, when the grasp of our 'civilisation' weakens…? Or will they be entirely swallowed by that ugliness of shops and trousers with which we enchain the earth, and become a memory and less than a memory?" He answered his own questions: "They are that already. The Indians have passed."

Brooke was unable to imagine that Indians might have the power, good sense and stamina to shape their own future. Influenced by Scott, as well as by the Social Darwinist tenets of his day, he wrote from a sincere and melancholy conviction that Aboriginal people could exert no control over their own destiny. He believed their fate lay in the hands of others—of enlightened men like Scott, if they were lucky, or of businessmen if they were not. *Shall we preserve... will they be entirely swallowed?* No, and no.

~

PAID TO PERFORM THEIR ancient dances and chants, free to wear their magnificent masks and regalia, Charles Nowell and Bob Harris found the 1904 St. Louis World's Fair a happy escape from life in Canada. The fair validated their identity as proud Kwakwaka'wakw. It confirmed the significance of their rituals. Thousands of people watched their performances—perhaps incredulous, certainly baffled, but seldom if ever hostile. The men gave lectures explaining the meaning of their stories, the symbolism of their costumes. They also spent a month at the Field Museum in Chicago, where Nowell enjoyed standing inside a big exhibit case and answering the questions of visitors (they often shook his hand and slipped him some extra money). To tourists and anthropologists alike, they were stars.

To Duncan Campbell Scott, they would eventually be criminals. Of all the Aboriginal peoples in British Columbia, the Kwakwaka'wakw had the reputation of being the most resistant to progress. Describing them, missionaries and Indian agents used terms like "intractable," "incorrigible," "difficult to civilize," and "inferior to any other in the Province in respect to morals and habits generally." The Kwakwaka'wakw lived in northern Vancouver Island and the adjacent parts of the mainland, many of them in coastal villages that outsiders found hard to reach. They spent much of their time in traditional, multi-family lodges; few of them had converted to Christianity; worst of all, from the government's standpoint, they continued to engage in the potlatch.

Generalizations about the potlatch are tremendously hard to make, partly because of the number and variety of Aboriginal peoples living near the Pacific coast. Each had a separate version of the potlatch with its own history, its own attributes, its own meanings. Yet the potlatch was a central part of all their lives. It functioned as both a spiritual and an economic event, one that could take place on a single day or stretch over many weeks. A potlatch entailed a feast involving dances, rituals and songs; it also served to redistribute wealth in the community. The more a person gave away, the greater his or her prestige, and the higher a rank or privilege that person could then claim. In the past, the property received and given at a potlatch had included slaves. Births, marriages, deaths and other rites of passage would all provide occasions for a potlatch, although the longest ceremonies tended to occur in winter. The tradition was by no means static—with the advent of a wage economy along the Pacific coast in the nineteenth century, potlatches altered, dwindling in some areas, growing in others.

To its defenders, the potlatch had many virtues. Those defenders were not all Aboriginal. "Unless the Dominion Government expect the Indians to suck their paws like bears all winter," wrote Charles Clifford, a leading businessman and politician in northern BC, "I do not see well, how they can get along without their feasts." Aside from the role they played as art and entertainment, potlatches also acted as a form of welfare. "Old people and infirm are fed and clothed during the long winter months, who otherwise would starve," Clifford stated. Aboriginal voices pointed out that potlatches allowed people to redeem their debts in public, thus avoiding shame. Moreover, as Douglas Cole and Ira Chaikin noted in their book *An Iron Hand Upon the People,* "they allowed an enlarged network for arranging marriages according to custom and provided a forum where matters affecting property, rank and precedence could be settled." The spiritual dimensions of the potlatch were spoken about less often. That doesn't mean they lacked importance.

Yet to its detractors, the potlatch was a despicable invention. And those detractors were not all white—Aboriginal people who had converted to

Christianity spoke up against the practice too. For one thing, it encouraged prostitution. Men often saw their wives and daughters as a means of accumulating wealth that could then be given away, and in the Skeena region, at least, older women used their daughters and nieces in the same manner. By the late nineteenth century, with the population of many Aboriginal nations shrinking fast, potlatches were a breeding ground for infectious disease. They also led to adults abandoning their jobs for weeks at a time, and to children missing long stretches of school. Indian agents looked with appalled hostility on the complex marriage customs of the Kwakwaka'wakw, which allowed women to be bought and sold. The potlatch was critical to the tradition: an old man who had distributed great wealth might expect a very young bride as a payment for the debt he would then be owed. Those who opposed the potlatch most strongly were not business leaders but social reformers.

Scott was not responsible for criminalizing the potlatch. Serious efforts to ban it dated back to 1884, when Sir John A. Macdonald was both prime minister and Superintendent-General of Indian Affairs. His amendment to the Indian Act aroused little stir in Ottawa—the leader of the Opposition, Edward Blake, called the potlatch an "insane exuberance of generosity." Outlawed at the same time was the *tamanawas* dance of some west coast shamanic societies, which involved arm-biting, dog-eating and the ritual simulation of cannibalism. In much of BC, potlatching carried on regardless of the law, leading to that further amendment of 1895 targeting the prairie dances as well. The Kwakwaka'wakw—and, to an extent, other peoples too, notably the Gitksan and the Nuu-chah-nulth—ignored the law. They appeared convinced that if only the government understood the potlatch, the practice would be tolerated, and many times they invited decision makers in Ottawa to come and see for themselves. These invitations were never accepted. "It seems a great pity," Scott observed in 1912, "that we cannot do something to break up this abominable and wasteful aboriginal custom." Soon, having taken over the department, he was ready to act.

The first wave of prosecutions took place in the Kwakiutl agency in 1914 and 1915. To Scott's annoyance the courts handed down nothing more than suspended sentences; there was even an outright acquittal by a Nanaimo jury that saw no harm in potlatching. And while war raged in Europe, Indian Affairs turned a blind eye to the practice. But late in 1918, Scott urged his agents to suppress potlatching once and for all. By now they enjoyed summary power under the Indian Act—that is, agents no longer had to submit a case of potlatching to a court; they could judge it themselves and decide on the punishment. A permanent RCMP detachment arrived in the Kwakwaka'wakw town of Alert Bay in December 1919, making the agent's job easier, and the first jail sentences were handed down a month later.

Even so, Charles Nowell did not hesitate to hold a mourning potlatch in January 1921 after his brother's death. Tom Nowell received the honour of both a church funeral and a totem-pole raising. Once the ceremonies were complete, Charles Nowell distributed hundreds of dollars to the guests. Because of this, he was arrested, sentenced to three months' imprisonment and shipped off to work on a prison farm near Burnaby. Seven other Kwakwaka'wakw had already served time for potlatching. Dozens more would follow.

The landmark case involved an enormous potlatch that was held around Christmas of 1921, on Village Island off the coast. The island is in the middle of a maze-like archipelago, and the wealthy chief who gave the potlatch, Dan Cranmer, thought it lay at a safe distance from the department's reach. After the speeches, feasts, dances and other ceremonies, he began to give stuff away: canoes, pool tables, gas boats, clothes, jewellery, blankets, sewing machines, musical instruments, teapots, basins, sacks of flour and more, much more. Then the RCMP arrived. More than three hundred people were attending the event; forty-five of them would be convicted, both men and women. Bob Harris, who had accompanied Charles Nowell to the world's fair, was not among the guests; he was on trial for perjury, having refrained from telling the full truth about yet another potlatch a year earlier. Harris was sentenced to three months' hard labour.

Indian Affairs rejoiced in the convictions. If the Kwakwaka'wakw potlatch system was dead at last, paganism and indolence had been dealt a severe blow.

Scott defined the purpose of his anti-potlatching amendment as "to prevent the Indians from being exploited as a savage or semi-savage race, when the whole administrative force of the Department is endeavouring to civilize them." The Village Island arrests cast a shadow on this statement. If any exploitation was involved in the potlatch, the Kwakwaka'wakw were doing it to themselves. But after the RCMP broke up the event, exploitation of a different sort occurred. The police seized more than 450 masks and other regalia; they lay piled in the Indian agent's woodshed before some of them were put on display in the Anglican parish hall at Alert Bay. A collector in New York bought thirty-three pieces; most of the rest were divided among the National Museum of Man in Ottawa, the Royal Ontario Museum in Toronto, and the Memorial Museum in Victoria.

In the entranceway of his Ottawa home, Hayter Reed had maintained a small collection of Aboriginal artwork: saddlebags, beaded slippers, clothing decorated with porcupine quills, as well as the CPR pass belonging to the Blackfoot chief Crowfoot. Duncan Campbell Scott had the good taste not to emulate Reed's placement of a moth-eaten buffalo head above his fireplace. He did collect Indian mementos, though. The music room, where he kept a grand piano, a few of his daughter's toys, and paintings by several of Canada's leading artists, also contained what a friend described as "Indian things, glinting silver and pieces of leather and woven geometric designs." It's possible—nobody appears sure—that a few of those "Indian things" were works of Kwakwaka'wakw art from Dan Cranmer's potlatch.

Just like the Blackfoot in southern Alberta, the Kwakwaka'wakw did not abandon their traditions in the face of Scott's law. Through the 1920s and '30s they continued to hold small potlatches in secret. So did the Nuu-chah-nulth. The cultural knowledge survived. Public support for the repressive law, always patchy and limited, dissolved over the ensuing decades, with even the mainstream churches expressing serious doubts about its fairness. Eventually potlatches became legal again, and after long negotiations with the museums in question, most of the artwork seized at Dan Cranmer's potlatch was returned to the Kwakwaka'wakw. It is now housed in new, purpose-built museums in Cape Mudge and Alert Bay.

Displays of Aboriginal art are now so common in Canada, people often find it hard to imagine the cultural oppression of the past. Yet in some quarters, Scott's distaste for "senseless drumming and dancing" lingers on. "Many Canada Day celebrations this year were marked by performances of traditional aboriginal drumming and dancing," Peter Foster wrote in the *National Post* in 2009. "Such displays—while an undeniable part of Canada's heritage—increasingly invoke uneasiness. That's because the state of aboriginal people in Canada is a national disgrace." Exactly how it would improve the state of Aboriginal people to remove their dancing and drumming from public view, Foster did not explain.

~

FOR SOME WEEKS ON his second treaty expedition in 1906, Scott was joined by his friend Edmund Morris. "Eddie," he was generally called. As a small boy in the 1870s he had lived in Winnipeg, where his father, Alexander Morris, served as lieutenant-governor of Manitoba and the North-West Territories. This was the same Alexander Morris who negotiated four of the western treaties, revised two others, and ringingly declared: "Let us have Christianity and civilization to leaven the mass of heathenism and paganism among the Indian tribes." He was a lawyer and a politician, callings which the youngest of his eleven children had no desire to follow. Edmund Morris studied art in New York, then spent three years in Paris before sailing home to Canada. The portraits he painted of Aboriginal people in traditional dress were eagerly bought by provincial and federal governments. He always gave his subjects a calm, resolute dignity.

Morris joined Scott again on a western trip in the summer of 1910—not that he always agreed with the policies for which his friend was responsible. In a letter he wrote to the *Manitoba Morning Free Press,* Morris discussed "the Indian problem" and asked, "[What are] we reducing them to by thrusting upon them our so-called civilization"? The verb "reducing" is worth noting. Within a few years of each other, and before the horrors of the First World War, Scott, Brooke and Morris all raised public questions about the true value of their civilization. Only Scott lived long enough to answer.

In 1913, Morris travelled east to Île d'Orléans to paint. His body was found washed up at the edge of the St. Lawrence River. It may have been an accident.

Scott's elegy to Morris is among his finest poems. Their friendship was a strong one although they met only occasionally—"Nothing of the mis-use," Scott writes, "That comes of the constant grinding / Of one mind on another." He recalls the sunrises and moonrises they saw in northern Ontario. Memory takes him then to the prairies, where Morris had once paid tribute to Crowfoot by marking a site of the great chief's tepee with a ring of stones. Recalling the work of his friend, whose portraits demanded close attention not to general traits but to specific details, Scott is willing to speak of Aboriginal people as individuals. He describes the evening he and Morris spent at Qu'Appelle with a Plains Cree elder named Sakimay. He evokes a day when the old chief Ne-Pah-Pee-Ness sat for Morris's por-trait—just one of the days, in truth, for Morris knew the chief well and painted him at least five times. And in his mind Scott conjures up someone else again:

> Here, Morris, on the plains that we have loved,
> Think of the death of Akoose, fleet of foot,
> Who, in his prime, a herd of antelope
> From sunrise, without rest, a hundred miles
> Drove through rank prairie, loping like a wolf…

The lines begin a beautiful passage made strange by the rhetorical tactic Scott is employing: asking a dead man to imagine the death of another.

"Lines in Memory of Edmund Morris" is a poem unusually frank, for Scott, about grief and disappointment. His contention that "Tears are the crushed essence of this world" leads eventually to a rueful admission of "the failures hidden in our sum of conquest." Akoose becomes a symbol of a willed triumph—yet Akoose is dead, resting "forever amid the poplars / Swathed by the wind from the far-off Red Deer / Where dinosaurs sleep, clamped in their rocky tombs." (The line marks one of the first appearances of dinosaurs in Canadian literature.) Somehow, by the superb alchemy of metaphor to which Scott could occasionally rise, the poem ends on a note of hope, as a kernel of the old, dying world, "deep enriched with effort and with love," escapes like a phoenix and flames forth "with presage, not of tears, but joy."

It took his friend's death to coax that vision out of Scott—a vision in which the painter joins Akoose, Crowfoot, Sakimay and Ne-Pah-Pee-Ness as emblems of a passing world. In their old age, in their death, in their remembered unthreatening strength, Scott could pay these men a graceful tribute. They were people whom at some level of his being he deeply admired, although only in the form of elegy could he bring himself to admit it. "Lines in Memory of Edmund Morris" would, in turn, be praised by Pelham Edgar in the generous obituary he wrote for Scott in 1947: "Never has aboriginal character been more faithfully portrayed." Alas, Edgar could not refrain from adding: "It is a permitted incongruity that the magnificent passages of nature description transcend the limitations of the Indian mind."

The year before Morris and Edgar travelled with Scott through northern Ontario, the poet's treaty journey had begun badly. Four days after a train dropped the group of men at an isolated CPR post, they rose early from their camp on Lac Seul and canoed against a strong wind to reach a Hudson's Bay Company post. Before arriving there, as Commissioner Stewart wrote in his journal, "we had heard the sound of a drum some distance up the lake." This was not the mimic thunder of a partridge's drumming; as they learned at the trading post, "this was a medicine drum that was being used at a 'Dog Feast' which was being held on the reserve about 8 miles distant. As certain of the proceedings connected with the feast are contrary to the law, we decided to go to the reserve and endeavour to put a stop to them." An hour's further canoeing brought the men to an Ojibwa white dog feast—a traditional practice that was forbidden by the same law which proscribed the western dances. Scott was leading a sizable party that included two policemen (one bearing the Union Jack) and a Hudson's Bay Company trader. "On landing," Stewart wrote, "Mr. Scott speaking for the Commissioners demanded to see the Conjurer."

Scott's own journal is, as always, terse. "Long conference with old medicine man, cunning old devil with swollen jaw. Powassan the head medicine man had sent them word to make the medicine. Can speak with McKenzie about this. Warned Inds not to dance. They promised to do what they could to stop it, but we must speak to Powassan." Stewart gives the name of the medicine man as Neotanaqueb; MacMartin, the third commissioner, spells it Neeohamaguet. The old man impressed Stewart by showing "great diplomacy in the manner in which he conducted his case. We could not but be surprised at the wisdom shown by him in the replies given to certain questions, and the manner in which he avoided answering others." The commissioners never did meet Powassan.

The Ojibwa were camped in about twenty tents and wigwams. The flag-bearing outsiders visited them all to lecture them on their folly in maintaining the white dog feast. No signing needed to be done that day, for the Aboriginal people in the region were already bound by a previous treaty. One of the policemen, writing his own account of the day's events, noted that the commissioners had told the Indians "their great Father the King would be shocked if he knew of their conduct." To soften the blow, the commissioners invited the Ojibwa to visit the trading post that evening for a legal feast.

It included a roast of caribou, Stewart says, "and was apparently much enjoyed" by the Aboriginal guests. Not, however, by Scott. "Very hot," his journal says. "Taken ill." Stewart is circumspect: "He was somewhat indisposed." MacMartin is more blunt: "I regret to record that Mr. Scott was taken ill suddenly this evening." Nobody else fell sick, and no reason for his illness could be found.

He recovered, of course. But he never forgot. And many years later, while in his day job he was preoccupied by conflicts involving the demands of the Six Nations and the persistence of Aboriginal culture in the West, he used the experience in one of his most troubling poems, "Powassan's Drum."

> He crouches in his dwarf wigwam
> Wizened with fasting,
> Fierce with thirst,
> Making great medicine

In memory of hated things dead
Or in menace of hated things to come.

The sound that recurs in every stanza is the medicine man's drum. To Aboriginal people, as Scott must have known, the drum is the heartbeat of life—but in this poem, Powassan's beat is one of pain and anger. The words "throb—throb—throb—throb" recur like a migraine.

So does the idea of hatred. The poem contains some marvellous images—"The stars in the earth shadow / Caught like whitefish in a net"—but what overrides the beauty is hatred. It induces a horrific vision of a headless Indian in a canoe, trailing his severed head "through the dead water." Powassan's magic in the shaking tent has created this "murdered shadow," and his magic culminates in a storm that blackens the sky and "crushes the dark world." What remains, at the heart of the storm and the end of the poem, is "the triumphant throb—throb—throb—throb—/ Throbbing of Powassan's Drum."

Visiting the prairies in 1910, Eddie Morris beside him, Scott could relax enough to appreciate the company of Indians and to recognize something of their worth. They were weak now, confined to small reserves, their numbers apparently falling; the menace they once posed to Canadian ambitions had faded. In a region suddenly lined by roads and dotted by tractors and grain elevators, Indians could inspire the poet to a lyricism tinged by nostalgia. His mood had been different in 1905 amid the uncut forests and undammed waterways north of Lake Superior. There a representative of the Canadian government might still feel like a trespasser, and there Scott sensed an Aboriginal power that had not disappeared. It met him as a challenge. There was nothing nostalgic about it. What he read in it was hatred, a hatred that turned inward and festered for the remainder of his long career.

⁓

A BLUSTERY NIGHT, THE wind shouting in the bare trees, gusting strongly enough to rub a couple of branches against the roof. The day's rain had stopped at last, and as the temperature fell, dark clouds scudded through a clearing sky. A giant puddle occupied the bottom of my driveway. I was alone in the house, finishing a novel on the sofa, nursing a Scotch.

"Good evening, Mr. Abley."

I stood up with a start, my heart beating a little faster than usual. He was walking slowly toward me from the far side of the room, the deep lines in his face etched by the lamplight.

"Good evening," I said. "I'm surprised to see you—it's wild out there. I hope the wind doesn't bring on a power failure."

"It would make some difference to you," he replied, "but none to me."

"Of course. I forgot. And I guess we should be safe—power failures are rare in the fall."

The lid of someone's garbage can was careening down the road, blown by a particularly strong blast of wind. I glanced out the window, distracted.

"Though winter is not far off, I suppose. Shall we sit down?"

He didn't sit in the usual manner—he simply materialized onto a chair. Why had I never noticed this before? I took a last long swig of my drink.

Scott was looking at me intently. He would probably have enjoyed a Scotch himself.

"You will be free of me soon," he said.

"Is free the right word?" I tried to force my lips into a smile.

"After this evening, you will be free to move on. To progress."

"That's an odd choice of expression," I said. "I've been thinking about progress, as it happens. I don't suppose you ever read a German-Jewish writer by the name of Walter Benjamin?"

Scott shook his head.

"Shortly before his death in 1940," I told him, "Benjamin wrote a wonderful description of a painting by Paul Klee. I know some of that description by heart. The painting shows an angel with wide eyes, his mouth hanging open, his wings spread out as though he's ready to leave. 'This is how the angel of history must look,' Benjamin says. 'His face is turned toward the past. Where we perceive a chain of events, he sees a single catastrophe, which keeps piling wreckage upon wreckage and hurling it before his feet.'"

"A single catastrophe," Scott repeated.

"Yes. Benjamin goes on to write, 'The angel of history would like to stay, awaken the dead, and make whole what has been smashed. But a storm is blowing from Paradise; it has got caught in his wings with such violence the angel can no longer close them. This storm irresistibly propels him into the future to which his back is turned, while the pile of debris before him grows skyward. This storm is what we call progress.'"

Scott sat in silence for a few moments, his eyes downcast. At last he looked up at me and said, "Can nothing that has been smashed be made whole?"

"Who am I to know?"

A further silence.

Finally he stirred and sighed. "I will say what I have to say, even though I don't suppose it will do me any good."

"We'll have to see," I replied. I didn't mean the remark to sound callous.

"Well then. On my last visit, you accused me of a lack of courage in my treatment of the Indians. I've been thinking about that remark, as you may suppose. And it puzzles me. Are you aware of the work I did to ensure that potlatching would be stopped?"

"I am."

"No doubt you think it was unfair."

"I think it was hugely presumptuous—this was the spiritual basis of an entire culture, and you tried to stamp it out."

"Indeed," he said. "Plenty of people in the Indian department—some of them in senior positions—were inclined to let the matter slide. Several of our officials on the coast preferred to do nothing. They said the potlatch was declining in force, as I admit it was in certain areas, and they heeded the voices of the businessmen who wanted it to carry on. It was making some of them substantial profits. I freely admit that on the whole, the general public in British Columbia was not averse to the potlatch."

"So why didn't you—"

His words were still coming toward me. "But I knew from my agents, as well as the missionaries, that the Kwakiutl potlatch was thriving, in fact growing. And unless we put a stop to it, progress would have been impossible to achieve in that most conservative and difficult of tribes. Had we allowed the Kwakiutl to persevere in their folly, the potlatch might well have emerged again elsewhere in the province. In this matter I did have the courage to act and, let me emphasize, not for the sake of winning praise from politicians. Only those of us who had the Indians' future at heart were determined to intervene."

"So," I said slowly, "with the residential school fiasco, you're ready to pass a lot of the blame onto the churches, but with the potlatch you're saying the churches were right."

"Agreed. You came out with the lofty phrase 'spiritual basis' just now, but the truth is, the potlatch was a cruel institution, especially for girls and young women, and it had become degraded over time. While the missionaries shared our ideals, they could do little until we took decisive action." He sat back and looked at me hard, oblivious to the gale outside. "It has taken many visits before I understood something about you, Mr. Abley. Permit me to explain. Back in the summer you accused me of failing to bring fresh enthusiasm to the department when I was placed in charge, and of failing to make significant changes in how it was run."

"I remember."

"And I pleaded innocent," Scott said. "When I did so, I was thinking about the potlatch, the sun dance, the thirst dance. Until I took control of the department, a singular lack of energy went into suppressing those customs. My predecessor, Frank Pedley, was not a man of consistently high ideals—I regret to say his attitude to morals was sometimes rather laissez-faire. He did not see, as I did, that if the potlatches and the prairie dances were allowed to flourish, they could threaten the rest of our work."

I was shaking my head and, no doubt, pulling a face.

"No, let me finish, please. You see, I tried to keep faith with the highest achievements, the shining ideals of our civilization. I suspect you do not give me credit for this. In fact I suspect this is something you have abandoned, even though you say you are a poet."

He gestured with his right hand toward the djembes on my floor, still blocking the piano from use.

"You may believe that by interfering with native culture we were stepping beyond our rightful powers. But I would respond that besides all the practical reasons for doing so—making sure Indian men went faithfully to the plough or the salmon cannery on a Monday morning, that kind of thing—we were hoping to raise them up to a full measure of civilization. We were hoping they would progress in the full sense of that word. I do not believe the sun dance is worthy of comparison with *Giselle* or *Swan Lake*. I do not believe the drumming you might hear at, let us say, a smudging ceremony is worthy of comparison with a symphony by Mozart. Music is the art of perfection, and all people—including the Indians—should have a chance to appreciate it."

"Absolutely right," I said.

He waited.

"But they should be free to make that choice for themselves. It can't be imposed on them. You're not some kind of cultural emperor, with the power to decide on behalf of everyone else what's worthy and what's not. 'Revolt is essential to progress': that's what you told the Royal Society of Canada when they installed you as their president. You were talking about poetry, I realize, but the idea has a broader resonance. 'There are many mansions in the house of poetry,' you said on the same occasion. Well, there are even more mansions in the great palace of music. Who are you to say that one kind of music is better than another?"

"Surely you would concede that Mozart—"

"I concede nothing," I said, for once overriding his interruption. "It so happens that my father was an organist. I was raised on J.S. Bach, and I'll always be glad of it. But if I'd been raised on Sufi chants or African-American gospel music or the ragas of India, I wouldn't be any less civilized. I think Aboriginal dances can hold just as much meaning and beauty as *Giselle*. And besides, we've reached a point in history where that word 'civilized' sends up loud alarm bells. Were the Nazis uncivilized? They revered the music of Wagner. I'm sure many of them loved Bach and Mozart too. Ads went up recently in the New York subway system saying 'In any war between the civilized man and the savage, support the civilized man.' That's not just a slogan I reject, Mr. Scott—it's a war I refuse to fight."

Silence. Through the far window I could see clouds scudding across the face of the moon. Against the cedar hedge by the driveway, debris was piling up.

"When you asked me on one of your earlier visits how the Indians of Canada are faring, I gave you some depressing facts. There's something else I didn't say, something you might find even more depressing. In 1951 the law against the potlatch and the sun dance was taken off the books. Since then, Aboriginal ceremonies have become so common, so *normal,* a lot of Canadians have no idea they were ever suppressed. I've been to powwows myself—they take place all over the continent. And though I've never had the good fortune to attend a potlatch, I did once see a totem pole being carved by a Kwakwaka'wakw artist. 'Kwakiutl,' as you would say. But Richard Hunt wasn't doing this on the west coast of Canada. He was carving the pole in the capital of Scotland, as an official artist at the Edinburgh Festival. Does that give you some idea of the esteem in which west coast Aboriginal culture is now held?"

Silence.

"You enjoyed visiting Victoria, didn't you? Mild winters, high tea at the Empress and all. It's a pity you couldn't see something that happened there in the summer of 2012. A new totem pole was raised on the grounds of Government House. That's where the lieutenant-governor lives—I expect you remember it well. The main carver was from the Kwakwaka'wakw people. But what made it truly special was this: one day the lieutenant-governor picked up a chainsaw, walked over to the pole, and helped carve a killer whale's tail. You see, the queen's representative in British Columbia was a member of the Sto:lo nation."

Silence.

"And some years ago, when Canada opened a new embassy in Washington, DC, the government wanted to showcase a major work of Canadian art. It turned to a Haida sculptor by the name of Bill Reid. He produced a wonderful bronze canoe holding thirteen figures, with both Eagle and Raven sitting in the same boat. Not to mention Bear Mother and Beaver, and a shaman perched in the middle. The canoe looks pretty crowded, but at least everyone's paddling in the same direction. Do you see what I'm saying, Mr. Scott? Maybe you don't, so let me show you."

I reached into the wallet in my pocket. Luckily it contained a twenty-dollar bill.

"There you go: *The Spirit of Haida Gwaii,* on the same piece of paper as the British queen."

He peered at the bill without a word. I put it back in my wallet.

"One last thing," I said. "If you could make a spectral trip back to your old stomping ground—Parliament Hill, I mean—you'd notice a new window above one of the entrances to the Centre Block. It shows an Aboriginal woman performing a jingle dance and an Inuit man drumming. It shows a grandmother sitting in a sacred lodge, smoking a pipe for her grandchildren. It shows a young mother holding a baby, with the words 'I love you, my child' written in Cree, Inuktitut, Mi'kmaq and Ojibwa. Another panel is much more sombre in colour. The children in it are wearing uniforms; their heads are shorn, their faces expressionless. The entire window commemorates the residential schools. The artist who designed it, Christi Belcourt, is Métis."

Silence. "So maybe Walter Benjamin was wrong after all," I said. "Maybe some things that are smashed *can* be made whole."

"Well," he said at last, "it's clear to me where you stand." He cleared his spectral throat. "I confess, I had been wondering why in all our meetings you concentrated almost entirely on the plight of the Indians. Before I arrived here, I realized you would need to learn about my work for the department. I knew I would have to defend myself. But I thought that, as a poet, you would naturally pay more attention to my literary work." There was a trace of self-pity now in his voice. "Instead you have hardly asked a thing about my poems and stories. All that seems to interest you is Indian Affairs."

"That's not completely true," I replied, "but it's how people know about you. It's the reason your name is still recognized. Your poems and stories speak for themselves—though I must admit, not many people listen. Don't take this personally. Very few Canadians today could quote a single line by Archibald Lampman or Pauline Johnson, or recall a single one of their poems. Their names are sinking toward oblivion. But not yours."

"You mean among Indian agitators and the like."

"Among students of Canadian history. Among some journalists, politicians, civil servants. But yes, a lot of Aboriginal people still recognize your name. They know exactly who you were."

"Do they?" he said. "Do they really? Perhaps my petition should have been to speak to one of them. Although I would have had to prepare myself to endure even more vitriol."

"I think it's right you appeared in my living room last winter," I said, "because the legacy of what happened to indigenous people in Canada isn't for indigenous people to face alone. It's not something I should be able to ignore. I was struck by a statement by John Milloy in his book about residential schools. He's a professional historian, and in the introduction to that book he explains that he tried to answer questions like 'How did it happen? How were Christianity and responsibility perverted?' It's crucial to know these things. But even if we do, it's not enough. You see, Milloy then adds: 'It must fall to the reader, to all of us, to go further, to answer the question, Why did it happen?' *Why,* Mr. Scott? Aboriginal people can deal with this from their own standpoint, and that's exactly what they're doing now. But I can't turn away. As an educated white Canadian, I need to face it too."

Scott stood up and walked over to the window of the darkened dining room. Through the bare, swaying twigs of the maple, the moon was free of cloud. He looked out for a few seconds. When he came back and sat down again in the living room, his features looked more pointed than usual. His voice was unusually low.

"Do you not get tired of guilt, Mr. Abley?"

"Yours? Or my own? I'm not sure what you mean."

"I mean the continual search for blame and guilt. There seems something wilful, something almost luxurious in your desire to feel ashamed of the past."

I reached for the yellow folder on the coffee table, not sure if the statement I wanted to find was among the papers there. After a few moments I located it. I looked up to see Scott staring at me, the lines around his mouth pointing down.

"Am I to face a barrage of statistics?"

I smiled despite myself. "Only a statement by a judge," I said. "Not Murray Sinclair. Not an Aboriginal person. I want to read you a few lines that Judge Thomas Berger wrote back in 1985. He's talking about Canada—but not about Canada alone."

Scott settled back in his chair, a resigned expression on his face.

"'The question is not one of guilt, present or past. The question is one of continuing injustice, and the distinctive feature of the injustices, past and present, done to indigenous peoples is the fact that these injustices were committed against peoples. These peoples are still with us, and the nations that committed these injustices are still with us.'"

"This man is astonishingly innocent," Scott said, "if he believes that history is always on the side of justice."

"Oh, I agree," I replied. "But don't we have to strive for it anyway? If we think about justice, we start to move beyond guilt. Guilt is a corrosive, negative emotion. Justice is a much more positive one."

"Quite so. You have your principles—I accept that. Please grant me mine, without assuming I was always in the wrong."

We sat in silence for a few moments. Soon, I knew, Scott would return to the shadowlands unreconciled. Was there anything I could do to lessen the blow?

"I'm sorry you take all the blame," I said.

He looked at me quizzically.

"Someone has to, I suppose. At least, insofar as it's helpful now in our search for justice to have a public example of what went so wrong in the past. We need a scapegoat, it seems, and you've become that scapegoat. I know it's not entirely fair. I know there were others in your department who wanted to come down even harder on the Indians than you did. I know you performed your work with integrity. You suffered terrible hurt in your personal life and you wrote some very fine poems. It's just that you made your way to the eye of a storm, the centre of a hurricane, and the hurricane did terrible damage. People are still trying to gather up the wreckage and set their lives in order. That's why you take so much blame."

He stood up, a changed mood in his eyes. For the first time I noticed his posture was a little stooped. Even his voice was softer.

"So can you find it in your heart to forgive me?"

I stood up too. I had been both wanting and fearing this question.

"I expect you've read my story 'Labrie's Wife,'" he said.

I nodded.

"Do you recall what happens at the end?"

"A young man walks away from the trading post alone."

"Well, yes," he said. "But that's not what I mean. The narrator looks at the young man and says, 'I understood in a flash. I pray God to forgive me for the sin of blindness, and for always being so dead to others in my own affairs.' The narrator sees his own failures at last."

"But it's too late. He can't retract the evil he's done."

"Neither can I," Scott said slowly. "But I will ask. If I was often guilty of the sin of blindness, can you grant me forgiveness?"

The wind was gusting again in the trees.

"No. I can't."

He sighed and looked away. I steeled myself to be resolute.

"Not because I don't want to, but because I'm the wrong person to ask. You brought no grief to my family, Mr. Scott. I don't get up every morning and struggle with the harm you did to my ancestors, harm that lingers in my family to this day. I've told you before, there are 1.4 million Aboriginal people in Canada. You need to ask forgiveness from them."

"They would never grant it."

"Not all. Not many. But I'm sure some of them would. You always underestimated them, you know."

Scott closed his eyes for a moment. When he reopened them he spoke in a colder tone. "You mean I always tried to do the best for them. No, no, don't bother to attack me again. I know what you're about to say." His voice had a bitter edge. "Above all, I tried to do the best for my country. I loved this country. I was a Canadian to the marrow of my bones, and my work was enriched with effort and with love. Sometimes I wonder, Mr. Abley, if you share my love."

"Of course I do," I said. "But I—"

"No more 'buts,'" he interrupted. "No more of these endless 'buts.' Our exchanges have come to an end."

He straightened his jacket and adjusted his glasses. Earlier I had thought I could see the tragic poet lurking in his face. Now I could no longer read his mood.

"I must leave," he said, "and it seems I have failed in my mission. Unless you have failed me."

"One or the other."

"Well then. I shall miss your dishevelled garden."

If this was an insult, it was one I deserved.

A branch was drumming against the roof again. "You've given me a lot to think about."

"Likewise," he said briefly.

I saw his pale eyes rove around my living room. His manner now seemed less severe than it had been a few moments earlier. Perhaps failure allowed him to relax. It seemed almost as if, resplendent in his tab collar, tie and silver cufflinks, he belonged to a weird and waning race.

"We may meet again," he said. "Quite soon, perhaps." I noticed without pleasure the trace of a smile curling across his narrow lips. "Your time will come, Mark Abley."

What had he just said?

"So this may be *au revoir*," I replied, my words catching in my throat, "not *adieu*."

He pulled his head slowly back, as though lifting his neck toward the ceiling. Headlights were glinting in the driveway. I heard a car door slam. He closed his eyes and the impalpable air gave a faint quiver.

"Maybe so. In the wilderness of the afterlife, who can say?"

Then his voice was no longer floating around me, though its echo seemed to fill a space the size of Canada.

A Note to the Reader

"CAN I TRUST THIS book?"

Whether you've just finished reading *Conversations With a Dead Man*, are somewhere in the middle, or are wondering whether to embark on it, you may want an answer to that question. Here is my response.

All of the chapters—except for the first—begin with a long section in which there is no ghost named Duncan Campbell Scott and no character named Mark Abley. In these sections every quotation is accurate, every fact verifiable. These sections are, if you like, "pure non-fiction" rather than "creative non-fiction." As this is a book intended for readers, rather than academic specialists, it is not weighed down by lengthy pages of footnotes. But all of the main sources are listed in the following pages, and most of the minor sources too.

In the nine conversations, I have allowed myself a certain amount of speculation. For example I do not know—nobody can know—if after being told what Scott is told in these exchanges, he would ask for forgiveness. It is, I admit, presumptuous of me to speculate.

But the details about Scott that emerge in the conversational sections are as accurate as I can make them. I have imagined, I have sometimes presumed, but I have not altered the known facts. His admiration for Mozart and Tennyson, his fury at the Japanese in World War II, the name of the cat who delighted Rupert Brooke, Scott's fondness for Madge Macbeth's apple cake and Armenian Bliss: all such details are on the record.

Even many of the apparently offhand remarks in the conversations are grounded in fact. In Chapter Five, for instance, Scott mentions that he and his first wife admired Spanish music and painting; and admittedly I can't be sure of this. But we know that Belle Botsford performed violin pieces by the Spanish composer Pablo de Sarasate, who was still alive when she and Scott arrived in Madrid in 1907; we know that Scott wrote a poem about listening to nightingales sing in Grenada, and included the lines "Ripples of fairy colour, / Rhythms of Spain" in his elegy to Claude Debussy; we know that he collected art; and we know that his early short story "A Night in Cordoba" culminates in a vision of a Spanish painter. So I stand by my hunch. The following remark, about bullfighting, is based on more direct evidence: in its copious Scott papers, Library and Archives Canada holds a pair of tickets issued in 1907 by the Plaza de Toros, Madrid.

Truth is the seedbed of imagination. I believe that a book, if it's to succeed as a work of creative non-fiction, has to be imaginative. I also believe it should stay close to the known facts.

ANY WORK ON THIS particular subject risks causing offence on grounds of terminology alone. I am not brave or crazy enough to adopt Drew Hayden Taylor's tongue-in-cheek acronym NAFNIP (Native/Aboriginal/First Nations/Indigenous People). In general I have preferred to use the word "Aboriginal," with some appearances of "indigenous" (a term I have not capitalized, although I realize many people strongly believe it should be). Some Aboriginal people are still happy to call themselves "Indian," but in general I've chosen to keep "Indian" for historical passages and for direct quotes from Scott and others. The term "First Nations" is inescapable when referring to present-day governments, but (knowing that many Aboriginal people dislike it) I've avoided it when writing about individuals. I'm not fond of "native" as a euphemism or synonym for "Aboriginal," and have tended to avoid it except in a few direct quotes. I have freely used "white," "Canadian," "European" and "settler," according to whichever term seemed appropriate on a sentence-by-sentence basis.

These decisions are personal, are made in good faith, and are unlikely to please everyone. But I hope the book will be judged on its ideas, not its terminology.

Sources

NEARLY ALL OF DUNCAN Campbell Scott's work has been out of print for many years. Fortunately, some of it is available in anthologies and much of it can be found on the excellent Canadian Poetry Press website. The entry point to all the Confederation Poets is http://www.canadianpoetry.ca/confederation/index.htm—it contains the work not only of Scott, Archibald Lampman, Pauline Johnson and other well-known figures of the time, but also of several more obscure writers. In Scott's case, all of the poems and many of the short stories he published in book form are available on this site, as is Leslie Ritchie's two-volume *Duncan Campbell Scott: Addresses, Essays, and Reviews* (2000).

However, the Canadian Poetry Press site does not provide a complete collection of Scott's work. It excludes one book of short stories, *The Witching of Elspie,* as well as his only novel, which was published in 1979 by Penumbra Press. John Flood edited the text but did not add a title; the book appeared as *Untitled Novel, ca. 1905.* The Canadian Poetry Press site also excludes three books of Scott's non-fiction. *John Graves Simcoe* (The Makers of Canada series, Morang & Co., 1905) and the short monograph *Walter J. Phillips* (Ryerson Press, 1947) require foraging in used bookstores or university libraries. Somewhat easier to find is a collection of the columns that Scott, Lampman and Wilfred Campbell wrote for the Toronto *Globe* in 1892–93; Barrie Davies edited and published these columns under the title *At the Mermaid Inn* (University of Toronto Press, 1979). Still available in print form is Scott's short-story collection *In the Village of Viger* (New Canadian Library, 2008, with an afterword by Tracy Ware).

The most important biographical source for this book is E.K. Brown's forty-page memoir, which prefaces *The Selected Poems of Duncan Campbell Scott* (Ryerson Press, 1951). Also essential for my purposes was *The Poet and the Critic,* edited by Robert L. McDougall (Carleton University Press, 1983), a collection of the letters that Scott exchanged with Brown in the last seven years of his life. John Coldwell Adams' book *Confederation Voices: Seven Canadian Poets* (2007) is available on the Canadian Poetry Press website, http://www.canadianpoetry.ca/confederation/John%20Cold-well%20Adams/Confederation%20Voices/chapter%205.html; Chapter V, on Scott, includes both biographical and critical material. Sandra Gwyn's two chapters on Scott and Lampman in *The Private Capital: Ambition and Love in the Age of Macdonald and Laurier* (McClelland & Stewart, 1984) are a delight. An effusive short memoir of Scott was written by his friend Leonard W. Brockington and appeared in *Saturday Night,* August 1, 1942. Another friend, Arthur Bourinot, wrote about Scott on several occasions, notably in the two selections of letters he privately printed (and heavily edited) in 1959 and 1960.

Turning to critical works, I made frequent use of two books: Stan Dragland's *Floating Voice: Duncan Campbell Scott and the Literature of Treaty 9* (Anansi, 1994) and E. Brian Titley's *A Narrow Vision: Duncan Campbell Scott and the Administration of Indian Affairs in Canada* (UBC Press, 1986). I gratefully acknowledge my debt to the wisdom and research of both authors. I gained insight too from Laura Smyth Groening's *Listening to Old Woman Speak: Natives and alterNatives in Canadian Literature* (McGill-Queen's University Press, 2004). The essays on Scott by his fellow poets Raymond Souster and Douglas Lochhead, both mentioned in this book, were published in *Powassan's Drum: Poems of Duncan Campbell Scott* (Tecumseh Press, 1985). A few notable essays appeared in *The Duncan Campbell Scott Symposium,* edited by K.P. Stich (University of Ottawa Press, 1980). I admire, without always agreeing with, D.M.R. Bentley's "Shadows in the Soul: Racial Haunting in the Poetry of Duncan Campbell Scott" (*University of Toronto Quarterly,* Spring 2006).

I consulted many of the annual reports of the Department of Indian Affairs. These are available online at http://www.lac-bac.gc.ca/databases/

indianaffairs/index-e.html. Three standard works of history, all excellent in their own way, are J.R. Miller's *Skyscrapers Hide the Heavens: A History of Indian-White Relations in Canada* (University of Toronto Press, 2000), Arthur Ray's *An Illustrated History of Canada's Native People: I Have Lived Here Since the World Began* (McGill-Queen's University Press, revised and expanded edition, 2011), and *Canada's First Nations: A History of Founding Peoples from Earliest Times* (Oxford University Press, fourth edition, 2009) by Olive Dickason and David T. McNab. Older, more trenchant and still worth reading is Boyce Richardson's *People of Terra Nullius: Betrayal and Rebirth in Aboriginal Canada* (Douglas & McIntyre, 1993).

Scott was so well known in Canadian cultural circles, and lived such a long life, that material related to him appears in many archives. I would like to acknowledge the help of staff at the following institutions where I examined Scott-related material: Library and Archives Canada (Scott-Aylen papers, Arthur Bourinot papers), Thomas Fisher Rare Books Library at the University of Toronto (Duncan Campbell Scott papers), Carleton University Library (Robert McDougall papers), McGill University Library (Duncan MacCallum and W.D. Lighthall papers), McCord Museum (Hayter Reed papers), Queen's University Library.

For particular chapters, further sources follow.

CHAPTER 1

Vincent Massey edited *Canadian Plays from Hart House Theatre,* vol. 1 (Macmillan, 1926); his description of Scott appears there. John Masefield's letter to Scott about his experience of reading "The Piper of Arll" is quoted in Stan Dragland's *Floating Voice*. Will Ferguson's shaming of Scott as one of the ten worst Canadians of all time can be found in *The Beaver* (August 2007).

Scott's essay "The Tercentenary of Quebec, 1608–1908," appears on the Confederation Poets website. The excerpt of his poetry that begins "Catch up the sands of the sea..." comes from "Lines in Memory of Edmund Morris." "Fragment of an Ode to Canada" opens *The Poems of Duncan Campbell Scott* (McClelland & Stewart, 1926).

CHAPTER 2

E.K. Brown, in his introduction to Scott's *Selected Poems,* called Belle "imperious"; it was the musician Harry Adaskin who praised her warmth of personality (*A Fiddler's World: Memoirs to 1938,* published by November House, 1977). The quote from Amaryllis appears in Sandra Gwyn's *The Private Capital.* Sandra Martin and Roger Hall edited *Rupert Brooke in Canada* (PMA Books, 1978), a book I have happily used in a few other chapters as well. Arthur Bourinot's lines come from "The Ever-Eager Heart," a tribute to Scott he delivered at what was then Carleton College in Ottawa in February 1948.

Ashley Stacey's article "Dealing with the Indian Problem" appeared in *Obiter Dicta,* February 13, 2012. The quotations about fur-trading forts come from the websites of Saskatchewan Parks, http://www.saskparks.net/FortCarlton, and the Old Forts Trail, http://www.oldfortstrail.com/fort_whoopup.php.

Christopher Powell's comments on genocide were in the *Winnipeg Free Press,* February 24, 2012. The Postmedia News article associating Scott with the phrase "kill the Indian in the child" was written by Teresa Smith and appeared in the *Vancouver Sun* on January 23, 2012. Basil H. Johnston's poignant quotation comes from his foreword to *Magic Weapons: Aboriginal Writers Remaking Community after Residential School* by Sam McKegney (University of Manitoba Press, 2007). The text of John Masefield's tribute to Scott appeared in the *Ottawa Journal,* February 21, 1948. Susan Crean's perceptive and polemical book *The Laughing One: A Journey to Emily Carr* was published by HarperCollins in 2001.

Essential reading on residential schools is John S. Milloy's *"A National Crime": The Canadian Government and the Residential School System, 1879 to 1985* (University of Manitoba Press, 1999). The *Saturday Night* quote about P.H. Bryce appears in Chapter 5 of that work. An earlier and more personal book on this painful topic is *Stolen from Our Embrace: The Abduction of First Nations Children and the Restoration of Aboriginal Communities* by Suzanne Fournier and Ernie Crey (Douglas & McIntyre, 1997). The interim 2012 report of the Truth and Reconciliation Commission, *They Came for the*

Children: Canada, Aboriginal Peoples, and Residential Schools, is freely available at http://www.attendancemarketing.com/~attmk/TRC_jd/Res-SchoolHistory_2012_02_24_Webposting.pdf. I expect the final report will also be available online via the TRC's superb website, www.trc.ca.

P.H. Bryce's pamphlet *A National Crime* (1922) is available at http://www.archive.org/stream/storyofnationalcoobrycuoft#page/n5/mode/2up. See the article by Megan Sproule-Jones, "Dr. Peter Bryce, Public Health, and Prairie Native Residential Schools" in *Canadian Bulletin of Medical History,* vol. 13, no. 2 (1996). The details about Father Balter of Saddle Lake come from *Medicine That Walks: Disease, Medicine, and Canadian Plains Native People, 1880–1940* by Maureen K. Lux (University of Toronto Press, 2001). A moving essay on residential schools by Richard Wagamese, "Returning to Harmony," appears in *Speaking My Truth: Reflections on Reconciliation and Residential School* (Aboriginal Healing Foundation, 2011), available at www.speakingmytruth.ca. That book also contains essays by Drew Hayden Taylor and Jose Amaujaq Kusugak, among others.

The couplet about Hull's bells appears in Scott's poem "The End of the Day," and his remark about romantic scenery is from a letter to A.J.M. Smith. His poem "Farewell to Their Majesties" comes from his last book, *The Circle of Affection.*

CHAPTER 3

The question posed at the end of the first paragraph is lifted from T.S. Eliot's poem "Gerontion." John MacLean's book *Canadian Savage Folk* can be read online at http://eco.canadiana.ca, a website that also provides access to many other important historical documents, including William Scott's long report about the Oka Indians. John Borland's reply to William Scott is available at http://openlibrary.org/books/OL14000326M/An_appeal_to_the_Montreal_Conference_and_the_Methodist_Church_generally.

The quote from Thomas J. Morgan can be found, along with much other interesting material, in *Documents of United States Indian Policy,* edited by Francis Paul Prucha (University of Nebraska Press, third edition, 2000).

John MacLean's remark about Poundmaker's surrender is quoted by Sarah Carter in *Capturing Women: The Manipulation of Cultural Imagery in Canada's Prairie West* (McGill-Queen's University Press, 1997). In both this and the next chapter I have relied on quotes by Sir John A. Macdonald that I found in Blair Stonechild's *The New Buffalo: The Struggle for Aboriginal Post-Secondary Education in Canada* (University of Manitoba Press, 2006). See also "John A. Macdonald and Aboriginal Canada" by Donald B. Smith, *Historic Kingston,* vol. 50 (2002).

Disrobing the Aboriginal Industry, by Frances Widdowson and Albert Howard, was published by McGill-Queen's University Press in 2008. The summary of children's abuse in residential schools appeared in Volume 1, Chapter 10, of the final report of the Royal Commission on Aboriginal Peoples, and the incident at Crowstand School is described in John Milloy's *"A National Crime."*

Scott's comments about the Mohawk Institute are taken from *The Mush Hole: Life at Two Indian Residential Schools,* compiled by Elizabeth Graham (Heffle Publishing, 1997). The letter from A.Y. Blain to Samuel Blake is to be found among the Blake correspondence in the General Synod Archives of the Anglican Church of Canada; my thanks to Donald B. Smith for alerting me to it. It was mentioned in his fascinating study *Honoré Jaxon: Prairie Visionary* (Coteau Books, 2008). Don Smith also gave me a copy of "The History, Policy, and Problems of Protestant Missions to the Indians of Canada" by T.B.R. Westgate, published in *The North American Indian Today* (University of Toronto Press, 1943), from which I drew the comparison between the funding of orphanages and the funding of Indian residential schools.

The quotes by Clifford Sifton and Frank Oliver come from David J. Hall's fine essay "Clifford Sifton and Canadian Indian Administration, 1896–1905" (first published in 1977 and reprinted in the anthology *As Long as the Sun Shines and the Water Flows,* UBC Press, 1983). J.E. Hodgetts' "Indian Affairs: The White Man's Albatross" appeared in his *Pioneer Public Service: An Administrative History of the United Canadas, 1841–1867* (University of Toronto Press, 1955). Madge Macbeth's satirical novel about politics in Ottawa is *The Land of Afternoon* (1924).

Scott's lines about the arrival of spring are taken from "A Nest of Hepaticas," and his lines about the moon, stars and nature are from his early poem "Off the Isle Aux Coudres."

CHAPTER 4

George Woodcock's essay on Scott's poetry appeared in *Canadian Writers and Their Works* (poetry series, vol. 2, ECW Press, 1983). Bill Wilson's column ran in the *Vancouver Province* on December 15, 2011; here I have used his own preferred spelling, Kwawkgewlth, rather than more standard spellings for his people. David McNab's essay "'A Lurid Dash of Colour': Powassan's Drum and Canada's Mission, the Reverend William and Duncan Campbell Scott" appeared in *Aboriginal Cultural Landscapes,* edited by Jill Oakes and Rick Riewe (Aboriginal Issues Press, 2004).

Alexander Morris's quote comes from his book *The Treaties of Canada with the Indians of Manitoba and the North-West Territories* (1880), available at http://eco.canadiana.ca. Tom Flanagan's *First Nations? Second Thoughts* was first published by McGill-Queen's University Press in 2000 and reprinted, with a new chapter, in 2008. Peter Russell's *How Agriculture Made Canada: Farming in the Nineteenth Century* (McGill-Queen's University Press, 2012) contains an excellent chapter on native farming on the prairies, which draws on the important earlier book *Lost Harvests: Prairie Indian Reserve Farmers and Government Policy* by Sarah Carter (McGill-Queen's University Press, 1990).

For issues relating to Aboriginal soldiers, Timothy Winegard's *For King and Kanata: Canadian Indians and the First World War* (University of Manitoba Press, 2012) is an indispensable work. Scott's essay of 1919 discussed in this chapter is entitled "The Canadian Indians and the Great World War"; it can easily be read online at http://www.canadianpoetry.ca/confederation/DCScott/address_essays_reviews/vol1/cdn_indians_great_war. html. The quoted passages come from near the end. For some reason, however, that version omits the crucial phrase about Indian soldiers mingling with men of other races. The complete essay can be read with more difficulty at http://archive.org/stream/canadawar03variuoft/canadawar-03variuoft.txt.

The comments about Scott by D.G. Jones can be found in *Butterfly on Rock* (University of Toronto Press, 1970). Northrop Frye's remarks on "The Forsaken" appear in *Northrop Frye on Canada,* edited by Jean O'Grady and David Staines (University of Toronto Press, 2003).

The International Symposium on the World's Indigenous Languages took place in Nagoya in August 2005. Buffy Sainte-Marie's speech at the University of Regina can be watched on YouTube. For Joe Oliver's remarks, see the article by David P. Ball in the *Vancouver Observer,* March 21, 2012, "Joe Oliver's speech coloured by 'racism': First Nations Grand Chief." Diamond Jenness's frank essay "Canada's Indians Yesterday. What of Today?" appeared in the *Canadian Journal of Economics and Political Science* 20 (1954).

André Picard's feature on Aboriginal health—and the federal government's disregard for it—ran in the *Globe and Mail* on April 10, 2012. Picard has returned to the subject since (e.g., December 20, 2012). See also *First Nations, Métis and Inuit Children and Youth: Time to Act,* a report by the National Council of Welfare (Fall 2007). I found the line from Janet Ajzenstat on the website of the Macdonald-Laurier Institute for Public Policy, www.macdonaldlaurier.ca/nominated-for-the-donner-book-prize. For statistics on children in government care, see a Canadian Press article, "First Nations children still taken from parents," July 31, 2011.

The second-last paragraph of this chapter shamelessly repeats the final sentence of F. Scott Fitzgerald's novel *The Great Gatsby.*

CHAPTER 5

Stephen Leacock's *The Dawn of Canadian History* can be read at http://www.gutenberg.ca/ebooks/leacock-dawn/leacock-dawn-00-h-dir/leacock-dawn-00-h.html.

In this chapter and elsewhere I used Barnett Richling's *In Twilight and in Dawn: A Biography of Diamond Jenness* (McGill-Queen's University Press,

2012). This is the source for the quote from Edward Sapir. Jenness's *The Indians of Canada* (National Museums of Canada, 1932) remained in print for decades and went through several later editions.

Francis Parkman's *The Oregon Trail* can be accessed at http://xroads.virginia.edu/~hyper/oregon/oregon.html. Parkman's work is also available in print form in a Library of America edition. A Scott poem that is unequivocally based on Francis Parkman is the lurid "Dominique de Gourgues"; in all likelihood, Parkman was also a source for the better-known (and better) poem "On the Way to the Mission." See Leon Slonim's article at http://www.uwo.ca/english/canadianpoetry/cpjrn/vol03/blond.htm.

David J. Hall's essay on Clifford Sifton, mentioned in Chapter 3 notes, is the source for the *Manitoba Free Press* quotation. The two articles that Edward Curtis wrote for *Scribner's* in 1906 are available online at http://www.unz.org/Pub/Scribners-1906may-00513.

The quote from Marius Barbeau is taken from an essay that appeared in an obscure Scottish newspaper in 1931, in the *Winnipeg Free Press* in 1932, and in *Scientific American* in January 1933. See *Marius Barbeau: Man of Mana* by Laurence Nowry (NC Press, 1995).

Emily Carr's rejection letter was quoted by Sandra Campbell in the original, very long manuscript of *Both Hands: A Life of Lorne Pierce of Ryerson Press* (McGill-Queen's University Press, 2013); it did not make the final cut. The description of Kateri Tekakwitha in death comes from Fr. Pierre Cholenec, writing in 1696; it has been widely quoted ever since.

Marcel Giraud's two-volume study *The Métis in the Canadian West* was published by the University of Alberta Press in 1986 in a translation by George Woodcock; its underlying attitudes are lethally dissected by Frank Tough in *Native Studies Review,* vol. 5, no. 2 (1989).

Eric Ball's fine study *Archibald Lampman: Memory, Nature, Progress* (McGill-Queen's University Press, 2013) introduces Scott as Euktemon. Most of Lampman's poetry, like Scott's, is available on the Canadian Poetry Press website, "At the Long Sault" (originally printed by Ryerson Press) being an important exception. That poem can, however, be read at https://tspace.library.utoronto.ca/html/1807/4350/poem1178.html. (Scott's newspaper column about Dollard des Ormeaux, part of the collaborative venture entitled "At the Mermaid Inn," can be read at http://www.canadianpoetry. ca/confederation/mermaid_inn/apr_9_1892.htm.)

For John Ralston Saul's arguments, see *A Fair Country: Telling Truths about Canada* (Viking, 2008).

A detailed though extremely polemical website about Jeffery Amherst can be found at http://www.nativeweb.org/pages/legal/amherst/ lord_jeff.html. The Scottish historian I quote is Bruce Philip Lenman, in his book *Britain's Colonial Wars, 1688–1783* (Longman, 2001).

F.R. Scott's "The Canadian Authors Meet" was written in the late 1920s. His lines about the world and the human race are from a later poem, the short "Creed." Duncan Campbell Scott's poem beginning "The slender moon" is entitled "The Voice and the Dusk."

CHAPTER 6

Madge Macbeth wrote a shrewd chapter on Scott in her memoir *Over My Shoulder* (Ryerson Press, 1953). Details about the historical fancy dress ball of 1896 appear at http://www.civilization.ca/cmc/exhibitions/hist/balls/ 0-1eng.shtml, a website that includes a photo of Hayter Reed's costume as Donnacona, and in Reed's private papers.

John S. Long's *Treaty No. 9: Making the Agreement to Share the Land in Far Northern Ontario in 1905* (McGill-Queen's University Press, 2010) is an indispensable gathering of material about the 1905 trip. Many details in this chapter are taken from that book. Both the 1905 and 1906 trips are crucial to Stan Dragland's arguments in *Floating Voice*.

Pelham Edgar's "Travelling with a Poet" appears in *Across My Path* (Ryerson Press, 1952), a gathering of his essays edited by Northrop Frye. I have again used David J. Hall's essay in *As Long as the Sun Shines and the Water Flows,* this time for Clifford Sifton's rebuff of Lord Minto. All the quotes in this chapter from the historian J.R. Miller come from his article "How the First Nations View the Crown," *Montreal Gazette,* January 11, 2013.

Stephen Harper's widely quoted remark about the lack of colonialism in Canada is put in context at http://www2.macleans.ca/2009/10/01/

what-he-was-talking-about-when-he-talked-about-colonialism. The contrasting statement by Paul Martin appeared in an article in the *Montreal Gazette,* December 1, 2012, under the headline "Colonial Legacy Haunts Us, Martin Says."

Peter Moon's feature about Fort Albany appeared in the *Globe and Mail* on October 19, 1996; the *National Post* column about Attawapiskat, written by John Ivison, ran on November 28, 2011. Richard Wagamese's article for the *Calgary Herald* appeared on April 15, 2012, under the headline "Why First Nations Cling to Their Reserves." The press report comparing Scott to a Yankee and a greyhound appears in the Scott-Aylen papers at Library and Archives Canada.

The lines quoted early in the chapter about partridges, fireflies and quintessential passion all come from "Spring on Mattagami." It appeared, with six others, in his small book *Via Borealis,* published in the same year the poems were drafted. A century later, poetry publishing is almost never so fast.

CHAPTER 7

Details about Dr. Joseph Jacobs of Kahnawake come from the McGill University archives. I'm grateful to Dr. Allan Sherwin for the information.

For details of the St. Louis World's Fair, see *Anthropology Goes to the Fair: The 1904 Louisiana Purchase Exposition* by Nancy J. Parezo and Don D. Fowler (University of Nebraska Press, 2007). A more theoretical approach is taken in *Human Zoos: Science and Spectacle in the Age of Colonial Empires,* edited by Pascal Blanchard et al. (Liverpool University Press, 2008).

I found the anecdote about Mackenzie King and the Beothuk in Kevin Major's *As Near to Heaven by Sea: A History of Newfoundland and Labrador* (Penguin, 2002). On Winston Churchill, see "Not His Finest Hour" by Johann Hari (*The Independent,* October 28, 2010). D.C. MacCallum's remark about French Canadians as a Celtic race is taken from an 1885 letter to the press in his private papers. His *Addresses* were privately printed by Desbarats in Montreal in 1901. Henry James's remarks about the Irish were quoted by Margaret Scanlan in her article "Terrorism and the Realistic Novel," *Texas Studies in Literature and Language,* vol. 34, no. 3 (1992).

The full text of Charles Darwin's *Descent of Man* is available online at http://www.gutenberg.org/ebooks/2300. I made use of Carl N. Degler's book *In Search of Human Nature: The Decline and Revival of Darwinism in American Social Thought* (Oxford University Press, 1991) for much of the discussion in this chapter, including the quotations from W.E.B. Du Bois and William Wilson Elwang. Another work on this broad topic is *Social Darwinism in European and American Thought, 1860–1945* by Mike Hawkins (Cambridge University Press, 1997).

The idea of "stolen generations" in Australia has become the focus of intense controversy among historians, writers and the interested public. On one side (the political right), see the copious writings of Keith Windschuttle. On the other, see Robert Manne's *Whitewash* (2003) and *In Denial: The Stolen Generations and the Right* (2001). The remarks by the Northern Territory's Chief Protector of Aborigines are quoted on the website of the Australian Human Rights Commission at http://www.humanrights.gov.au/publications/bringing-them-home-8-history-northern-territory.

The Robert Byrd quote comes from a brilliant article by Ta-Nehisi Coates, "Fear of a Black President," in *Atlantic Monthly* (September 2012). Charles Dickens' unfortunate essay "The Noble Savage" can be found at http://www.gutenberg.org/cache/epub/872/pg872.html.

Amelia Paget's *People of the Plains* was published by the Toronto firm of William Briggs in 1909, with illustrations by Edmund Morris.

CHAPTER 8

Robert McDougall's essay "The Story of Elise Aylen" appears in his book *Totems: Essays on the Cultural History of Canada* (Tecumseh Press, 1990). The letters from Scott that Elise Aylen preserved are to be found in the copious Scott-Aylen papers at Library and Archives Canada. John Watkins is mentioned frequently in the later pages of Robert McDougall's *The Poet and the*

Critic, his edition of the letters exchanged between Scott and E.K. Brown. For Watkins' diplomatic career and sad end, see his *Moscow Despatches: Inside Cold War Russia* (James Lorimer, 1987), edited and introduced by Dean Beeby and William Kaplan.

Mildred Valley Thornton's *Indian Lives and Legends* appeared in print only in 1966, when it won a Canadian Authors' Association prize. It was reissued by Hancock House in 2003, under a title Scott would not have appreciated: *Potlatch People: Indian Lives and Legends of British Columbia.*

I enjoyed reading Charlotte Gray's *Flint and Feather: The Life and Times of E. Pauline Johnson, Tekahionwake* (HarperCollins, 2002). Scott's brief mention of Pauline Johnson is from his review essay "A Decade of Canadian Poetry" (1901), available on the Canadian Poetry Press website. Her essay "Sons of Savages" appeared in *The Boy's World,* May 19, 1906.

Brian Titley's *A Narrow Vision* has much to say about the Six Nations controversy, and I also made use of Yale Belanger's article "The Six Nations of Grand River Territory's Attempts at Renewing International Political Relationships, 1921–1924" (*Canadian Foreign Policy* 13, no. 3, 2007). Both Frederick Loft and Deskaheh are given excellent treatment by Donald B. Smith in the *Dictionary of Canadian Biography,* available online at www.bio graphi.ca. Donald Smith is also the author of *Chief Buffalo Child Long Lance: The Glorious Impostor* (Red Deer Press, 1999). A fine thesis by Scott R. Trevithick (University of Calgary, 1998) on the deposing of the Confederacy Council in 1924 is available at http://www.collectionscanada.gc.ca/obj/ s4/f2/dsk2/tape17/PQDD_0001/MQ34920.pdf. Ronald Wright's *Stolen Continent: The "New World" through Indian Eyes Since 1492* (Viking, 1992) includes many details about Iroquois and Six Nations history. The information about Scott's Mohawk name is taken from Stan Dragland's *Floating Voice.* Archibald Lampman's beautiful line about October comes at the end of his poem "September."

Hayter Reed's change of heart concerning white responsibility for Indian troubles is reflected in his unpublished address to the St. James Literary Society of Montreal in April 1928, preserved in his private papers. For Reed's foolishness about farming, see Peter Russell's *How Agriculture Made Canada* as well as Scott's unusually informal address "Some Features of Indian Administration in Canada," which he delivered in October 1916 to an American audience. That address has been published only in the *Report of the Thirty-Fourth Annual Lake Mohonk Conference on the Indian and Other Dependent Peoples;* once again I am grateful to Don Smith for the reference. Richard Pratt, who coined the phrase "Kill the Indian...and save the man," delivered a paper at the same conference entitled "Our Forlorn Indians."

Scott's remarks on Joseph Brant and altruism appear in his essay "Indian Affairs, 1763–1841," available on the Canadian Poetry Press website.

CHAPTER 9

For details about dancing and the Calgary Stampede, I again referred to Brian Titley's *A Narrow Vision.* I also relied on Hugh A. Dempsey's article "The Indians and the Stampede," included in *Icon, Brand, Myth: The Calgary Stampede,* edited by Max Foran (Athabasca University Press, 2008). A few details also came from James H. Gray's *A Brand of Its Own: The 100 Year History of the Calgary Exhibition and Stampede* (Western Producer Prairie Books, 1985). The remarks by Father Hugonard are quoted in Brian Titley's *A Narrow Vision.* Yale Belanger's article "'An all round Indian affair': The Native Gatherings at Macleod, 1924 and 1925" appeared in *Alberta History* (Summer 2005).

The standard book on the history of potlatch suppression is *An Iron Hand upon the People: The Law against the Potlatch on the Northwest Coast* by Douglas Cole and Ira Chaikin (Douglas & McIntyre, 1990). See also Christopher Bracken's smart and quirky book *The Potlatch Papers: A Colonial Case History* (University of Chicago Press, 1997). Details on Hayter Reed's collection of Indian artifacts come from a yet unpublished manuscript by his granddaughter, Kate Reed, entitled *A Woman's Touch.* Did some items from Dan Cranmer's potlatch end up in Scott's office and his home? Stan Dragland discusses the possibility in *Floating Voice.* The evidence is suggestive but, it seems, not conclusive. Peter Foster's article appeared in the *National Post,* July 3, 2009.

Information about Edmund Morris can be found in *Edmund Morris "Kyaiyii" 1871–1913* by Geoffrey Simmins and Michael Parke-Taylor (Norman Mackenzie Art Gallery, 1984), and in the *Dictionary of Canadian Biography.* Morris still awaits, however, a detailed study worthy of the man. On "Powassan's Drum," see Stan Dragland's *Floating Voice* as well as D.M.R. Bentley's essay "Shadows in the Soul."

Walter Benjamin's late, brief essay "On the Concept of History" exists in several translations and has been published in various editions. I slightly adapted the version on www.sfu.ca/~andrewf/CONCEPT2.html. Scott's remarks about music and poetry come from "Poetry and Progress," his presidential address of 1922 to the Royal Society of Canada. It is available on the Canadian Poetry Press website. For the raising of a totem pole outside Government House in Victoria, see the article by Tom Hawthorn in the *Globe and Mail,* September 10, 2012. Thomas Berger's statement about justice comes from his book *Village Journey* (Hill and Wang, 1985) and is quoted by John Long in *Treaty No. 9.*

Acknowledgments

THIS BOOK OWES ITS existence to my wife, Ann Beer. I say this because of her unrelenting and impassioned commitment to justice and honour for Aboriginal people, and also because of her surprising belief in me. For their patience, love and support, thanks also to our daughters, Kate and Megan.

I'm grateful to Denis Sampson for reading seven chapters of an early draft and offering his usual wise comments. Another friend, Doug Gibson, was my first sounding board when I was struggling with the form of the book, and gave me good advice later. Charles Foran, Eric Siblin and Taras Grescoe read a draft of the entire manuscript, providing generous and much-needed words of encouragement at a difficult time. David Staines later did the same, offering both encouragement and good advice. I was particularly delighted by the thoughtful and passionate response to a draft manuscript of this book by Daniel David, a proud member of the Mohawk nation. Other friends who helped in one way or another include Katia Grubisic, Gary Geddes and Adrian King-Edwards. Special thanks to Megan McLeod, thanks to whom I was able to hear Judge Murray Sinclair speak in Winnipeg.

Duncan Campbell Scott's nephew and executor, John Aylen Sr., together with his late wife Andrée welcomed me into their Ottawa home and spoke to me about Scott from the standpoint of a loving and respectful family. I thank their son, John Aylen Jr., for the introduction. Elsewhere in Ottawa, David Manicom and Teresa Marquis kindly took me to see Beechwood Cemetery.

Donald B. Smith introduced me to Dr. Allen Sherwin, who told me about the Kahnawake doctor Joseph Jacobs. With typical generosity, Don also provided dozens of other leads and details. My office table still groans under the weight of material he sent me. As a professional historian, he must have found much in this manuscript that annoys him, but nonetheless he read a complete draft and saved me from various errors. I am deeply grateful to him, and also to Kate Reed, who gave me much information about the life and times of her grandfather, Hayter Reed. Other helpful suggestions came from experts in various fields: David McNab, Eric Ball, Brian Titley, Susan Walsh, Dean Beeby, William Kaplan, Amy Tector, Sam Solecki and Michael Gnarowski. Ryan Van Huijstee enlightened me on a vexing issue of terminology.

I'm glad to acknowledge the support of the Conseil des arts et des lettres du Québec, which awarded me a modest writing grant during the final stages of writing this book.

Scott McIntyre lit the flame that made *Conversations with a Dead Man* possible. I have profound respect for his work as a publisher. Jackie Kaiser helped keep the fire alight. Howard White, Anna Comfort, Corina Eberle, Katherine Carey and the staff of Harbour Publishing and Douglas & McIntyre helped turn a manuscript into a book. Audrey McClellan provided adroit and intelligent editing. I thank them all.

Index

Stewart, Samuel, 138, 209, 210
Stolen From Our Embrace (Crey), 66
Sto:lo, 66, 216
Stoney, 124, 172, 198, 201
Strahl, Chuck, 141
Student of Weather, A (Hay), 70
Sulpician priests, 55–56
sun dance, 32, 105, 198–99, 201, 214, 216
Swain, Jimmy, 133

tamanawas dance, 204
Teetotaler's Hand-Book, The (William
      Scott), 27
Tekakwitha, Kateri, 110, 146
Tennyson, Alfred, 165–66
They Came for the Children, 46
thirst dance, 198–99, 201, 214
Thomson, R.H., 142
Thornton, Mildred Valley, 179, 189
Three Persons, Tom, 198
"Tie Me Kangaroo Down, Sport" (Harris),
      163
Titley, E. Brian, 79–80, 139, 184
Toronto Sunday World, 183
Touchwood Hills residential school, 39
Treaty Nine, 127–28, 138–39, 141
Treaty No. 9 (Long), 137, 139
Truth and Reconciliation Commission of
      Canada, 46, 74–75, 137
Tsuu T'ina (Sarcee), 108, 109, 198, 201

United Nations Declaration on the Rights of
      Indigenous Peoples, 141

Victory Stampede, 200
Village Island, 205–6
Voudrach, Paul, 75

Wabinoo, Charles, 136, 179
Wagamese, Richard, 140

Wahta Mohawk Territory, 56
Wallace, Russell, 82
Watkins, John, 177
Weadick, Guy, 198, 200
"White Man's Burden, The" (Kipling), 147
Widdowson, Frances, 60, 187
Wilson, Bill, 82
Winnipeg, 72–73, 100
Woodcock, George, 78

Yellow Horse, Chief, 200